RESPONSIBLE AI

RESPONSIBLE AI

RESPONSIBLE AI

BEST PRACTICES FOR CREATING

TRUSTWORTHY AI SYSTEMS

Qinghua Lu, Liming Zhu, Jon Whittle, and Xiwei Xu

✦Addison-Wesley

Boston • Columbus • New York • San Francisco • Amsterdam • Cape Town • Dubai
London • Madrid • Milan • Munich • Paris • Montreal • Toronto • Delhi • Mexico City
São Paulo Sydney • Hong Kong • Seoul • Singapore • Taipei • Tokyo

For information about buying this title in bulk quantities, or for special sales opportunities (which may include electronic versions; custom cover designs; and content particular to your business, training goals, marketing focus, or branding interests), please contact our corporate sales department at corpsales@pearsoned.com or (800) 382-3419.

For government sales inquiries, please contact governmentsales@pearsoned.com.

For questions about sales outside the U.S., please contact intlcs@pearson.com.

Visit us on the Web: informit.com/community

Library of Congress Control Number: 2023915722

ISBN-13: 978-0-13-807392-3

ISBN-10: 0-13-807392-9

Printed by Ashford Colour Press Ltd

Pearson's Commitment to Diversity, Equity, and Inclusion

Pearson is dedicated to creating bias-free content that reflects the diversity of all learners. We embrace the many dimensions of diversity, including but not limited to race, ethnicity, gender, socioeconomic status, ability, age, sexual orientation, and religious or political beliefs.

Education is a powerful force for equity and change in our world. It has the potential to deliver opportunities that improve lives and enable economic mobility. As we work with authors to create content for every product and service, we acknowledge our responsibility to demonstrate inclusivity and incorporate diverse scholarship so that everyone can achieve their potential through learning. As the world's leading learning company, we have a duty to help drive change and live up to our purpose to help more people create a better life for themselves and to create a better world.

Our ambition is to purposefully contribute to a world where

- Everyone has an equitable and lifelong opportunity to succeed through learning

- Our educational products and services are inclusive and represent the rich diversity of learners

- Our educational content accurately reflects the histories and experiences of the learners we serve

- Our educational content prompts deeper discussions with learners and motivates them to expand their own learning (and worldview)

While we work hard to present unbiased content, we want to hear from you about any concerns or needs with this Pearson product so that we can investigate and address them.

Please contact us with concerns about any potential bias at https://www.pearson.com/report-bias.html.

The authors have been influenced and inspired by many leading thinkers in the fields of AI, Responsible AI, and related areas. We would like to acknowledge many of these individuals here. This book has in part been shaped by conversations with the following people, writings of theirs we have pored over, or ideas of theirs we have listened to. Thanks to all of them for all the contributions they have made to making AI more responsible.

Colleagues we have worked with:

- John Grundy
- Rashina Hoda
- Waqar Hussain
- Aurelie Jacquet
- Arif Nurwidyantoro
- Gillian Oliver
- Harsha Perera
- Mojtaba Shahin

- Rifat Ara Shams
- Judy Slatyer
- Stela Solar
- Toby Walsh
- Chen Wang
- Zhenchang Xing
- Didar Zowghi

Leaders we have been inspired by:

- Yoshua Bengio
- Nick Bostrom
- Joy Buolamwini
- Kate Crawford
- Virginia Dignum
- Kay Firth-Butterfield
- John C. Havens
- Dan Hendrycks
- Ben Hutchinson
- Tim Hwang
- Fei-Fei Li
- Margaret Mitchell

- Andrew Ng
- Bashar Nuseibeh
- Meredith Ringel Morris
- Francesca Rossi
- Stuart Russell
- Ed Santow
- Iyad Rahwan
- Irene Solaiman
- Max Tegmark
- Cat Wallace
- Jennifer Wortman Vaughan

Contents

Preface

Writing a book is not a minor undertaking. The authors of this book know this from experience: Collectively, we've labored through the trials of book-writing multiple times, and we've also had many failed attempts and false starts along the way. When an idea for a new book comes along, then, it is a brave soul that not only agrees to write it, but immerses him/herself into it, body and soul. Nevertheless, that's what happened with this book. The topic of Responsible AI is so important to society, so topical in the current zeitgeist, and so needed, that it would be folly not to take on the challenge.

But this is not just any book on Responsible AI. There are quite a few books covering the topic already. Some of these are deeply technical books that look only at the technology aspects of AI systems, such as how to manipulate AI models and their data to try and ensure responsible AI. Other books are more philosophical in nature, citing examples where AI has already had an unfortunate impact on society, or exploring what terrible potentials of AI there are in the future.

This book, however, lies somewhere in the middle. It fills a gap between the highly technical advice and more philosophical thinking. It aims to provide concrete guidance to the AI practitioner, to the AI development teams, and to those who care about governing AI systems when they are developed, such as senior managers and boards. The emphasis is on *concrete* guidance. There are many AI ethics principles available nowadays, but there is still a lack of information on how to convert these principles into practice. This book, which can be thought of as a reference volume, provides a set of tried and tested patterns for doing just that. We gathered these patterns from an in-depth search of existing literature and practice: We didn't make them up, but bring together solutions that have been tried out in anger and we collect them in one place.

We hope that this book will serve its purpose, to inform and guide the reader toward responsible AI. Indeed, in a perfect world, our book—like all good reference books—will sit on the reader's shelf many years into the future, to be picked up when a reminder is needed of how best to handle a particular ethical issue in AI. There's no doubt that AI will evolve significantly and rapidly in the coming years. But the fundamentals of how to design, implement and use systems responsibly are somewhat more stable. And so, we also hope that these patterns, although undoubtedly they will be added to over the years, will stand the test of time.

Register your copy of *Responsible AI: Best Practices for Creating Trustworthy AI Systems* at informit. com for convenient access to downloads, updates, and corrections as they become available. To start the registration process, go to informit.com/register and log in or create an account. Enter the product ISBN 9780138073923 and click Submit. Once the process is complete, you will find any available bonus content under "Registered Products."

Acknowledgments

Writing a book is a long journey that requires the assistance and support of many. We would like to thank Stuart Powell, Shujia Zhang, Didar Zowghi, and Francesca da Rimini for their contributions to the case studies. We also appreciate Judy Slatyer, Aurelie Jacquet, Yue Liu, Boming Xia, and Pamela Finckenberg-Broman for their help with the pattern chapters.

Pearson did a professional and efficient job in the production process. This book has greatly benefited from their expertise.

We are grateful to the management of CSIRO's Data61. Without their generous support, this book would not have been written.

About the Authors

Dr. Qinghua Lu is a principal research scientist and leads the Responsible AI science team at CSIRO's Data61. She received her PhD from University of New South Wales in 2013. Her current research interests include responsible AI, software engineering for AI/GAI, and software architecture. She has published 150+ papers in premier international journals and conferences. Her recent paper titled "Towards a Roadmap on Software Engineering for Responsible AI" received the ACM Distinguished Paper Award. Dr. Lu is part of the OECD.AI's trustworthy AI metrics project team. She also serves a member of Australia's National AI Centre Responsible AI at Scale think tank. She is the winner of the 2023 APAC Women in AI Trailblazer Award.

Dr./Prof. Liming Zhu is a Research Director at CSIRO's Data61 and a conjoint full professor at the University of New South Wales (UNSW). He is the chairperson of Standards Australia's blockchain committee and contributes to the AI trustworthiness committee. He is a member of the OECD.AI expert group on AI Risks and Accountability, as well as a member of the Responsible AI at Scale think tank at Australia's National AI Centre. His research program innovates in the areas of AI/ML systems, responsible/ethical AI, software engineering, blockchain, regulation technology, quantum software, privacy, and cybersecurity. He has published more than 300 papers on software architecture, blockchain, governance and responsible AI. He delivered the keynote "Software Engineering as the Linchpin of Responsible AI" at the International Conference on Software Engineering (ICSE) 2023.

Prof. Jon Whittle is Director at CSIRO's Data61, Australia's national centre for R&D in data science and digital technologies. With around 850 staff and affiliates, Data61 is one of the largest collections of R&D expertise in Artificial Intelligence and Data Science in the world. Data61 partners with more than 200 industry and government organisations, more than 30 universities, and works across vertical sectors in manufacturing, health, agriculture, and the environment. Prior to joining Data61, Jon was Dean of the Faculty of Information Technology at Monash University.

Dr. Xiwei Xu is a principal research scientist and the group leader of the software systems research group at Data61, CSIRO. With a specialization in software architecture and system design, she is at the forefront of research in these fields. Xiwei is identified by the Bibliometric Assessment of Software Engineering Scholars and Institutions as a top scholar and ranked 4th in the world (2013–2020) as the most impactful SE researchers by JSS (*Journal of Systems and Software*), a well-recognized academic journal in software engineering research.

Credits

PART I

BACKGROUND AND INTRODUCTION

What is responsible artificial intelligence (AI)? Why do we need responsible AI? How complex is the operationalization of responsible AI? How many different perspectives need to be taken into account? These are the questions we answer in Part I.

In Chapter 1, "Introduction to Responsible AI," we introduce the history and motivation of responsible AI and give a definition from a systems perspective. We also discuss who should be responsible for responsible AI.

In Chapter 2, "Operationalizing Responsible AI: A Thought Experiment—Robbie the Robot," we go through a thought experiment using Robbie the Robot to explain what organizations need to think about when it comes to responsible AI, including governance considerations, process considerations, and product considerations.

1

Introduction to Responsible AI

Ever since the dawn of the modern computing age, pioneers have been just as concerned about computers' impact on society as they have about the technical development of the field. The first electric programmable computer, Colossus, was invented by Tommy Flowers in 1943. Around the same time, Norbert Wiener first started to lay out ideas and principles that eventually would define a new field of academic research, now known as computer ethics. Wiener was among the first to foresee the radical transformation of society that computers would bring about, and to predict not just the good that computers would do in the world, but also the downsides: "[We are] here in the presence of another social potentiality of unheard-of importance for good and for evil."[1]

The ripple of interest in computer ethics, first started by Wiener, was eventually picked up more broadly. Within little more than two decades, the Association for Computing Machinery, the world's largest computing society, published its first Code of Ethics, designed to provide guidance to software practitioners on how to act ethically when building software systems. In 1976, Walter Maner coined the term *computer ethics*. The theory and practice of building and adopting computer systems responsibly now had a name. Almost a decade later, the first computer ethics textbook appeared in print.[2]

Even in those early days of computer ethics, artificial intelligence (AI)—both the opportunities it could bring as well as its potential harm to society—was uppermost in mind. The 1950s were a heady decade for computing. As well as the birth of computer ethics, the field of AI officially came into being at the Dartmouth Conference. Even back then, much of the deep thinking around what

---

1. N. Wiener, *Cybernetics: Or Control and Communication in the Animal and the Machine* (John Wiley, 1948).

2. D. G. Johnson, *Computer Ethics* (Prentice Hall, 1985).

it meant for AI to be ethical had already been started. But it was largely a side issue. AI had not yet matured enough to bring issues of ethics into focus. The rubber hadn't yet hit the road.

When the rubber did hit the road, it hit with a vengeance. Advances in big data, computing power, and AI algorithms have moved AI from an experiment to a vehicle for large-scale transformation in just about every industry. AI is no longer a futuristic idea; it is here now. As a result, the ethical challenges of AI are here now as well. This is why we've seen a surge in the development of principles, frameworks, standards, and even tools, for ethical AI. For the most part, however, these largely remain at the stage of high-level guidance. What we will see in the next decade is a focus on how to make those principles and frameworks real: *how to operationalize the principles into practice.*

This is where this book comes in. While not yet having all the answers, this book is the first attempt to gather all the knowledge about operationalization of AI ethics principles in one place. In particular, we view things through the lens of engineering large-scale AI systems. Responsibility is a consideration that must be taken into account at all levels when engineering an AI system. For example, it is not sufficient only to consider responsibility in the data for an AI system or in the machine learning model. The software infrastructure that goes around the AI—such as the user interface and the software architecture—can also lead to ethical issues if not considered as well. Similarly, whereas ethicists, philosophers, lawyers, and social scientists have a lot to offer in terms of high-level ethical considerations, ethics must also be considered in an organization's structure and in the design of software systems (not just the AI part).

This is why this book takes a system engineering perspective to responsible AI. It offers guidelines and best practices not just for the AI—which is typically a small part of a larger system—but also for the system engineering process and organizational governance. Without this holistic approach, we will never see a society where the benefits of AI are realized without also opening Pandora's box and unleashing the chaos of negative consequences on the world.

What Is Responsible AI?

As with many terms that refer to emerging technologies, the term *responsible AI* is loosely defined. Indeed, a set of terms is currently being used in the community to mean largely the same thing: *responsible AI, ethical AI, trustworthy AI, AI for Good, values-driven AI,* and, more broadly, *digital humanism.* At their heart, all these terms have the same underlying objective: to inform how we can develop, adopt, and maintain AI systems in a way that has a positive benefit on society.

Unfortunately, there are far too many examples where AI—or more broadly, automation (we come back to this distinction later)—has led to negative societal impacts. These range from life-threatening negative impacts, such as driverless cars leading to road deaths[3] and autonomous

---

3. BBC News, "Uber Car 'Had Six Seconds to Respond' in Fatal Crash," May 2018, https://www.bbc.com/news/technology-44243118.

drones killing humans,[4] through serious but not life-threatening impacts such as AI-based discriminatory sentencing at parole boards,[5] inaccurate assessments in automated debt recovery systems,[6] and bias in automated exam grading systems,[7] all the way to less serious—but still important—cases such as price gouging by automated airline pricing systems in the aftermath of natural disasters[8] or discriminating against minority neighborhoods when offering retail pricing discounts using AI algorithms.[9]

In response to many examples of "AI gone wrong," governments, corporations, and independent citizen groups from all over the world have come together to define constraints on how AI systems should behave. For the most part, the outcome of these efforts is a statement of principles such as the Australian AI Ethics Principles,[10] which define eight high-level principles that AI systems should adhere to, as illustrated in Table 1.1. Many countries have now formalized sets of ethical principles, as have bodies such as the Institute of Electrical and Electronics Engineers (IEEE), the International Organization for Standardization (ISO), the World Economic Forum (WEF), and the Organization for Economic Co-operation and Development (OECD). Companies have come together to define a position on ethical AI, either by defining in-house guidelines, or by joining consortia such as the Partnership on AI. In some cases, countries have even legislated the responsible use of AI, with perhaps the best known and potentially most impactful example being the European Union's AI Act, recently passed by the European Parliament.[11]

---

4. "Autonomous Drones Have Attacked Humans. This Is a Turning Point," *Popular Mechanics*, November 2, 2021, https://www.popularmechanics.com/military/weapons/a36559508/drones-autonomously-attacked-humans-libya-united-nations-report/.

5. "Can the Criminal Justice System's Artificial Intelligence Ever Be Truly Fair?" *Massive Science,* May 13, 2021, https://massivesci.com/articles/machine-learning-compas-racism-policing-fairness/.

6. "Robodebt: A Conspiracy or a Stuff Up" *The Guardian,* November 15, 2022, https://www.theguardian.com/australia-news/audio/2022/nov/15/robodebt-a-conspiracy-or-a-stuff-up.

7. "How an AI Grading System Ignited a National Controversy in the U.K.," *Axios*, August 19, 2020, https://www.axios.com/2020/08/19/england-exams-algorithm-grading.

8. "'Price Gouging' and Hurricane Irma: What Happened and What to Do," *New York Times*, September 17, 2017, https://www.nytimes.com/2017/09/17/travel/price-gouging-hurricane-irma-airlines.html.

9. "Amazon Same-Day Delivery Less Likely in Black Areas, Report Says," *USA Today*, April 22, 2016, https://www.usatoday.com/story/tech/news/2016/04/22/amazon-same-day-delivery-less-likely-black-areas-report-says/83345684/.

10. D. Dawson et al., "Artificial Intelligence: Australia's Ethics Framework," Report EP191846, CSIRO, Australia, 2019, DOI: 10.25919/ydfm-5p75.

11. Artificial Intelligence Act. Proposal for a regulation of the European Parliament and the Council laying down harmonized rules on artificial intelligence (Artificial Intelligence Act) and amending certain union legislative acts. EUR-Lex-52021PC0206, 2021.

Table 1.1   Australian Government's AI Ethics Principles

Principle	Description
Human, societal, and environmental well-being	AI systems should benefit individuals, society, and the environment.
Human-centered values	AI systems should respect human rights, diversity, and the autonomy of individuals.
Fairness	AI systems should be inclusive and accessible, and should not involve or result in unfair discrimination against individuals, communities, or groups.
Privacy protection and security	AI systems should respect and uphold privacy rights and data protection, and ensure the security of data.
Reliability and safety	AI systems should reliably operate in accordance with their intended purpose.
Transparency and explainability	There should be transparency and responsible disclosure so people can understand when they are being significantly impacted by AI and can find out when an AI system is engaging with them.
Contestability	When an AI system significantly impacts a person, community, group, or environment, there should be a timely process to allow people to challenge the use or outcomes of the AI system.
Accountability	People responsible for the different phases of the AI system lifecycle should be identifiable and accountable for the outcomes of the AI systems, and human oversight of AI systems should be enabled.

In this book, we mainly use the term *responsible AI* to capture the intent of the preceding objectives. Rather than trying to define this term too precisely, we mean it to represent the development of AI systems that respect the principles in Table 1.1. While there are many ethical AI frameworks and principles, there is a great deal of agreement on the core principles—see, for example, Fjeld's thorough analysis of AI ethics frameworks across the world[12]—and the eight in Table 1.1 can largely be taken as representative. Put another way, in this book, we frame responsible AI as follows:

> *Responsible AI is the practice of developing and using AI systems in a way that provides benefits to individuals, groups, and wider society, while minimizing the risk of negative consequences.*

What Is AI?

Now that we have defined *responsible* AI, it remains to define AI itself. AI is a contested term that, despite decades of research and practice, has eluded a precise definition. Australia's National AI Centre defines AI as follows:

> *AI systems embrace a family of technologies that can bring together computing power, scalability, networking, connected devices and interfaces, and data. AI systems can be trained to perform a specific task such as reasoning, planning, natural language processing, computer vision, audio*

---

12. J. Fjeld et al., *Principled Artificial Intelligence: Mapping Consensus in Ethical and Rights-Based Approaches to Principles for AI* (Berkman Klein Center Research Publication, 2020).

processing, interaction, prediction and more. With Machine Learning, AI systems can continue to improve a specific task according to a set of human-defined objectives. AI systems can be designed to operate with varying levels of autonomy.

This definition broadly aligns with what is commonly termed *narrow AI* (or *weak AI*)—that is, AI systems that are designed to perform a specific task, such as recommending a movie, performing a patient diagnosis, or detecting an object of a particular kind in an image. Narrow AI contrasts with *general AI* (or *strong AI*), which is used to denote an AI system that has general intelligence on par with (or even beyond) that of human beings. As of the time of writing, the state of the art is an impressive collection of narrow AI, typically machine learning trained for a specific task. While many of these examples of narrow AI are striking—and some, such as large language models that mimic human conversation, are approaching a level of generality—true general AI is well beyond current capability. Let's make no mistake: AI can do many things, but no one has yet come close to inventing an AI that is conscious or can learn in the way a human does.

The EU's AI Act takes a different approach to the definition of AI. It aims to define a list of technologies that can be considered as AI: "*AI means software that is developed with one or more of the techniques and approaches listed in Annex I and can, for a given set of human-defined objectives, generate outputs such as content, predictions, recommendations, or decisions influencing the environments they interact with.*"[13] In this case, the annex identifies three types of AI technologies:[14]

- Machine learning approaches, including supervised, unsupervised, and reinforcement learning, using a wide variety of methods including deep learning;

- Logic- and knowledge-based approaches, including knowledge representation, inductive (logic) programming, knowledge bases, inference and deductive engines, (symbolic) reasoning, and expert systems;

- Statistical approaches, Bayesian estimation, and search and optimization methods.

While this definition is not universally agreed upon, it is reminiscent of another way of describing AI, based on two broader classes of technology: symbolic versus nonsymbolic (or connectionist) AI. Symbolic AI was the dominant technology in the early days of AI and takes the approach of building knowledge into an AI system, typically as a set of rules, and supporting reasoning over this knowledge. Nonsymbolic AI, on the other hand, as typified by neural network and other machine learning approaches, relies on large datasets and sophisticated pattern matching so that the AI system can "learn" to recognize features in data given enough input data to allow it to distinguish between features.

AI can be classified into symbolic AI and nonsymbolic AI. To illustrate the difference in everyday terms, suppose you wish to create an AI system that would predict what kind of food you will order

13. Artificial Intelligence Act. Proposal for a regulation of the European Parliament and the Council laying down harmonized rules on artificial intelligence (Artificial Intelligence Act) and amending certain union legislative acts. EUR-Lex-52021PC0206, 2021.

14. European Commission. Laying down harmonized rules on artificial intelligence (Artificial Intelligence Act) and amending certain union legislative acts, 2021.

at a restaurant in any particular context. A symbolic AI system designer would encode rules such as "if it's before 7 a.m., toast and eggs" or "if it's a weekend and I'm with friends, zucchini fritters." With enough rules, a symbolic AI system can reason over the knowledge database to predict food choices over time, even in situations without a specific rule to describe them. On the other hand, a nonsymbolic AI would rely on a large dataset of food choices over time. In effect, the AI would "follow" its user for a period of time, noting all the food choices and contexts. Given enough time, the AI could then learn from these examples to predict future food choices.

In the end, there is no perfect definition of AI. Indeed, AI is not a binary concept. It is not the case that a system is an AI or not. Rather, AI should be viewed as a spectrum: some systems are more intelligent than others. In some situations, this is obvious. So, for example, an AI that filters out spam is clearly less intelligent than a conversational agent that can have realistic interactions with a human. Indeed, some systems that purport to be AI might be better described as "automation"—that is, mechanical programs that simply follow a well-defined set of rules. However, even distinguishing between AI and automation is not as simple as it might first seem. Symbolic AI, for instance, is based on a set of rules. It typically, however, involves searching through a rule database and the outputs can be nondeterministic. This is different from automation, which often (although not always) produces the same output for a given input.

The key point is that, as far as *responsible* AI is concerned, it really does not matter how we define AI. The whole issue is a red herring. Why? Because every software system should be designed responsibly. It is not just AI that can have negative consequences on society. Software systems can make decisions with negative impact even if those systems are only following simple, deterministic rules. Given this, perhaps we should have titled this book *Responsible Software Systems*. Arguably, yes, we should have—but then we would not have been able to leverage the current zeitgeist that is AI!

Developing AI Responsibly: Who Is Responsible for Putting the "Responsible" into AI?

This book argues that responsibility in AI is a systems-level concern. That is, there is no one set of stakeholders that has ownership of responsible AI. It is not solely down to the AI experts who develop the models and algorithms—although they certainly play a large part. Neither is it solely down to ethicists. Many companies have experimented with bringing in AI ethics experts or committees of ethicists. While these roles can certainly contribute to developing AI more responsibly, they are certainly not the only ones. It's not even the purview of managers to ensure that AI is developed and used responsibly. Clearly, managers are critical, but they can't do the work alone.

AI systems will be developed and applied responsibly only if stakeholders of all types and at all levels take responsibility for the effort (pun intended!). This means actors at all levels of an organization developing or using AI as well as users, industry bodies, and governments. There is no one single solution. Everyone needs to play a part. And the solution is likely to be a collection of different approaches, both technical and nontechnical. We agree with Borenstein et al. and others who have called for more interdisciplinarity in the design of AI systems: "In terms of who is currently involved, it is largely computer scientists and engineers… [However,] sociology, economics, philosophy, the law, gender and race studies, and public policy (among other fields) have valuable insights to share."[15] We would go further, however, and stress not just the importance of bringing social scientists in, but also designers, product managers, and governance professionals. And it's important to make sure that each discipline understands its role. If too much emphasis is placed on one group of stakeholders, there is a danger that responsibility for AI will be deferred to others. For example, software engineers might wrongly assume that the ethics team will deal with responsible AI. Or middle managers might think that ethical considerations are "above their pay grade" and will be handled by senior management.[16]

In short, everyone is responsible for responsible AI—which makes it, unfortunately, a fiendishly difficult problem to address. It also means that for a company adopting or developing AI, the buck ultimately stops with the CEO and company board.

About This Book

When it comes to developing AI responsibly, the good news is that there is now widespread recognition of the need to consider ethical considerations in AI. High-profile cases of irresponsible AI in the media—such as those mentioned earlier in this chapter—have highlighted the need to take these issues more seriously. As a result, the academic community and industry have responded. For example, the premier international conference for AI researchers, International Joint Conference on AI (IJCAI), introduced a special track on AI for Good in 2022, and also trialed a process for ethical review of submitted research papers to flag any problematic uses of AI in the submissions. More generally, AI experts are now writing more and sharing more about approaches for responsible AI: a CSIRO report in 2022, for example, highlighted ethical AI as one of six future trends for the development of AI.[17]

The not-so-good news is that there are now thousands of papers written on responsible AI, which present hundreds of possible solutions. Many companies have developed their own ethical AI frameworks. And there are already tens of books written specifically on the topic of ethical AI. (The irony of writing another one is not lost on us!) As a result, practitioners wishing to rely on best practices for responsible AI don't know where to start.

One of our main aims with this book is to provide a comprehensive reference for those interested in developing AI systems responsibly. We have combed the literature so you don't have to, and we have distilled best practices in responsible AI as a set of patterns that you can use and adapt to your own context. Each of these patterns describes a high-level solution to a challenge encountered

15. J. Borenstein et al., "AI Ethics: A Long History and a Recent Burst of Attention," *Computer* 54, no. 1 (2021): 96–102, DOI: 10.1109/MC.2020.3034950.

16. W. Hussain et al., "Human Values in Software Engineering: Contrasting Case Studies of Practice," *IEEE Transactions on Software Engineering* 48, no. 5 (2022): 1818–33.

17. S. Hajkowicz et al., *Artificial Intelligence for Science—Adoption Trends and Future Development Pathways,* CSIRO Data61, Brisbane, Australia, 2022.

when designing, implementing, and/or managing AI systems. You can think of each pattern as a template that provides a starting point addressing a key issue related to responsible AI. The template won't solve your problem for you, but it will give you a framework that can be adapted to suit your own needs. Each template goes beyond the current high-level principles that categorize current approaches to responsible AI. Indeed, the patterns provide possible ways of implementing those principles in practice. The patterns explicitly call out which principles they help to implement; in this book, we use the Australian AI Ethics Principles as reference, but you can easily adapt the patterns to other well-known ethics principles.

The complete set of patterns—and there are 62 of them in this book—can be used in combination to develop AI systems in a more responsible way. It is not expected that all AI systems will use all patterns; rather, it is up to you to decide which combination of these patterns is most useful for your particular situation. If you like, you can think of the pattern catalogue as a source of inspiration.

The book is divided into chapters, with the bulk of those representing a catalogue of patterns sorted by theme.

In Chapter 2, we go through a thought experiment using Robbie the Robot to explain the things to think about when it comes to responsible AI, including governance considerations, process considerations, and product considerations.

Chapter 3 provides more detail about what it means to operationalize responsible AI in practice and gives an overview on the Responsible AI Pattern Catalogue. We explain how responsible AI is a holistic challenge, which must be addressed from a range of different perspectives: governance, product, and process.

Governance concerns how AI systems are managed, either at a team level, within an organization, or at a society level via industry associations or government regulations. Governance is less concerned with the technical specifications of an AI system (and how that relates to responsible AI) and more concerned with how people, systems, and practices are managed to ensure that issues of responsible AI are properly identified, monitored, and mitigated at all times. Chapter 4 presents a catalogue of patterns specifically designed to address issues of governance of AI systems.

Process concerns relate to how AI systems are conceived, designed, operated, and tested. The process of developing an AI system can be divided into the traditional phases of systems engineering: requirements, design, implementation, testing, and operation. Each of these phases can affect how ethical an AI system turns out to be. The literature already contains many possible solutions focused on each of these different process phases. Chapter 5 collects best practices together as a set of process patterns, each pattern specifically addressing one or more phases of the systems engineering lifecycle.

Product patterns are solutions for the systems-level design of responsible AI systems. Problems related to responsible AI can appear at any stage in the design process—whether that's sketching out in high-level terms how an AI system will operate, or whether it's lower-level decisions about which off-the-shelf components will be used to implement the system. Chapter 6 collects together some of the better-known patterns for addressing product design challenges of responsible AI systems. Chapter 7 provides a comprehensive reference of reusable solutions for designing and building AI systems in a responsible way. The reference architecture is composed of three parts, including the deployed AI system, the operation infrastructure that provides auxiliary functions to the AI system, and the software supply chains that generate the software components that compose the AI system. Chapter 8 summarizes the principle-specific techniques to address the responsible AI concerns around models and data, primarily on fairness, privacy, and explainability, which are emerging quality attributes for AI systems. These techniques can be embedded as product features of AI systems and viewed as product patterns.

How to Read This Book

Much of this book—namely, Chapters 4–8—form a reference manual. As such, we do not necessarily recommend reading this book from start to finish. Chapter 2 is an easy introduction, using a fun example to illustrate key concepts. Chapter 3 describes the approach and background on the importance of considering responsible AI from all perspectives. Chapter 7 provides a reference architecture; —that is, it shows how combinations of the patterns from Chapters 4–6 and 8 can be used together to address a particular AI system. Patterns are not meant to be used individually, and no single pattern can provide a complete solution. Indeed, there is no guarantee that, even if all patterns are used, an AI system will be "fully responsible." Rather, as a creator of an AI system, you must use your judgment to select those patterns that make more sense in your particular context. The reference architecture gives some hints on how to do this in terms of which types of combinations typically go together.

A good place to start in this book, after reading Chapters 2–3, is Chapters 9–11. Each of these chapters presents a real-world case study of responsible AI in practice. Each case study is written by a group of guest authors who describe a particular example illustrating how they addressed responsible AI concerns in practice and relate their experience to the pattern catalogue in terms of which patterns were (or could have been) used in the case study. Chapter 9 introduces a risk-based RAI approach adopted by Telstra, Australia's largest telecommunications company. In Chapter 10, Reejig, a workforce intelligence platform startup company, shares their ethical talent AI approach and explains how Reejig manages the bias issues present in datasets and algorithms through a three-stage debiasing strategy. Chapter 11 presents guidelines on diversity and inclusion in AI developed by CSIRO, Australia's national science agency. There are a few examples illustrating how the guidelines are mapped to the patterns. This chapter is highly valuable because it sheds light on how organizations can promote diversity and inclusion in AI by leveraging the guidelines and the Responsible AI Pattern Catalogue.

Finally, Chapter 12 takes a step back and looks at where responsible AI as a field is likely to go in the next few years. It's an exciting time to be working in AI and even more exciting to be at the forefront of developing AI systems responsibly. We hope that this book will provide you with concrete ideas for how to develop your own AI systems responsibly so that we all together adopt AI to build a world that is positive and uplifting for our future generations.

2

Operationalizing Responsible AI: A Thought Experiment—Robbie the Robot

Before we delve into the details of how to operationalize responsible AI principles, this chapter presents an example, designed to illustrate the complexity of responsible AI, and the broad range of stakeholders that need to be involved in the process. We hope you will find this example both fun and illustrative.

A Thought Experiment—Robbie the Robot

To illustrate just how complex the operationalization of responsible AI principles is—and how many different perspectives need to be taken into account—let's walk through a thought experiment. For this experiment, we use Robbie the Robot, the nonspeaking robot introduced by Dr. Susan Calvin in Isaac Asimov's classic book *I, Robot*.

Robbie is a children's robot, designed to play with and take care of kids. Without the ability to speak, Robbie finds other ways to communicate. As Susan Calvin says in the prelude to the chapter on Robbie: "Robbie had no voice. He was a nonspeaking robot. Robbie was made to take care of children. He was a nanny...."[1]

---

1. I. Asimov, *I, Robot* (Gnome Press, 1950), 1st Edition, page 11, 2 December 1950.

The first chapter in *I, Robot* then goes on to tell a story of a young girl, Gloria, and her friendship with Robbie. We first find them playing hide-and-seek in Gloria's garden. Gloria is incredibly fond of Robbie, remarking at one point in the chapter: "He was *not* only a machine. He was my *friend!*"[2] But Gloria's mother, Mrs. Weston, is suspicious of Robbie. Although Robbie has been with the family for two years—and there have been no issues—Mrs. Weston gradually starts to worry that Robbie might do something unexpected, and might even harm Gloria.

> "I don't want a machine to take care of my daughter. Nobody knows what it's thinking." She tells her husband. And then: "I wasn't worried at first. But something might happen and that…that thing will go crazy and…"[3]

In the end, Mrs. Weston sends Robbie back to the manufacturer, US Robots. This action upsets Gloria, who really misses him. To try to show Gloria that Robbie is just "some pieces of metal with electricity," Mr. and Mrs. Weston take Gloria to the factory where Robbie was made and is now being used to manufacture other robots. Things don't go according to plan, however. When Gloria sees Robbie, she runs toward him, not noticing a huge tractor on the factory floor, which would have run her over were it not for Robbie, who, seeing Gloria in danger, rescues her. Mr. and Mrs. Weston are forced to take Robbie back to the house, and Gloria is reunited with her best friend.

Although the story of Robbie was originally published in 1940, and predicted a future where children would have robot nannies, we still don't. And to create one remains fiendishly difficult, both from a technical perspective (we still struggle to get robots to carry out seemingly simple tasks such as playing a game of hide-and-seek) and from a perspective of responsibility (how can Mrs. Weston be confident that Robbie won't go "crazy" and hurt her daughter?). The trope of kids befriending robots has since been explored extensively in popular entertainment, in movies such as *The Iron Giant, Big Hero 6,* and *Earth to Echo*. In many of these stories, the robot AI does indeed go "crazy" and bad things happen; the recent movie *M3GAN* is a good example in the horror genre.

Who Should Be Involved in Building Robbie?

In the remainder of this chapter, we use Robbie the Robot as an example to consider where responsible AI issues come up. Let's consider things from the perspective of US Robots, the company that created Robbie.

As discussed earlier in this chapter, a diverse set of stakeholders need to be involved in building, using, and managing an AI system such as Robbie the Robot. Each stakeholder has knowledge that will contribute to making sure that Robbie is designed responsibly. Table 2.1 lists some of the stakeholders that US Robots should include, as well as the key contributions each of these stakeholders can make when it comes to designing Robbie in a responsible way.

---

2. I. Asimov, *I, Robot* (Gnome Press, 1950), 1st Edition, page 16, 2 December 1950.

3. I. Asimov, *I, Robot* (Gnome Press, 1950), 1st Edition, page 15, 2 December 1950.

Table 2.1   Stakeholders of Robbie

Stakeholder Type	Role	Responsible AI Contribution	Type of Contribution
US Robots Company Board	To manage the reputation and market risks of developing Robbie	Ensures that a risk management framework is set up and monitored to assess, mitigate, and manage risks associated with Robbie's deployment in family settings	Governance
Government	To ensure the safety of the general public	Enacts laws that regulate how family robots are designed, manufactured, and used	Governance
Industry Bodies	To produce standards for robotics companies to follow	Creates standards for family robots that member organizations agree to follow	Governance
Parent Groups	To advise parents on the use of Robbie and to lobby government on appropriate legislation	Sets up information sharing for parents, e.g., workshops, web portals	Governance
VP Ethics	US Robots executive who ensures the company has a reputation for responsible AI	Defines and rolls out training and practices for responsible AI across the company; may include independent testing of Robbie features before release	Process
COO	US Robots executive responsible for effective and efficient processes within the company	Implements recommendations from the VP Ethics to ensure company practices include responsible AI considerations	Process
Product Manager	Team member who makes decisions as to which features go into Robbie (e.g., what its objectives are, what the constraints are)	Sets up and manages a process to get customer input on desired features and works with technical experts on feasibility	Process
Project Manager	Team member who manages the development of Robbie over time, ensuring delivery of features according to an agreed-upon schedule	Ensures that the project plan includes key check-in points to consider issues related to responsible AI	Process
Technical Manager	Team member who manages the technical teams developing Robbie to deliver agreed-upon features	Ensures best-practice responsible AI guidelines (coding practices, appropriate use of off-the-shelf components) are used	Product
Data Scientist	Team member who manages the data that Robbie is trained on to carry out tasks	Ensures, as far as possible, that training data is representative of the broader population and not biased to one segment of society	Product
AI Expert	Team member who develops AI models to process data	Monitors AI model performance for bias	Product
Software Engineer	Team member who manages the integration of Robbie into US Robots' larger software systems as required	Ensures that best-practice responsible AI software patterns are used	Process
General Public	Users of Robbie	Provides feedback to US Robots to ensure that any responsible AI issues are fixed	Governance
Suppliers	Other manufacturers or AI technology/solution providers	Ensures the supplied product components are without any responsible AI issues	Governance

As Table 2.1 shows, responsible AI is complex: many stakeholders need to be involved. The good news, however, is that this is no different to any complex systems engineering task. Building skyscrapers, flying airplanes, implementing large-scale government information systems—these are all examples of complex engineering projects that society operates routinely today. And, over time, society has agreed upon sets of rigorous processes and methods to ensure that such systems are safe, secure, and operate as expected. The only difference with responsible AI is that AI is a fast-moving technology, so we do not yet have a full set of rigorous practices. (This book, of course, partially fills that gap!)

What Are the Responsible AI Principles for Robbie?

The first step in ensuring that Robbie implements AI responsibly is for US Robots to agree to a high-level set of responsible AI principles. These could be Australia's AI Ethics Principles, as described in Chapter 1, or they could be something company- or context-specific. In his book, Asimov famously captured the operating principles of US Robots as the Three Laws of Robotics, codified in the Handbook of Robotics, 2058 AD:

1. A robot must not harm a human. And it must not allow a human to be harmed.

2. A robot must obey a human's order, unless that order conflicts with the First Law.

3. A robot must protect itself, unless this protection conflicts with the First or Second Laws.[4]

These Robot Laws were encoded in Robbie's positronic brain to ensure that they would be followed. For a modern engineering firm creating a robot like Robbie, these laws could well serve as high-level principles to follow. But to encode them in the design and operation of a robot, they need to be made more concrete (i.e., the laws must be operationalized).

To some extent, Asimov's laws can be related to modern AI ethics principles. Table 2.2, for example, maps them to Australia's AI Ethics Principles. Note that some of Asimov's laws map in a fairly straightforward manner. It becomes quickly clear, however, that Asimov's laws are actually quite narrow. Other than the safety of humans, they say nothing about what is considered societally appropriate behavior by Robbie. For example, one would expect Robbie, as a child's companion, to act and teach in a way that is considered proper. In modern-day AI systems, in contrast, there is a lot of concern about whether AI systems will exhibit behavior that is discriminatory, biased, unfair, or socially unacceptable. None of this concern is captured in Asimov's laws. Arguably, this kind of behavior could be included under the First Law, but this depends on the definition of *harm*, which in Asimov's book is largely focused on physical safety.

---

4. I. Asimov, *I, Robot* (Gnome Press, 1950), 1st Edition, page 9, 2 December 1950.

Table 2.2 Mapping Asimov's Laws to Australia's AI Ethics Principles

AI Ethics Principle	Description	Sample Problematic Behaviors in Robbie Context	Covered by Asimov's Laws?
Human, societal, and environmental well-being	AI systems should benefit individuals, society, and the environment.	Robbie causes problems with children, such as child safety or psychological dependency.	Partially—First Law covers physical safety but not broader well-being issues.
Human-centered values	AI systems should respect human rights, diversity, and the autonomy of individuals.	Robbie does not encourage children to assert their right of freedom of speech.	No—Laws say nothing about human rights.
Fairness	AI systems should be inclusive and accessible, and should not involve or result in unfair discrimination against individuals, communities, or groups.	Robbie treats children from different backgrounds differently.	No—Laws say nothing about diversity in end users.
Privacy protection and security	AI systems should respect and uphold privacy rights and data protection, and ensure the security of data.	Robbie collects data from the child and shares with the company.	No—Laws do not cover privacy.
Reliability and safety	AI systems should reliably operate in accordance with their intended purpose.	Robbie fails to rescue Gloria from the tractor due to a malfunction.	Partially—Second Law somewhat covers "intended purpose" but does not explicitly address malfunctions.
Transparency and explainability	There should be transparency and responsible disclosure so people can understand when they are being significantly impacted by AI, and can find out when an AI system is engaging with them.	Robbie fails to tell Mrs. Weston that he has been cheating Gloria at hide-and-seek.	Partially—Second Law guarantees that Robbie explains his actions but only if explicitly asked.
Contestability	When an AI system significantly impacts a person, community, group, or environment, there should be a timely process to allow people to challenge the use or outcomes of the AI system.	Mrs. Weston is unable to get Robbie to teach Gloria in a way that she wants.	Partially—Second Law guarantees a challenge of Robbie's outcomes but only if explicitly asked.
Accountability	People responsible for the different phases of the AI system lifecycle should be identifiable and accountable for the outcomes of the AI systems, and human oversight of AI systems should be enabled.	US Robots fails to put appropriate procedures in place to ensure Robbie follows the three laws.	No.

Robbie and Governance Considerations

Putting aside Asimov's Laws for a moment, as they are clearly incomplete for our purposes, let's move forward assuming the AI ethics principles in Table 2.2 are our driver.

Table 2.1 identifies six stakeholders relevant to Governance. Let's consider just one of these, the company board. Like any board, the main purpose of the board of US Robots is to set the strategic direction of the company and to ensure that the company is operating within all relevant laws, ethically, and in a way that safeguards the reputation and financial sustainability of the company.

Imagine, then, the position of the CEO of US Robots. She's just had a brilliant idea: to create a new robot, which will be called Robbie, that will act as a child's nanny. It could be a big money-spinner for the company and could really place US Robots on the map as a global leader in robotics technologies. The only remaining question is what will the board think? In many ways, the board's main job is to think about what can go wrong and make sure that the CEO has a plan to deal with any potential threats. In the case of Robbie, the board can imagine a *lot* that can go wrong. Robbie could accidentally hurt a child; he's a heavy piece of metal, after all, and could easily put one of his heavy metal feet in the wrong place. Or Robbie could inflict psychological damage on a child by inadvertently creating an emotional dependency. How will Robbie protect children from harm caused by others? Are Robbie's computer vision systems good enough to identify all harmful objects correctly, or will he miss one? Robbie can't speak, so there is less risk that he will fill the child's head with inappropriate thoughts, but there's still a risk of not being inclusive; he'll need to be programmed with all the different customs and traditions of children from different ethnic and religious backgrounds. And what if Robbie breaks the law? Will the company ultimately be responsible? What HR practices should the board ensure are in place to reprimand engineers who build the wrong mechanisms into Robbie?

It isn't the board's job to provide answers to all of these questions. That is the CEO's job. The board, however, needs to make sure that the questions are asked—and that someone has the answers.

Fortunately, the board is a sophisticated one. Board members gather all the relevant experts together and come up with a plan of action. The board directs the CEO to do the following:

- Develop a responsible AI risk assessment (see G.12. RAI Risk Assessment). One way to do this is to start with the AI ethics principles in Table 2.2 and then imagine all the things that can go wrong. Each of them represents a risk; the board agrees to a risk likelihood and impact severity in each case, and considers mitigation actions that can be put in place to reduce the overall risk rating.

- Introduce ethics training across Project Robbie (see G.13. RAI Training). The board is aware that their workforce is diverse. It includes graduates fresh out of college who are up to speed with the latest technological developments but, as primarily technical specialists, may not have any background or training in the social impacts of technology. The company also includes many staff who have worked for the company for years; they have a good sense of the company's core customer needs but may not be up to speed on the latest technological developments and, in particular, the ethical risks associated with them. So, the board decides that everyone working on Project Robbie should undergo mandatory ethics training.

- Set up an ethics committee as a subcommittee of the board (see G.10. RAI Risk Committee). The board realizes that it has too many things to worry about to leave ethics to the board itself. So it delegates responsibility to an ethics committee, whose job is to oversee the implementation of Robbie in a responsible way. But to make sure that the board has visibility and remains accountable, the ethics committee will be composed of a subset of board members and will be chaired by the most relevant board member. It is at this point that the board members realize they do not have enough ethics expertise on the board, so they go back and revise their board skills matrix to include ethics, and the chair goes out to recruit a new board member with the requisite experience who can chair the subcommittee. No work on Project Robbie will commence until this is done.

The CEO explains to the board that Project Robbie is complex, at a scale unlike anything the company has tackled before. "We can't build Robbie by ourselves," the CEO explains, and she goes on to explain that US Robots will need to procure components of Robbie from other providers. The board agrees, but to ensure that Robbie remains an exemplar of responsible AI, the board insists that all acquired components go through a rigorous responsible AI evaluation process before considering their use, including how they will interact with other components (see G.15. RAI Bill of Materials).

The board is happy with its decisions. It's been a busy few weeks for board members, figuring out how all of this is going to work, but they are content with the outcome. They are happy to support this new idea from the CEO, and they agree that it could be a new future for the company. But they are also as confident as they can be that Robbie will be developed in a responsible way and that, in particular, there won't be any adverse events that will come back to haunt the company.

The latest board meeting is about to finish. Everyone is happy. Until, almost as an afterthought, the CEO raises a question.

"Have we done enough?" she asks the chair.

"What do you mean? We're implementing all these measures."

"Yes," continues the CEO. "But are they enough? Is there more we can do?"

"I can't think of anything," says another board member.

The board chair reflects for a moment and then, like the wise experienced executive that she is, she says: "I can't think of anything either. But that doesn't mean there isn't anything. Maybe we are just not seeing it. Let's do two things. First, we'll get an independent review of our plan by experts in the field to make sure it holds water. Second, we'll have a quarterly review at board meetings to make sure it's working and there's nothing we're forgetting."

The board meeting ends, and the exciting work on creating Robbie, the children's nanny robot, begins.

Robbie and Process Considerations

Is the company's work on responsible AI done? After all, the board and the CEO have put in place rigorous mechanisms to assess and track the risks associated with Robbie's development. Things should be fine, right?

Of course, the company's work is far from done. In fact, it is just beginning. Governance considerations have been taken care of, but what about process issues? The CEO summons her VP Ethics and COO.

"I have some exciting news," starts the CEO. "The board has just approved that we can go ahead with Robbie!"

"That's fantastic," says the VP Ethics. "But now we have some *real* work to do."

The CEO, VP Ethics, and COO agree to put a working group together, containing key experts and stakeholders from across the company, to define a process approach to developing Robbie. It takes a few months, and some in the company are frustrated that development on Robbie can't start until the process considerations are resolved, but the CEO is firm: "We must get the processes right before starting."

The working group reports back to the CEO, who takes the recommendations to the board. Recommendations include

- **Verifiable Responsible AI Requirements** (see P.2. Verifiable RAI Requirement): The first issue the working group addresses is that the definition of AI Ethics is too vague to measure. The working group's recommendation is that the business analyst team develop a set of verifiable ethical AI requirements. For example, the group says, the ethical AI principle, transparency, could partially be satisfied by a requirement that Robbie includes a parent app where parents can review all Robbie's interactions with their children.

- **A Rigorous Data Lifecycle** (see P.3. Lifecycle-driven Data Requirement): The working group realizes that Robbie needs to respect different cultural traditions (as captured in one of the verifiable ethical AI requirements!). So the group defines a process for careful management of the data lifecycle—what data is collected, how it is managed, who has access, and so on—so that the data loaded into Robbie initially, as well as the way that Robbie collects additional data through sensing, is diverse and treats people from different cultural backgrounds equally.

- **Responsible Design** (see P.7. RAI Design Modeling): The working group also recommends that the responsible AI requirements are considered throughout the design process. They suggest a suite of processes for designing features that ensures the designers put responsible AI first, not let it be an afterthought.

- **Responsible AI Simulation** (see P.8. System-Level RAI Simulation): The working group strongly recommends that the company's simulation platforms, which it currently uses to simulate robotic interactions before deployment, are updated to build in ethical AI considerations. The working group is excited by the prospects here; they suggest using an AI simulator to run what-if scenarios and measure compliance to the verifiable ethical requirements over as many scenarios as possible. "We're using AI to test AI," they muse.

- **Software Engineering Process** (see P.10. RAI Governance of APIs, P.12. RAI Construction with Reuse, P.16. Extensible, Adaptive, and Dynamic RAI Risk Assessment): The working group takes a good look at the company's existing software engineering processes. Group members quickly realize that responsible AI is not built in. So the working group consults with relevant stakeholders and comes up with adaptations to existing engineering processes to make sure that responsible AI is the primary consideration. Changes include the reuse of AI assets (to ensure that best-practice responsible AI is reused across the development), AI risk assessment at all levels of development (not just done once and forgotten), and a new process for testing Robbie's APIs to ensure there are no privacy leaks.

The board invites the working group to a special meeting of the board, where it runs a rigorous process to test the assumptions and recommendations of the working group. The careful probing of the board leads to some improvements, but, ultimately, the board members are happy. The board chair, however, wants visibility of the process implementation.

"Let's introduce regular review points," she says. "We'll do this quarterly so we can see how well the new process is working out, and if there need to be any changes."

Robbie and Product Considerations

At this point, many of the developers and AI experts within US Robots are getting very excited. They've been hearing about this new robot project for months. There are rumors, but there never seems to be any indication of a timeline for starting work on the project. Until, one day, the CEO sends an internal communication to the teams:

> Dear Team,
>
> I am very pleased to inform you that the board has now approved a start date for the development of our latest robot, Robbie. Robbie will be a children's companion robot. It will revolutionize the way that families interact with robots. This is an opportunity to change the world! But we must do this responsibly. And so, we have spent the last few months being rigorous about how we will ensure that Robbie does no harm.
>
> We are now ready to embark on this adventure, and I look forward to working with you all on what will be a challenging but exciting initiative.

US Robots is abuzz with enthusiasm.

But the development teams know there is a lot of hard work ahead. They also know that the first, and most important, consideration is to make sure Robbie is developed ethically. The teams have been undergoing mandatory ethics training for many weeks now. There have been constant communications from the executive team about the importance of responsible AI—not just in the Robbie project, but in all projects. And line managers have asked all their staff to write clear objectives in their annual plans about how they will contribute to responsible AI.

The product manager and project manager for Robbie get together to agree on a way forward. They have been briefed on the new process, with responsible AI built in, that they will follow. But many system-level design decisions still need to be made. And the product and project managers are insistent that these also should put responsible AI first. They decide to do the following:

- Ensure responsible AI is built into Robbie's supply chain (see D.1, RAI Bill of Materials Registry). Robbie's development will be highly dependent on external providers, both of hardware and software components. A project as complex as Robbie can't be delivered by a single company, even one as large as US Robots. "We need to make sure all external components are developed to the same high standards when it comes to responsible AI," says the product manager, sensibly.

- Build in *kill switches* at multiple levels (see D.5. AI Mode Switcher). The project manager is concerned that, even if rigorous responsible AI practices are properly followed, situations outside the team's control may still come up once Robbie is active. "We should build in *kill switches*, both local and remote ones, so that, if anything doesn't look right, we can shut down different parts of the AI before things get out of hand."

- Build redundancy into critical AI systems (see D.6. Multi-Model Decision-Maker). The product manager: "Any time that Robbie could potentially put a child in harm's way—even if that potential is very remote—we should make sure multiple AI models are running in parallel. This will give us confidence that Robbie is only making critical decisions if all the models agree." The project manager: "We could go further than that, and if the models disagree, activate a *kill switch*."

- Quarantine new features (see D.9. RAI Sandbox). The product manager: "We'll need to introduce new features once Robbie is active in society. There's no way around this; at the very least, it will be needed to fix issues without recalling all versions of Robbie. The project manager agrees and replies, "We should quarantine new features when they are rolled out by isolating it from other critical AI components wherever possible—at least until it's fully tested in the field."

Summary

As you can see, when it comes to responsible AI, there is a lot to think about. Responsible AI isn't the job of a single group of people. Rather, it needs to be embedded at all levels across a company. Neither is responsible AI something you do once and then forget. It is a constant challenge to review and re-review the approach. And, of course, there is a tension between the need to be responsible—and therefore, cautious—and the need to get features out the door and into a product. All of these considerations need to be taken seriously.

The example in this chapter is obviously an idealized scenario. There is no mention of the downsides of introducing governance, process, and product measures to ensure responsible AI. In practice, these measures cost money, and these costs may need to be balanced with the need to get a product out to market—although this, in itself, is an important decision to discuss in the context of responsible AI. One might argue that for-profit companies only care about profit, so many of these measures won't be implemented. However, public and government opinion about responsible AI is clearly changing. It is becoming a competitive advantage to be responsible. And we are likely to see companies measured for it in the same way that they are measured—either formally through Environmental, Social, Governance (ESG) metrics or informally through reputation—for impacts on society.

Good luck, Robbie! We hope that US Robots has done a good job in building your AI responsibly.

PART II

RESPONSIBLE AI PATTERN CATALOGUE

In Part II, we present a Responsible AI Pattern Catalogue for operationalizing responsible AI. Should be overview of the responsible ai pattern catalogue for operationalizing responsible AI. This pattern catalogue includes a collection of patterns that captures the reusable solutions about responsible AI in a structured way for AI system stakeholders to reference. The patterns are classified into three categories: governance patterns, process patterns, and product patterns.

Chapter 4, "Multi-Level Governance Patterns for Responsible AI," discusses the governance patterns for establishing multilevel governance for responsible AI. The patterns are grouped into three levels, including industry-level governance patterns, organization-level governance patterns, and team-level governance patterns.

In Chapter 5, "Process Patterns for Trustworthy Development Processes," we introduce the patterns that can be used at different stages of the AI system development process, including requirements, design, implementation, testing, and operation.

Chapter 6, "Product Patterns for Responsible-AI-by-Design," discusses the product patterns for building responsible-AI-by-design into AI systems. Such patterns can be embedded into the AI systems as product features or a piece of structural design that is across multiple architectural elements.

Chapter 7, "Pattern-Oriented Reference Architecture for Responsible-AI-by-Design," presents a product-pattern-oriented reference architecture for responsible AI systems. The reference architecture can serve as a design guideline to assist architects and developers in designing the architecture of a responsible AI system.

Chapter 8, "Principle-Specific Techniques for Responsible AI," summarizes the principle-specific techniques to address the responsible AI concerns around models and data. The chapter focuses primarily on the techniques to address fairness, privacy, and explainability, which are emerging quality attributes for AI systems.

PART II

3

Overview of the Responsible AI Pattern Catalogue

In this chapter, we explore important aspects of operationalizing responsible AI and give an overview of the Responsible AI Pattern Catalogue.

The Key Concepts

The Multifaceted Meanings of *Responsible*

The word *responsible* has a plurality of meanings that are interrelated but different. If you were to look up the word *responsible* in any dictionary, you would find a half dozen of these meanings. Even when we precisely defined *responsible AI* in Chapter 1, these everyday meanings of *responsible* often play an implicit but important role in understanding the goals and approaches to responsible AI. We categorize these meanings into three main categories:

- **Normative:** Capable of being trusted to be good. As in "a responsible adult," the word has a normative sense of being both good and trustworthy. This is the primary meaning we were invoking when we defined responsible AI as minimizing negative consequences, with the resulting AI system capable of being trusted.

- **Possessive:** Having responsibilities, duties, and obligations. For example, in the statement "The management and developers are both responsible for producing trustworthy AI systems," the meaning points to the responsibilities of the AI system producers. The distribution of responsibilities among different AI producer roles, even to AI users and AI systems, is an important point we discuss later.

- **Descriptive:** Being the primary cause of something and so able to be blamed or credited for it. For example, in the statement "The defective AI software is responsible for the incident," the meaning implies that a cause has been attributed to some AI producers or systems so that they may be blamed for the harm caused.

The word *responsible* in *responsible AI* has a normative meaning that implies being trustworthy and good. This leads people to use responsible AI to mean both *AI for Good* (e.g., using AI to advance the United Nations' Sustainable Development Goals) and *trustworthy AI* (capable of being trusted to perform its task). As a result, AI for Good projects are often considered inherently responsible, and less scrutiny is given to their trustworthiness. However, good intentions do not guarantee a trustworthy AI system, as unintended negative consequences can occur in both well-intentioned AI for Good projects and profit-driven projects.

While the normative meaning is the ultimate goal of responsible AI, the possessive meaning is reflected in most responsible AI principles in the form of accountability, explainability, and answerability of AI systems. Individuals and organizations that play roles in producing an AI system must share responsibility for its actions. They need to justify and explain why they chose to develop an AI system in the first place, as well as the decisions and actions the AI system takes. These justifications and explanations should be tailored to the audience's literacy level in technology and AI.

When we seek to improve an AI system and take corrective measures, it is essential to understand the cause of harm to an individual, a group, or society as a whole. The descriptive meaning of *responsible* refers to the attribution of cause involving an AI system or its components and the associated roles or organizations. This meaning is reflected in the principles of transparency, contestability, accountability, and explainability in both general and specific contexts and incidents.

Although the various meanings of the word *responsible* can sometimes cause people to talk past each other, the sum of all its relevant meanings covers different aspects of the noble goals of responsible AI, including good intentions, harm reduction, trustworthiness for the AI system, and identification of the causes of harm to enable corrective measures. These goals are reflected in various responsible AI principles.

Varied Understandings of *Operationalization*

What about the term *operationalization*? Many people express frustration that high-level principles are not practical enough and demand that they be operationalized. However, in the fields of regulation, policy-making, and standards, a principle-based approach is gaining popularity, especially in rapidly evolving technology domains where a prescriptive and ready-to-use approach may soon become obsolete. A principle-based system allows for technology-neutral, context-independent, and future-proof guidance to be put forward, while still enabling context-specific interpretation and practices during operationalization. Therefore, a principle-based approach to responsible AI is necessary. However, we must improve our ability to operationalize these principles, which is complicated by several factors.

One of the factors that makes it difficult to create a simple, prescriptive approach to operational-izing responsible AI is the diverse range of stakeholders involved in building, using, monitoring, and understanding these systems. These stakeholders include AI experts, software engineers, DevOps engineers, product managers, technical managers, executives, boards, investors, AI system procur-ers, AI system users, impacted individuals, regulators, social scientists, ethicists, legal professionals, civil societies, and the general public. Operationalizing responsible AI requires more than just the practices of AI experts; it requires governance at all levels, including incentives from procurers and investors, monitoring from regulators, civil societies, and the general public, and the ability of AI users and impacted individuals to understand, examine, and contest any issues.

All these stakeholders require different concrete practices that operate at varying levels of abstrac-tion and are tailored to their concerns and level of AI literacy. Ideally, these practices should be connected to provide complementary means of assurance, control, and monitoring to achieve the ultimate goal. Simply exposing all the practices for responsible AI to anyone, even experts, would be overwhelming. Conversely, developing practice areas in isolation creates risk management silos (such as responsible AI and data privacy or cybersecurity), overlapping competing efforts, and over-looked gaps.

Let's examine a few examples of these levels in more detail.

At the AI expert level (such as data scientists and engineers), algorithmic approaches that use mathematical analysis of data, algorithms, and models help to quantify properties such as fairness, bias, re-identification/privacy, and security risks. However, this approach is often limited to a nar-row set of properties amenable to mathematical definitions and analysis. Additionally, there are two key challenges: (1) different stakeholders disagree on the correct definition and metrics for these properties, such as fairness, which is too multifaceted and context-specific to be reduced to a few metrics; and (2) property guarantees at the data, algorithm, or model level do not lead to system-level guarantees because many more parts of a complex system (including non-AI components and human interactions) come into play in causing the final impact and risks. Nevertheless, quantifying these data-, algorithm-, or model-level properties as inputs to broader risk assessments is crucial. Technical experts in safety, security, and reliability, and increasingly in fairness, privacy, and explain-ability, have accumulated a wealth of knowledge in minimizing risks at the data, algorithm, or model level.

At the next level, software engineers and technical managers require software engineering prac-tices for embedding data, AI algorithms (such as deep learning algorithms), and machine learning models into larger components and systems that interact with many other non-AI systems and humans to fulfill the system-level responsible AI requirements. They need to verify and validate these requirements during development and postdeployment to minimize negative consequences. Verifying, validating, and monitoring non-AI complex systems are already notoriously difficult, and the additional challenges of AI and the amorphous responsible AI requirements make these tasks even more challenging. We expand on these challenges in later sections.

Moving up further, executives and boards require different practices, methods, and tools to manage and govern responsible AI risks. For example, they may need a list of informed questions to ask and best practices in assessing the answers at a very high level of abstraction. They may also need an updated risk management framework that can consider AI risks and some high-level measures and metrics that they could monitor through dashboards and regular reports.

Finally, at the industry/society level, regulators, civil societies, impacted individuals, and concerned members of the public have their own unique needs. Regulators and civil societies are often resource-constrained and do not have full access to the AI system of concern. Impacted individuals and concerned individuals are primarily nontechnical, so they need their own practices and tools to protect themselves, identify and report issues, and contribute meaningfully to the overall health of the responsible AI ecosystem. Ideally, the various responsible AI practices across the algorithm, system, governance, and industry or society level reinforce each other. In reality, risk management silos and practice silos often exist, not to mention the lack of best practices and tools in some areas.

Another important aspect to consider is the need for clarity on what constitutes concrete practices. What may seem concrete at one level may be very abstract at another. For instance, the list of questions a board can ask may be very concrete relative to high-level abstract principles for the board, but it may be seen as abstract by management and technical teams who need more detailed guidance for their work.

Checklists and information-sharing templates, such as model cards and data sheets, are often proposed as concrete practices. However, checklists and templates work only if practitioners have an agreed-upon and trustworthy technical approach for completing each item on the list. Checklists are primarily intended as memory aids or prompts for discussion, requiring good techniques to ensure the quality of the steps taken rather than ad hoc or superficial steps taken at an individual's discretion. When empirical studies show checklists working effectively, the reason is that high-quality and standardized practices are being faithfully executed behind each check mark. Conversely, when people criticize a compliance checklist mentality, they typically mean that there is no substance or scrupulous practitioners behind each check mark.

These examples illustrate the key element of operationalization: the need for high-quality, reusable, lower-level practices to connect with higher-level practices such as checklist items, governance questions, templates, and guidelines.

The connections are not just here to provide guidance and substance across levels. The outputs of one practice may need to be shared with other stakeholders within an organization, with regulators, communities, or across supply chains. You have to ensure that the outputs of one practice are understandable and processable by the receiving side. More importantly, the information needs to be trustworthy, and the receiving side needs to trust the supplier to some degree. This brings up another two often misunderstood concepts: trust and trustworthiness.

The Duality of Trust and Trustworthiness

Trust and *trustworthiness* are often used interchangeably and intuitively in responsible AI. But they are different. Let's use a simple example. Imagine you have a friend named Bob.

Trust is like your subjective belief that Bob will do what you expect him to do. For example, if you lend him your favorite book, you trust that he will take care of it and return it back to you.

Trustworthiness is more about how likely it is that Bob will actually do what you expect. If Bob has always returned things he borrowed in the past, then he's likely to be trustworthy.

In the context of AI systems, trust is how much you subjectively believe that an AI system will work the way you expect it to. For instance, if you have a self-driving car, you trust that it will drive you to your destination safely.

Trustworthiness of an AI system is more about how well the system has been designed and built to actually do what it's supposed to do. If your self-driving car has been built with good practices, then it's more likely to be trustworthy.

However, trust and trustworthiness might not always match up. You might trust the AI system too much (overtrusting) or too little (undertrusting) compared to how trustworthy it actually is.

For example, you might think your self-driving car will perfectly avoid all accidents (overtrusting), but no system can guarantee that 100 percent. On the other hand, you might believe that the car will get you into an accident (undertrusting), but if it was well designed and tested, this is less likely to happen.

In any case, you would probably use the self-driving car only if your trust in it is above a certain level. If your trust in the system is low compared to what it can actually do, the reason could be that the system wasn't designed or built properly, or it could be that you have unrealistic expectations of what the technology can do.

Many practitioners and responsible AI approaches solely focus on ensuring the system's trustworthiness by achieving the desired properties in alignment with responsible AI principles. However, the preceding definition highlights the importance of a truster's realistic expectations and subjective estimation. When it comes to expectations, an AI system may have a high level of trustworthiness, but it may not meet the reasonable or unreasonable expectations of the truster. For example, even if an autonomous car system performs three times better than humans on average, the public may expect it to be ten times better than humans and have zero chance of making mistakes in exceptional cases, such as hitting a rule-abiding pedestrian. Subjective estimation is also critical, and many factors can affect it. A lack of first-party or third-party evidence that the truster can truly comprehend may lead to a lack of appreciation for the trustworthiness of an AI system.

In summary, responsible AI approaches should not solely focus on ensuring a system's trustworthiness but also consider the truster's expectations and subjective estimation. Failing to do so can lead to unjustified trust or mistrust in the system. To address this issue, essential practice areas and reusable solutions should be developed to help communicate, convince, and calibrate subjective trust to make it justified. However, this seemingly reasonable goal has been a daunting task for humans for millennia due to the irrationalities of human minds and the challenges in social-technical communication.

Why Is Responsible AI Different?

After exploring the meaning of *responsible* and *operationalization* and delving into the intricacies of trust and trustworthiness, an essential question remains: is responsible AI any different from responsible software or responsible technologies in general? Has society not been attempting to build responsible software/tech for a long time? As Chapter 1 highlighted, computer ethics has been considered since the dawn of computing. While we know that AI systems differ from traditional systems, do they differ enough to require new approaches?

The first clue comes from the observation that many responsible AI principles recur across various frameworks. However, there are several reasons for the need of responsible AI principles:

- First, scale matters.

  For instance, imagine if your medical records were still on paper and in your doctor's cabinet; while there may be a risk of improper access and theft, the impact scale would be relatively small. If these records were then digitalized but scattered across individual doctors' computer systems, the risk would increase as hackers could remotely access them. Now imagine all these records being automatically uploaded into a central system whenever they become available. All doctors can remotely request them (for legitimate reasons to help you), but the central system may be compromised via any connected system in each doctor's office, potentially exposing millions of records. AI may seamlessly connect your medical records across periods, clinics, and even nonmedical data to apply analytics and provide personalized treatment to millions of people. The benefits are enormous, but the potential risks related to security breaches and privacy are also alarming, simply due to the automation and application of AI at scale. This example highlights the need for additional attention to at-scale risks across the board, regardless of any unique AI characteristics.

- Second, AI exacerbates many challenges such as explainability.

  AI solutions are often more complex than traditional systems due to their highly probabilistic, harder-to-explain, and black box nature. The uncertainty and inscrutability make assuring traditional reliability, security, and safety more difficult, not to mention the more amorphous requirements related to well-being and human values. The inscrutability also makes transparency and accountability requirements less meaningful, as simply opening up everything that no one fully understands will not help.

- Third, AI presents unique challenges.

  Compared to traditional software systems, AI systems involve higher degrees of uncertainty and more risks due to its autonomous and opaque decision-making. Generally, AI solves problems autonomously, providing seemingly effective solutions that humans may not fully comprehend. AI can even propose new problems to solve. This paradigm differs radically from the traditional approach of identifying and solving problems using tools that are reasonably understood. With some human agency and autonomy in problem-solving being taken away, retaining meaningful control over the process and the result becomes challenging.

Let's further expand on the preceding points, starting with requirements. Humans have always discovered and specified requirements, including responsible AI requirements. In contrast, in ML-driven approaches, requirements are often hidden in the labeled or unlabeled training data. For labeled data, they are samples of expected input-output pairs that serve as proxies for our requirements and expectations. For unlabeled data in unsupervised learning, we assume there might be hidden patterns that happen to satisfy our requirements. Rather than uncovering the implicit requirements to be confirmed by humans, AI methods only discover a version of the implementation—the learned models. These learned models may seem consistent with the training data but are often inscrutable to humans. The latent requirements, especially responsible AI requirements, lead to concerns about value alignment and unintended consequences. Even more concerning, AI could discover that manipulating and changing human expectations is far easier than finding a solution to satisfy them. A classic example is a recommender engine that manipulates humans into liking extreme content, thus making future predictions easier.

Next, let's consider designing and building responsible AI requirements into the system via quality control. Existing software development best practices have an impressive array of methods to explicitly build quality into software, verified or validated against an explicit set of functional and quality requirements and supported by design rationales. This approach is being extended to ethical AI, where we attempt to imbue AI systems with prescriptive human values and ethics. However, these by-design approaches are not working very well for AI-generated black box solutions where there are fewer meaningful places to inject quality control. This issue is almost inevitable when we hope for the best by merely providing AI training datasets and high-level optimization goals—a hodgepodge of human bias, follies, ingenuity, and underspecified aims. Additionally, some responsible AI requirements are amorphous due to their context-dependent and nonquantifiable nature. For example, fairness is highly dependent on culture, usage context, and an individual's subjective judgment. Human values are harder to be translated to quantifiable system-level and algorithm-level properties to be explicitly built in.

Then how do we apply ethical-by-design approaches and control tactics when AI designs for us with solutions we do not fully comprehend? It requires us to think beyond the existing paradigm and introduce responsible AI practices that should possess attributes that help achieve the following:

- Define responsible AI outcomes and guardrails in contrast to the traditional approaches of specifying problems, ethical requirements, and specifications. AIs solve problems autonomously for us, sometimes even proposing new problems to be solved. We need new methods to engage with diverse users and communities to better select problems, define outcomes, and specify more inclusive goals and guardrails for AI. We can leave the rest to AI, but with better-assured bounds.

- Understand AI-generated solutions rather than setting or solving problems. We need new practices and (AI) tools that different stakeholders can use to interpret, explain, and simplify cryptic AI-based solutions, including their responsible AI characteristics. More importantly, these methods should go beyond the algorithmic level to cover end-to-end lifecycles and help governance and communication with nonexpert stakeholders.

- Embed radical observability and monitorability for governance, not just for error detection and diagnosis. With impenetrable solutions and latent/implicit requirements to check against, we need new approaches to observability and monitorability, especially for the postdeployment of high-risk AI systems. We need new practices for "meaningful" human intervention rather than humans being symbolic liability sponges. We need new approaches to monitor the quality of data input for AI, which is different from traditional rule-based data validation and data quality. Finally, we may have to invent new approaches to studying and controlling mysterious machine behaviors from the outside, just like how social/behavioral scientists study humans and societies without a complete understanding of the human brain.

In the following chapters, you will find product, process, and governance practices in the vein of general software/technology governance tailored to AI systems by adding the preceding attributes.

A Pattern-Oriented Approach for Responsible AI

In this book, we adopt a pattern-oriented approach and build a Responsible AI Pattern Catalogue,[1] as illustrated in Figure 3.1, for operationalizing responsible AI from a systems perspective. In software engineering, a pattern is a reusable solution to a problem commonly occurring within a given context in software development. Many solutions contribute to multiple responsible AI principles. Rather than staying at the ethical principle or algorithm level, we focus on patterns that practitioners and broader stakeholders can undertake to ensure that responsible AI systems are responsibly developed throughout the entire lifecycle with different levels of governance. In this book, the term *patterns* is defined in a broader sense to include not just traditional design patterns, but also any reusable practices within product design, development processes, and governance procedures.

To describe the pattern, we use the classic design pattern template,[2] including summary, context, problem, solution, consequences, related patterns, and known uses. When we use the pattern template, these reusable practices can be effectively captured, documented, and communicated to stakeholders in a structured manner, reflecting contexts and trade-offs that are super important in responsible AI best practices. While we do not explicitly introduce "forces," we discuss them indirectly through the "context" and "problems" associated with each pattern. Furthermore, we list additional information about each pattern in the appendix, including pattern type, objective, target users, impacted stakeholders, lifecycle stages, and relevant principles.

In the template, the type of objective is classified into trust and trustworthiness. When the objective is trustworthiness, the patterns are designed to help that AI system meet responsible AI principles and requirements. On the other hand, when the objective is trust, the patterns aim to provide evidence about processes or products, thereby enhancing trust. It is important to note that while patterns cannot fully address all trust and trustworthiness issues, their primary objective is to work toward achieving them.

---

1. https://research.csiro.au/ss/science/projects/responsible-ai-pattern-catalogue/.

2. E. Gamma et al., *Design Patterns: Elements of Reusable Object-Oriented Software* (Pearson Deutschland GmbH, 1995).

The target users and impacted stakeholders are identified based on the three-level classification of stakeholders in the AI ecosystem, which is discussed in Chapter 4. Furthermore, the relevant principles are determined by referencing the Australian government's AI Ethics Principles.[3] Additionally, the lifecycle stages are identified from the traditional software engineering process, including requirements, design, implementation, testing, and operation.

The approach has the following characteristics.

Across multiple angles: Governance, process, and product. Not only should you use product patterns to directly enforce responsible AI principles within the AI product and verify or validate them, but you should also incorporate process and governance patterns to complement these efforts further:

- **Governance patterns** for establishing multi-level governance for responsible AI;

- **Process patterns** for setting up trustworthy development processes; and

- **Product patterns** for building responsible-AI-by-design into AI systems.

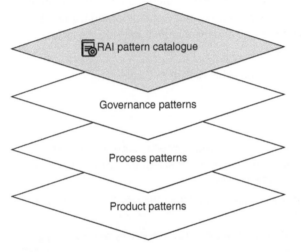

Figure 3.1
Overview of responsible AI pattern catalogue.

Across multiple organization levels and connected: Industry/community, organization, and teams. The patterns we are introducing here are at different levels, so you can situate your practice areas in the bigger picture and see how you fit in and how different practices and patterns influence and reinforce each other from a team, organization, and industry or community level.

---

3. https://www.industry.gov.au/publications/australias-artificial-intelligence-ethics-framework/
australias-ai-ethics-principles.

Across system lifecycle and connected: Requirements, design, implementation, testing, deployment, and postdeployment monitoring. Across the lifecycle of AI systems, different patterns and practices can be applied at other times, with the outputs of one practice becoming the input of another.

Across the supply chain, system, and operation layer and connected: We connect most of the patterns through a system reference architecture across AI supply chain, AI system, and operation/deployment infrastructure layer.

Benefiting multiple connected risks: Individual responsible AI risks should be managed in silos by using risk-specific solutions. The patterns in this book often help multiple risks together to raise the responsible AI posture of the organization significantly.

Acknowledging drawbacks and additional risks introduced: Adopting pattern-oriented risk mitigation may introduce additional risks and costs. We recognize them by incorporating drawbacks in the patterns and connecting with other related ways to tackle the challenges further.

Clear differentiation of trust and trustworthiness: We recognize that the importance of gaining stakeholder trust goes beyond the objective trustworthiness of the systems. Gaining trust is about diverse and inclusive engagement, setting realistic expectations, and communicating trustworthiness evidence in a way that stakeholders can understand and meaningfully critique. We include trust and trustworthiness dimensions in our patterns.

Tables 3.1 through 3.3 provide an overview of the Responsible AI Pattern Catalogue.

Table 3.1   Governance Pattern Overview (see Chapter 4)

Category	Pattern Name	Summary
Industry-Level Governance	RAI Law and Regulation	RAI laws and regulations cover enforceable rules and policies that are issued by an executive authority or regulatory agency of a government to ensure the responsible development and use of AI systems within that jurisdiction.
	RAI Maturity Model	RAI maturity model is used to assess an organization's RAI capabilities and its readiness to utilize AI responsibly.
	RAI Certification	RAI certification can be used as the attestation that an AI entity has met certain specified criteria.
	Regulatory Sandbox	A regulatory sandbox allows for the testing of innovative AI products in a real-world setting.
	Building Code	A building code is a set of rules that establishes the minimum standards for the development and use of an AI system.
	Independent Oversight	Independent oversight involves having an external group review the development and use of AI systems to ensure that they are in compliance with established laws, regulations, or standards.
	Trust Mark	A trust mark is a seal that indicates that an AI system has been endorsed as being compliant with RAI standards.
	RAI Standards	RAI standards are often presented in the form of voluntary documents that provide specifications, procedures, and guidelines to develop responsible AI systems.

Category	Pattern Name	Summary
Organization-Level Governance Patterns	Leadership Commitment for RAI	Achieving leadership commitment to RAI within an organization requires the management team to actively invest their time and effort into building RAI practices within an organization.
	RAI Risk Committee	An RAI risk committee is a group of individuals who are responsible for reviewing and approving proposals of AI projects to ensure the adoption of AI is done in a responsible manner.
	Code of RAI	A code of RAI is a set of guidelines that employees within an organization are expected to follow when developing or operating AI systems.
	RAI Risk Assessment	An RAI risk assessment is conducted to measure the likelihood and consequence of the potential RAI risks associated with the development and use of AI systems.
	RAI Training	RAI training is designed to improve the level of awareness and skill of employees in implementing RAI.
	Role-Level Accountability Contract	A role-level accountability contract is a document that describes the specific roles and responsibilities of individuals or organizations involved in the various stages of the AI system lifecycle.
	RAI Bill of Materials	An RAI bill of materials maintains a list of components used to create an AI software product.
	Standardized Reporting	Organizations should establish standardized processes and templates for informing different stakeholders about the development process and product design of AI systems.
Team-Level Governance Patterns	Customized Agile Process	Agile development processes can be adapted and customized by incorporating RAI principles.
	Tight Coupling of AI and Non-AI Development	The AI and non-AI development sprints and standup meetings need to be closely coordinated.
	Diverse Team	Building a diverse project team can effectively eliminate bias and promote diversity and inclusion in AI systems.
	Stakeholder Engagement	Keeping stakeholders engaged throughout the AI project is essential to building AI systems responsibly.
	Continuous Documentation Using Templates	Continuous documentation is important to track development activities and ensure that the continuously evolving AI systems are responsible.
	Verifiable Claim for AI System Artifacts	A verifiable claim is a statement that supports developers in making an AI system's ethical properties publicly verifiable.
	Failure Mode and Effects Analysis (FMEA)	Failure mode and effects analysis involves conducting a bottom-up risk assessment to identify and analyze RAI risks.
	Fault Tree Analysis (FTA)	Fault tree analysis is a top-down risk assessment method that is used to analyze the root causes of potential RAI risks associated with the development and use of an AI system.

Table 3.2   Process Pattern Overview (see Chapter 5)

Category	Pattern Name	Summary
Requirement Patterns	AI Suitability Assessment	The development team should assess the suitability of using AI in the software system they plan to build.
	Verifiable RAI Requirement	RAI requirements should be expressed in a verifiable way to make the development of AI systems compliant with AI ethics principles.
	Lifecycle-Driven Data Requirement	Data requirements must be clearly defined throughout the data lifecycle, taking into account the ethical considerations and responsibilities of all stakeholders.
	RAI User Story	RAI requirements can be elicited and incorporated into the product backlog in the form of RAI user stories.
Design Patterns	Multi-Level Co-Architecting	Multi-level co-architecting is necessary to ensure the smooth integration of various components, including co-designing AI and non-AI components, as well as co-designing different components within the AI model pipeline.
	Envisioning Card	Envisioning cards are created to assist the development team incorporating human values into the design processes of AI systems.
	RAI Design Modeling	RAI design modeling can be useful for capturing and analyzing ethical principles in the design process.
	System-Level RAI Simulation	System-level RAI simulation is a cost-effective way to comprehend the characteristics and behaviors of AI systems, and to assess potential RAI risks before deploying them in the real world.
	XAI Interface	Explainable AI can be viewed as a human-AI interaction problem and achieved by human-centered interface design.
Implementation Patterns	RAI Governance of APIs	An RAI knowledge base can be built to support the compliance checking for APIs.
	RAI Governance via APIs	Developers can provide AI services in the cloud and control the interactions with these services via APIs.
	RAI Construction with Reuse	It is highly desirable and valuable to ethically reuse the AI artifacts across different applications.
Testing Patterns	RAI Acceptance Testing	RAI acceptance testing is conducted to determine if the ethical requirements of an AI system are met.
	RAI Assessment for Test Cases	All the test cases for RAI acceptance testing should pass RAI assessment.
Operations Patterns	Continuous Deployment for RAI	New versions of AI systems can be seamlessly deployed into production environments by utilizing various deployment strategies that ensure fulfillment of RAI requirements.
	Extensible, Adaptive, and Dynamic RAI Risk Assessment	It is essential to continuously perform risk assessment and mitigation for RAI systems.
	Multi-Level Co-Versioning	Multi-level co-versioning can capture the relationships and dependencies of AI system artifacts at different levels.

Table 3.3   Product Pattern Overview (see Chapter 6)

Category	Pattern Name	Summary
Supply Chain Patterns	RAI Bill of Materials Registry	The RAI bill of materials registry keeps a formal machine-readable record of the supply chain details of the components used in building an AI system.
	Verifiable RAI Credential	Verifiable RAI credentials can be issued by trusted authorities and verified by users or AI systems.
	Co-Versioning Registry	A co-versioning registry can track the co-evolution of components or AI artifacts at different levels.
	Federated Learner	A federated learner preserves data privacy by training models locally on the client devices and formulating a global model on a central server based on the local model updates.
System Patterns	AI Mode Switcher	Adding an AI mode switcher to the AI system offers users efficient invocation and dismissal mechanisms for activating or deactivating the AI component when needed.
	Multi-Model Decision-Maker	A multi-model decision-maker is used to employ different AI models to perform the same task or enable a single decision.
	Homogeneous Redundancy	Deploying redundant AI components is a solution to deal with the highly uncertain AI components that may make unethical decisions or the adversary hardware components that produce malicious data or behave unethically.
Operation Infrastructure Patterns	Continuous RAI Validator	A continuous RAI validator continuously monitors and validates the outcomes of AI systems against the RAI requirements.
	RAI Sandbox	An RAI sandbox can be applied to isolate AI components from non-AI components by running the AI components separately in a safe and isolated environment using virtual machines.
	RAI Knowledge Base	An RAI knowledge base makes meaningful entities and concepts, and their relationships in design, implementation, deployment, and operation of AI systems.
	RAI Digital Twin	An RAI digital twin could be used to perform system-level simulation to understand the behaviors of AI systems and assess potential ethical risks in a cost-effective way.
	Incentive Registry	An incentive registry records the rewards that correspond to the AI system's ethical behavior and outcome of decisions.
	RAI Black Box	Embedding a RAI black box in an AI system is to investigate why and how an AI system caused an accident or a near miss.
	Global-View Auditor	A global-view auditor provides global-view accountability by finding discrepancies among the data collected from multiple AI components or AI systems and identifying liability when negative events occur.

We hope these multi-layer, multi-aspect, multi-stage, and connected patterns can help you better navigate the landscape and achieve responsible AI systems more successfully.

4

Multi-Level Governance Patterns for Responsible AI

The governance of AI that enables responsible AI (RAI) encompasses the structures, processes, and mechanisms that ensure the development and use of AI systems align with AI principles, AI standards, and existing and upcoming laws. As illustrated in Figure 4.1, we have identified a range of RAI governance patterns and classified them into industry-level governance patterns, organization-level governance patterns, and team-level governance patterns, following Shneiderman's classification.[1] Please note that the patterns are not arranged following a specific order. The selection of patterns can be based on the pattern users, context, and problem description. Additionally, AI risk assessment tools, such as CSIRO's Responsible AI Question Bank,[2] can be employed to recommend patterns as risk mitigation solutions.

AI system stakeholders are individuals or groups that can impact or are impacted by the development and use of AI systems. Identifying AI system stakeholders is crucial in AI governance, because different stakeholders may have varying needs and concerns regarding RAI. As shown in Figure 4.2, AI system stakeholders can be categorized into three groups: industry-level stakeholders, organization-level stakeholders, and team-level stakeholders.

---

1. B. Shneiderman, "Responsible AI: Bridging from Ethics to Practice," *Communications of the ACM* 64, no. 8 (2021): 32–35.

2. https://arxiv.org/abs/2305.09300.

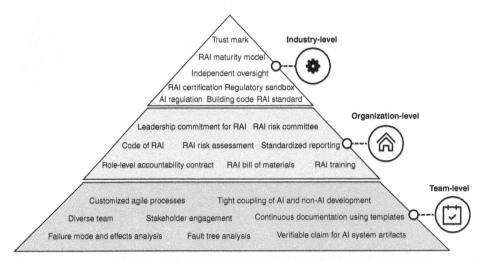

Figure 4.1
Multi-level governance patterns for RAI.

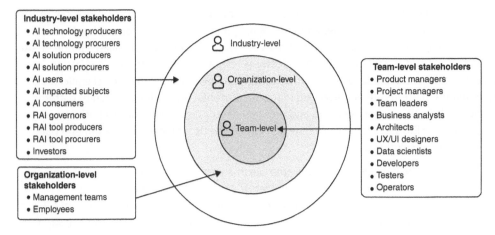

Figure 4.2
Stakeholders for RAI governance.

The industry-level stakeholders include

- **AI technology producers:** Those who develop AI technologies for others to build on top to produce AI solutions (e.g., parts of Google, Microsoft, and IBM). AI technology producers may embed RAI in their technologies and/or provide additional RAI tools.

- **AI technology procurers:** Those who procure AI technologies to build their in-house AI solutions (e.g., companies or government agencies buying and using AI platforms and tools). AI technology procurers may care about RAI issues and embed RAI into their AI technology procurement process.

- **AI solution producers:** Those who develop in-house and blended solutions on top of technologies and need to make sure the solutions adhere to RAI principles, standards, or regulations (e.g., parts of MS/Google providing Office/Gmail "solutions"). AI solution producers may offer the solutions to AI consumers directly or sell to others. They may use RAI tools (provided by tech producers or third parties) and RAI processes during their solution development.

- **AI solution procurers:** Those who procure complete AI solutions (with some further configuration and instantiation) to use internally or offer to external AI consumers (e.g., a government agency buying from a complete solution from vendors). They may care about RAI issues and embed RAI into their AI solution procurement process.

- **AI users:** Those who use an AI solution to make decisions that may impact a subject (e.g., a loan officer or a government employee). AI users may exercise additional RAI oversight as the human in the loop.

- **Investors:** those who have interests or concerns in the responsiblle development and use of AI, which can influence a company's performance and risk profile.

- **AI impacted subjects:** Those who are impacted by some AI-human dyad decisions (e.g., a loan applicant or a taxpayer). AI impacted subjects may contest the decision on dyad AI ground.

- **AI consumers:** individuals who consume AI solutions (e.g., voice assistants, search engines, recommender engines) for their personal use (not affecting third parties). AI consumers may care about the dyad AI aspects of AI solutions.

- **RAI governors:** Those who set and enable RAI policies and controls within their culture. RAI governors could be functions within an organization in the preceding list or external (regulators, consumer advocacy groups, community).

- **RAI tool producers:** Technology vendors and dedicated companies offering RAI features integrated into AI platforms or machine learning operations (MLOps) or AI for operations (AIOps) tools.

- **RAI tool procurers:** Any of the preceding stakeholders who may purchase or use RAI tools to improve or check solutions' or technology's RAI aspects.

The organization-level stakeholders include

- **Management teams:** Individuals at the higher level of an organization who are responsible for establishing an RAI governance structure in the organization and achieving RAI at the organization level. The management teams include board members, executives, and (middle-level) managers for legal, compliance, privacy, security, risk, and sustainability.

- **Employees:** Individuals who are hired by an organization to perform work for the organization and are expected to adhere to RAI principles in their work.

The team-level stakeholders are made up of a variety of roles in the development teams, who are responsible for developing and deploying AI systems, including product managers, project managers, team leaders, business analysts, architects, UX/UI designers, data scientists, developers, testers, and operators. The development teams are expected to implement RAI in their development process and embed RAI into the product design of AI systems.

Industry-Level Governance Patterns

This section focuses on the governance patterns that RAI governors can utilize to establish industry-level governance. The target users of these industry-level governance patterns are RAI governors, while the impacted stakeholders include AI technology producers and procurers, AI solution producers and procurers, and AI tool producers and procurers. The industry-level governance patterns outlined in this section pertain to all the stages of the AI system lifecycle and relate to all the AI ethics principles.

G.1. RAI Law and Regulation

RAI laws and regulations cover enforceable rules and policies that are issued by an executive authority or regulatory agency of a government to ensure the responsible development and use of AI systems within that jurisdiction.

Context

A number of laws and regulations already apply directly or indirectly to AI systems. However, the processes and requirements to ensure compliance are not always certain. Also, some laws may need to be updated. There is an urgent need for clear guidance to make sure that AI systems are developed and used responsibly in compliance with existing and upcoming laws (e.g., discrimination laws).

Problem

How can we ensure AI systems are developed and used appropriately?

Solution

Enforceable AI laws and regulations aim to ensure that AI systems are developed and used in a way that is ethical and beneficial to the society at large within that jurisdiction—that is, that citizens and their rights are protected and innovation is supported. Governments across the world, such as the

European Union and Canada, have been working on establishing comprehensive regulatory frameworks for AI to reach these goals. Organizations that build AI systems must meet certain criteria before they can enter the AI development market—for example, build AI using methodology for RAI-by-design into AI systems and have governance capabilities in place to ensure ongoing compliance with laws and implement standards and ethical codes. The specific criteria may vary based on the level of risk or the domain in which the AI systems are used.

Benefits

Here are the benefits of following an RAI law and regulation pattern:

- **Compliance:** RAI laws and regulations can help ensure the development and use of AI systems adhere to ethical principles and align with ethical and human values.

- **Legal recourse:** RAI laws and regulations can mandate practices that reduce AI risks, such as processes for limiting bias and protecting privacy, and increase public confidence in the responsible development and deployment of AI.

Drawbacks

Here are the drawbacks of using an RAI law and regulation pattern:

- **Long time to enact:** It is common for regulation to take years to go into effect after it is first proposed. The length of time can be related to a variety of factors, such as the time to consult with a wide range of stakeholders and the need to carefully consider the potential consequences.

- **Lack of interoperability and portability:** AI systems are often developed across multiple jurisdictions. There may be discrepancies or a lack of interoperability between RAI laws and regulations from different jurisdictions.

Related Patterns

Here are the related patterns of the RAI law and regulation pattern:

- G.4. Regulatory sandbox: Since RAI laws and regulations can take a significant amount of time to enact, regulators can introduce an agile regulatory sandbox as an interim measure. This sandbox allows innovative AI products to be tested in a live environment for a limited time and within a specified space under the supervision of a regulator.

- P.11. RAI governance via APIs: AI technologies can be delivered as cloud-based services, and the interaction with these services can be governed through APIs in order to enforce RAI laws and regulations.

Known Uses

Here are some RAI laws and regulations that are underway:

- The European Union (EU) AI Act was proposed in April 2021 to set out the rules for developing and using AI systems within the territory of the EU.[3]

- The Algorithmic Accountability Act of 2022 was introduced in the US Senate and in the US House of Representatives. [4]

- In October 2022, the US White House Office of Science and Technology Policy issued the Blueprint for an AI Bill of Rights.[5]

- Regulations on Internet Information Service Algorithmic Management Regulations went into effect in China on March 1, 2022.[6]

G.2. RAI Maturity Model

An RAI maturity model is used to assess an organization's RAI capabilities and its readiness to utilize AI responsibly.

Context

AI is a transformative technology that is expected to have a significant impact on society and industry. Many organizations view AI as a top strategic priority. According to the 2022 Gartner CIO and Technology Executive Survey, almost half of organizations have either already deployed AI technologies or plan to do so within the next year. However, as organizations seek to adopt AI, they may encounter challenges that could impact their business if they are not aware of their own RAI maturity.

Problem

How can the RAI maturity of organizations be effectively assessed?

---

3. https://artificialintelligenceact.eu.

4. https://www.congress.gov/bill/117th-congress/house-bill/6580/text?r=2&s=1.

5. https://www.whitehouse.gov/ostp/ai-bill-of-rights/.

6. http://www.cac.gov.cn/2022-01/04/c_1642894606364259.htm.

Solution

An RAI maturity model is used to assess an organization's RAI capabilities and readiness to implement AI.[7] The model includes dimensions such as impact, governance, development, and people, which represent the capabilities that contribute to an organization's RAI maturity. To assess an organization's RAI maturity, all of the dimensions should be evaluated to determine the overall level of RAI maturity.

Benefits

Here are the benefits of the RAI maturity model pattern:

- **Accelerated AI adoption:** By using the RAI maturity model, organizations can assess their AI dimensions that contribute to the adoption of AI technology.

- **Increased AI capability:** The RAI maturity model helps organizations assess their current capabilities and readiness in relation to responsible AI. By using the model as a guide, organizations can take steps to address deficiencies and increase their overall RAI capabilities.

Drawbacks

There are some potential drawbacks to using an RAI maturity model pattern:

- **Complexity:** The RAI maturity model can be complex with many dimensions and criteria that need to be evaluated. This can make it challenging for organizations to understand and use the model effectively.

- **Limited quality:** The effectiveness of the RAI maturity model relies on the quality of the model. The maturity model should clearly define the assessment dimensions and provide a method for rating the maturity for each dimension.

Related Patterns

Here are the related patterns of the RAI maturity model pattern:

- G.3. RAI certification: The assessment results of the RAI maturity model could be used to certify an organization's RAI capability and support the issuance of an ethical certificate.

- G.5. Building code: RAI certification could use building codes as the inspection standard.

---

7. S. A. Alsheibani, Y. P. Cheung, and C. H. Messom, "Towards an Artificial Intelligence Maturity Model: From Science Fiction to Business Facts," *Pacific Asia Conference on Information Systems,* 2019; P. Fukas et al., "Developing an Artificial Intelligence Maturity Model for Auditing," *European Conference on Information Systems,* 2021.

Known Uses

Here are the known uses of the RAI maturity model pattern:

- Microsoft's Responsible AI Maturity Model describes five maturity levels: latent, emerging, developing, realizing, and leading.[8]

- Boston Consulting Group defines four stages of RAI maturity: lagging, developing, advanced, and leading.[9]

- Salesforce identifies four stages in their maturity model for building a responsible AI practice: ad hoc, organized and repeatable, managed and sustainable, and optimized and innovative.[10]

G.3. RAI Certification

RAI certification can be used as the attestation that an AI entity (i.e., system, component, development process, developer, operator, or organization) has met certain specified criteria, such as mandatory regulatory requirements or voluntary AI ethics principles.

Context

AI is a high-stakes technology that faces challenges in gaining societal acceptance and permission to operate. Building trust in AI could help unlock the market for AI technology and increase its adoption. Trustworthiness refers to the ability of an AI system to adhere to AI laws, regulations, and ethics principles, while trust is the subjective estimate of a stakeholder regarding the trustworthiness of AI systems. It is important to note that even if an AI system is deemed trustworthy, this does not necessarily mean the stakeholders automatically trust it.

Problem

How can we assess and verify the responsible practices of AI entities?

Solution

Trust can be improved by providing stakeholders with evidence of compliance with laws and standard in the context of the application of the AI. To provide such evidence, certification can be designed to recognize that an organization or individual has the ability to develop or use an AI system in a responsible manner, or that the development process or design of an AI system or

---

8. https://www.microsoft.com/en-us/research/publication/responsible-ai-maturity-model/.

9. https://www.bcg.com/publications/2021/the-four-stages-of-responsible-ai-maturity.

10. https://www.salesforceairesearch.com/static/ethics/EthicalAIMaturityModel.pdf.

component is compliant with standards or regulations. To obtain certification, a trusted third party typically conducts an assessment. If the assessment results show that the entity (i.e., system, component, development process, developer, operator, or organization) meets the specified criteria, it is granted certification. This certification serves as evidence that the entity has met the necessary standards and requirements for responsible AI practices.

Benefits

There are several benefits of the RAI certification pattern:

- **Improved trust:** RAI certification can help improve trust in AI systems by providing evidence of ethical compliance.

- **Accelerated AI adoption:** RAI certificates can be used as proof of compliance, which can accelerate the adoption of AI systems.

- **Implementation of AI ethics principles:** Obtaining RAI certification can incentivize the stakeholders to adhere to AI ethics principles in order to meet the requirements for certification.

Drawbacks

Here are some drawbacks of the RAI certification pattern:

- **Forgery:** RAI certificates may be forged, making it difficult to verify their authenticity.

- **Complexity:** The certification process can be complex, costly, and time consuming. This complexity may be a barrier for some organizations or individuals seeking RAI certification.

- **Lack of standardization:** There can be multiple RAI certification programs, which may lead to inconsistency.

- **Untrusted certification authority:** There is a risk of not having trusted certification authorities to manage the certification process. This can result in a lack of confidence in the authenticity and effectiveness of the certification.

Related Patterns

Here are some patterns related to the RAI certification pattern:

- G.2. RAI maturity model: RAI certification can use the RAI maturity model as the framework for assessing an organization's level of preparedness for implementing AI.

- G.7. Trust mark: A trust mark is a special form of RAI certification that is designed to be easily attached to AI products.

- G.8. RAI standards: RAI certification can be used to recognize that the development process or design of an AI system is compliant with RAI standards.

- G.13. RAI training: RAI training can be provided to individuals to develop the skills necessary to obtain RAI certification.

- G.22. Verifiable claim for AI system artifacts: RAI certificates can be designed and verified in the form of verifiable claim.

Known Uses

Here are the known uses of the RAI certification pattern:

- Malta AI-ITA certification is the world's first national AI certification scheme for AI systems to be developed in a responsible manner.[11]

- CertifyAI provides third-party certification to AI solutions across four distinct levels: basic, silver, gold, and platinum.[12]

- Responsible AI Institute provides an independent certification program for AI systems to demonstrate alignment with responsible AI requirements.[13]

G.4. Regulatory Sandbox

A regulatory sandbox allows for the testing of innovative AI products in a real-world setting, with relaxed regulatory requirements, on a time-limited basis, at a smaller scale, and with appropriate safeguards in place.

Context

As AI becomes more widespread in society, both organizations and individuals have called for clearer rules to ensure that it is developed and used responsibly. RAI laws and regulations refer to government rules and policies that oversee and advance AI technology. While the policies and rules are necessary to both advance AI and mitigate related RAI risks, they often take a long time to enact.

Problem

How can we facilitate the trial of innovative AI products in the market?

---

11. https://www.mdia.gov.mt/innovative-technology-arrangement-guidelines/.

12. https://www.certifyai.net.

13. https://www.responsible.ai/.

Solution

One way to facilitate the testing of innovative AI products in the market is to create a regulatory sandbox, which enables the testing of innovative AI products in a real-world setting under relaxed regulatory requirements but with appropriate safeguards in place on a time-limited and small-scale basis.[14] Depending on the experiment, the sandbox may provide appropriate regulatory support by temporarily easing certain regulatory requirements for the duration and space of the sandbox. The sandbox can include safeguards to assess and mitigate RAI risks. Once the AI products exit the sandbox after the experiment, they must fully comply with RAI regulatory rules.

Benefits

Here are the benefits of the regulatory sandbox pattern:

- **Reduced time to market:** AI systems can be brought to market faster under more flexible regulatory requirements.

- **Real-world trial:** Companies can legally test their AI products in the market with real consumers and determine whether the AI product is appealing to them.

- **Accelerated regulations:** The regulatory sandbox allows for agile regulation, keeping pace with AI innovation.

Drawbacks

Here are the drawbacks of the regulatory sandbox pattern:

- **Increased cost:** Additional costs may be associated with applying for a regulatory sandbox.

- **Inconsistency with large-scale deployment:** AI products tested in a regulatory sandbox may not perform responsibly when deployed at a larger scale or in a different context.

Related Patterns

G.1. RAI law and regulation: A regulatory sandbox can be implemented temporarily while RAI laws and regulations are being developed.

Known Uses

Here are the known uses of the regulatory sandbox pattern:

- EU's AI Regulatory Sandbox was included in the EU's Artificial Intelligence Act proposal submitted in April 2021.[15]

---

14. J. Schaich Borg, "Four Investment Areas for Ethical AI: Transdisciplinary Opportunities to Close the Publication-to-Practice Gap," *Big Data & Society* 8, no. 2 (2021). doi.org/10.1177/20539517211040197.

15. https://www.eipa.eu/publications/briefing/sandboxes-for-responsible-artificial-intelligence/.

- The UK Information Commissioner's Office (ICO) introduced a Regulatory Sandbox for products and services that use personal data.[16]

- The Australian government released the Enhanced Regulatory Sandbox for innovative financial services that do not have to meet current regulatory requirements.[17]

- Singapore's FinTech Regulatory Sandbox allows financial companies to test innovative financial products and services in a live environment with relaxed regulatory requirements.[18]

G.5. Building Code

A building code is a set of rules that establishes the minimum standards for the development and use of an AI system.

Context

AI systems can be more uncertain and riskier than traditional software due to their autonomous and opaque decision-making processes. The level of uncertainty and risk may vary depending on the specific AI technologies and application domains being used. As AI technology continues to evolve and become more prevalent, there is a need for clear and consistent guidelines for developers to follow to ensure that AI systems are developed and used responsibly.

Problem

What are ways to ensure that AI systems are trustworthy and meet certain minimum responsible AI standards?

Solution

A building code is a set of rules that ensures the development and use of AI systems conform to certain minimum standards.[19] Building codes are usually developed by standards organizations or governments and may be formally enacted as law in a particular jurisdiction. Developers must comply with building codes to obtain developmental approval or liability insurance for their AI systems.

---

16. https://ico.org.uk/for-organisations/regulatory-sandbox/the-guide-to-the-sandbox/.

17. https://asic.gov.au/for-business/innovation-hub/enhanced-regulatory-sandbox/.

18. https://www.mas.gov.sg/development/fintech/regulatory-sandbox.

19. F. E. Landwehr, "A Building Code for Building Code: Putting What We Know Works to Work," *Proceedings of the 29th Annual Computer Security Applications Conference*, 2013, 139–47.

Benefits

Here are the benefits of the building code pattern:

- **Reduced RAI risk:** Building codes can help reduce the RAI risks in the development and use of AI systems.

- **Increased trust:** Building codes improve trust among users and the public through clear guidelines on how AI systems should be built and deployed.

Drawbacks

Here are the drawbacks of the building code pattern:

- **Progress delay:** The construction of an AI system or the sale of an AI product in the market may be delayed until approval is granted by a local authority.

- **Inefficiency:** Enacting a building code may take a long time.

Related Patterns

G.2. RAI certification: RAI certification could use building codes as the inspection standard.

Known Uses

Here are the known uses of the building code pattern:

- The IEEE Building Code for the Internet of Things provides guidelines for developing the Internet of Things and smart cities in the form of questions.[20]

- The IEEE Building Code for Medical Device Software Security was released by the IEEE Cybersecurity Initiative to help develop secure medical device software.[21]

- The IEEE Building Code for Power System Software Security specifies the rules required to ensure the security of power system software.[22]

G.6. Independent Oversight

Independent oversight involves having an external group review the development and use of AI systems to ensure that they are in compliance with established laws, regulations, or standards.

---

20. https://cybersecurity.ieee.org/blog/2017/10/04/building-code-for-the-internet-of-things/.

21. https://ieeecs-media.computer.org/media/technical-activities/CYBSI/docs/BCMDSS.pdf.

22. https://ieeecs-media.computer.org/media/technical-activities/CYBSI/docs/BCPSSS.pdf.

Context

AI failures and incidents can lead to significant consequences, such as harm to individuals, economic or reputation loss for organizations, and negative societal impacts. In addition to immediate negative effects, they can also erode public trust in AI technology, making it more difficult for organizations to develop and adopt AI. Auditing is crucial to identify risks associated with the development and use of AI systems, helping to build public confidence in the technology.

Problem

How can we audit AI systems and conduct investigations in a trusted manner, particularly when failures or issues arise?

Solution

Independent oversight refers to the process of having an independent review board audit the development and use of AI systems to ensure that they are in line with laws/regulations and established standards. The independent review board is typically composed of experts with no conflicts of interest with the organizations being reviewed. The activities of independent oversight include planning review, continuous monitoring, and analysis of failures or near misses. The goal of independent oversight is to provide an objective and unbiased assessment of the development and operation activities and to help identify any issues that may need to be addressed.

Benefits

The independent oversight pattern offers several benefits, including

- **Confidence:** By establishing a trusted audit process, independent oversight can help build confidence in AI.
- **Reduced RAI risk:** The additional expertise and audit provided by an independent oversight can help reduce the RAI risks associated with AI systems.

Drawbacks

The drawbacks of the independent oversight pattern include

- **Lack of independence:** A key factor of the success in independent oversight is the independence of the oversight body. If the oversight body has conflicts of interest, the review may be inadequate or biased. This can undermine the credibility and effectiveness of the oversight and result in problems being misidentified or overlooked.
- **Limited expertise:** Finding qualified and experienced experts to serve on independent review boards can be challenging, particularly in emerging areas of AI.

Known Uses

Here are the known uses of the independent oversight pattern:

- The US Department of Commerce established the National Artificial Intelligence Advisory Committee (NAIAC) in 2021 to advise the president and federal agencies on AI-related issues.[23]

- The US National Transportation Safety Board is an independent US government agency that investigates every civil aviation accident and significant accidents in other types of transportation in the US.[24]

G.7. Trust Mark

A trust mark is a seal that indicates that an AI system has been endorsed as being compliant with RAI standards.

Context

As AI technology has been rapidly evolving, it has been incorporated into a wide range of software systems across various domains, such as entertainment and home automation. However, the autonomous and unpredicted nature of AI systems has raised public attention and concerns. Many consumers may not have professional knowledge about AI and may find it difficult to understand the sophisticated algorithms that power the systems. This lack of understanding makes it challenging for consumers to make decisions about the use of AI products and services.

Problem

How can consumers confidently trust the AI systems they use without having professional knowledge about AI?

Solution

One way to improve public confidence in AI and address ethical concerns is to use a trust mark, a visible seal of endorsement that signifies that an AI system meets certain RAI standards. Trust marks can be easily understood by all consumers and can provide assurance that an AI system has been designed and developed in a responsible manner. To ensure that trust marks make sense, it is important to establish agreed-upon standards for AI development and to have these standards reviewed by independent auditors. To be effective, the trust mark should be designed in a way that is easily understood by all consumers, such as through a label or visual representation indicating fulfillment with the trust mark requirements.

---

23. https://www.ai.gov/naiac/#ABOUT-NAIAC.

24. https://www.ntsb.gov/.

Benefits

The trust mark pattern offers several benefits, including

- **Public confidence:** By providing a visible symbol of endorsement, trust marks help improve consumers' confidence in AI systems and address ethical concerns.

- **Branding:** Trust marks can be particularly valuable for small AI companies that may not be well known in the market.

- **Understandability:** Trust marks are designed to be easily understandable by all consumers, including those with limited knowledge about AI.

Drawbacks

There are a couple of potential drawbacks to the trust mark pattern:

- **Lack of awareness:** Consumers may not be aware of trust marks or how to identify them when assessing an AI system.

- **Lack of trust:** Some consumers may not trust that the AI systems with trust marks are necessarily more responsible than those without one.

Related Patterns

G.3. RAI certification: A trust mark can be a simplified form (e.g., stamp) of RAI certification.

Known Uses

Here are the known uses of the trust mark pattern:

- The Australian Data and Insights Association (ADIA) Trust Mark ensures that their member organizations are compliant with the ethical standards.[25]

- The Privacy Trust Mark is awarded by New Zealand's Privacy Commissioner to a product or service for recognition of excellence in privacy.[26]

- The Data Protection Trustmark (DPTM) was developed by Singapore's Personal Data Protection Commission (PDPC) and Info-Communications Media Development Authority (IMDA) to help organizations demonstrate compliance with the Personal Data Protection Act (PDPA).[27]

---

25. https://dataandinsights.com.au/trust-mark/.

26. https://www.privacy.org.nz/resources-2/applying-for-a-privacy-trust-mark/.

27. https://www.pdpc.gov.sg/overview-of-pdpa/data-protection/business-owner/data-protection-trustmark.

G.8. RAI Standards

RAI standards are often presented in the form of voluntary documents that provide specifications, procedures, and guidelines to develop responsible AI systems.

Context

AI systems often use data or components from multiple jurisdictions, which may have different regulatory requirements on their use. For example, one jurisdiction may have more strict rules around data privacy, whereas another may have more lenient rules. These differences can create conflicting requirements for the use of the data or components within the AI system, which can make it difficult to ensure that the AI system is compliant with all relevant laws and regulations.

Problem

How can we ensure AI systems are trustworthy while avoiding the interoperability issue between jurisdictions?

Solution

To facilitate interoperability between jurisdictions, RAI standards can be developed to describe repeatable processes for creating responsible AI systems that are recognized internationally. The process of developing AI standards usually begins with the submission of a development proposal by the professional community. Once a proposal is approved, it is assigned to a technical committee, which manages working groups to draft the standard. The draft standard is then made available to the public for comments before it is finalized and released. RAI standards can be used on a voluntary or mandatory basis, and may be referenced in AI legislation by governments.

Benefits

Here are the benefits of the RAI standards pattern:

- **Consistency:** By providing a consistent statement about the level of trustworthiness users can expect from AI systems, RAI standards can help ensure that users can trust the AI systems that meet the standards.

- **Interoperability:** RAI standards can facilitate interoperability between different regulation approaches and ensure that AI systems are developed and used responsibly across jurisdictional boundaries.

Drawbacks

Here are the drawbacks of the RAI standards pattern:

- **Barrier for innovation:** Once organizations begin following an RAI standard, there may be less emphasis on new design or process methods.

- **Difficulty of modification:** Modifying a well-adopted standard may be challenging if issues are identified or if new AI technologies require updates to the standards.

Related Patterns

G.3. RAI certification: RAI certification can be granted to AI systems that meet certain RAI standards and demonstrate their commitment to AI ethics principles.

Known Uses

Here are the known uses of the RAI standards pattern:

- The ISO/IEC JTC 1/SC42 Artificial Intelligence Technical Committee has been developing a set of international standards for AI—for example, ISO/IEC 42001 Information Technology – Artificial Intelligence – Management System.[28]

- The IEEE Artificial Intelligence Standards Committee has released three AI standards: IEEE 3652.1-2020, "IEEE Guide for Architectural Framework and Application of Federated Machine Learning,"[29] IEEE 2830-2021, "IEEE Standard for Technical Framework and Requirements of Trusted Execution Environment-Based Shared Machine Learning,"[30] and IEEE P7000, "IEEE Standards for Model Process for Addressing Ethical Concerns During System Design."[31]

Organization-Level Governance Patterns

Implementing RAI within an organization requires the establishment of effective AI governance. This effort can involve setting up founding principles, an RAI risk committee, a governance structure, governance metrics, external committees, organization-wide training, initiatives to promote diversity and dissent, and so on. In this section, we describe the organization-level governance patterns that can be used by the management teams to promote RAI within their organizations. These patterns are intended for use by management teams and are designed to benefit a wide range of stakeholders, including employees, AI users, AI consumers, and AI impacted subjects.

---

28. https://www.iso.org/standard/77304.html.

29. https://standards.ieee.org/ieee/3652.1/7453/.

30. https://standards.ieee.org/ieee/2830/10231/.

31. https://ethicsinaction.ieee.org/p7000/.

G.9. Leadership Commitment for RAI

Achieving leadership commitment to RAI within an organization requires the management team to actively invest their time and effort into building RAI practices within an organization.

Context

AI has the potential to transform organizations through a wide range of applications, such as analyzing business data or optimizing hiring processes. However, successful AI adoption relies heavily on the management team's commitment to building responsible AI within an organization.

Problem

How can the management team ensure commitment to build RAI within an organization?

Solution

Leadership commitment is crucial for effective organization-level governance of RAI. Management teams can demonstrate their commitment to RAI within an organization in several ways. For example, the management team can establish clear founding ethics principles and governance structure for the organization.[32] They can also make RAI a key part of CEO contracts and performance reviews, appoint an executive responsible for RAI, set up an organization-level risk committee, promote a culture of RAI within the organization, and provide training and guidelines on RAI practices to employees.

Benefits

The leadership commitment pattern can have several benefits for an organization, including

- **Formation of a culture:** Continuous leadership commitment is the foundation of a strong organizational culture that values and promotes RAI.

- **Realization of vision:** Strong leadership commitment to RAI can help ensure that an organization's vision for RAI is realized.

- **Visible sponsorship:** Through visible support for and promotion of RAI, leadership commitment can build the organization's capacity for RAI practices.

---

32. B. Shneiderman, "Bridging the Gap Between Ethics and Practice: Guidelines for Reliable, Safe, and Trustworthy Human-Centered AI Systems," *ACM Transactions on Interactive Intelligent Systems (TiiS)* 10, no. 4 (2020): 1–31.

Drawbacks

There are some drawbacks with the leadership commitment pattern:

- **Additional efforts:** Establishing and maintaining leadership commitment to RAI can require significant time and effort.

- **Extra cost:** Implementing the leadership commitment may require additional financial and resource costs.

Related Patterns

Here are the related patterns of the leadership commitment pattern:

- G.10. RAI risk committee: An RAI risk committee is an important component of the RAI governance structure that is established through leadership commitment.

- G.11. Code of RAI: The management team plays a key role in enforcing the code of RAI within an organization.

Known Uses

Here are the known uses of the leadership commitment pattern:

- IBM has established an AI ethics board to support a culture of RAI throughout IBM.[33]

- Axon has assembled an independent AI ethics board to provide guidance on the development of the company's AI products and services.[34]

- Schneider Electric has appointed its first chief AI officer to advance the company's AI strategy.[35]

G.10. RAI Risk Committee

An RAI risk committee is a group of individuals who are responsible for reviewing and approving proposals of AI projects to ensure the adoption of AI is done in a responsible manner.

---

33. https://www.ibm.com/au-en/artificial-intelligence/ethics.

34. https://www.axon.com/company/ai-and-policing-technology-ethics.

35. https://www.iteuropa.com/news/schneider-electric-appoints-new-caio-and-opens-new-ai-hub.

Context

The RAI considerations surrounding the development and use of AI are complex and constantly evolving. Simply adhering to legal requirements is not enough to effectively manage the RAI risks and maintain public trust in AI. Additionally, legislation often lags behind technology advances, making it difficult for organizations to stay up to date.

Problem

What are ways to establish responsible AI governance within an organization?

Solution

An RAI risk committee is a governance body that is responsible for establishing standard processes for decision-making and for approving and monitoring AI projects within an organization. Review by an RAI risk committee is typically required for all the AI projects within an organization and can be regulated by governments. The committee should be composed of individuals with diverse areas of expertise, such as ethics, law, AI, software engineering, and domain-specific knowledge. It is important to consider potential conflicts of interest or biases within the committee. To avoid such situations, organizations can either include at least one external member on the RAI risk committee or establish an independent, external RAI risk committee.

Benefits

Here are the benefits of the RAI risk committee pattern:

- **Enforced internal governance:** An RAI risk committee can establish governance standards at the organization level.
- **Feedback and guidance:** The committee can provide feedback and guidance to the project team after reviewing proposals.

Drawbacks

Here are the drawbacks of the RAI risk committee pattern:

- **Limited capability and capacity:** Due to a lack of internal expertise in the area of RAI, organizations may have to rely on traditional risk management professionals to assess the potential risks associated with RAI.
- **Bias:** A limited range of expertise within an organization can potentially lead to biases or conflicts of interest in decision-making processes.

Related Patterns

Here are the related patterns of the RAI risk committee pattern:

- G.9. Leadership commitment for RAI: An RAI risk committee is a component of the RAI governance structure established by the management team.

- G.12 RAI risk assessment: An RAI risk committee is a group of individuals who are responsible for performing the RAI risk assessment process and making decisions based on the results of the RAI risk assessment.

Known Uses

Here are the known uses of the RAI risk committee pattern:

- Adobe has created an AI ethics committee that includes experts around the world with different background and experience.[36]

- Sony has an established AI ethics committee since 2019 to ensure the development and use of AI is socially and ethically appropriate according to the Sony Group AI Ethics Guidelines.[37]

G.11. Code of RAI

A code of RAI is a set of guidelines that employees within an organization are expected to follow when developing or operating AI systems.

Context

The adoption of AI is a central aspect of the digital transformation process for organizations. AI has been used across the value chain to create additional value. However, there is a risk that AI may make incorrect decisions or behave in a manner that is inappropriate, such as causing harm to humans or making poor purchasing decisions.

Problem

What are ways to guide AI-related activities within an organization?

---

36. https://www.adobe.com/about-adobe/aiethics.html.

37. https://www.sony.com/en/SonyInfo/sony_ai/responsible_ai.html.

Solution

A code of RAI is a set of principles and guidelines that guides employees in the development and use of AI systems. The code of RAI defines the intended purpose of these systems and the way that employees are expected to develop and use AI systems. For example, the code outlines the ethical boundaries that employees should not cross.

Benefits

Here are the benefits of the code of RAI pattern:

- **Guidance for employees:** A code of ethics provides employees involved in AI-related activities with clear guidance regarding the development and use of AI systems.
- **Same rules:** When an organization has a code of ethics, everyone from the executive team to the development team follows the same rules, which helps promote the organization's values and establish the organizational culture.

Drawbacks

Here are the drawbacks of the code of RAI pattern:

- **High-level guidelines:** While reading the code of RAI may provide employees with a general understanding of RAI principles and guidelines, it does not necessarily lead to a change in behavior.
- **Difficult to enforce:** The black box nature of AI makes it extremely difficult to determine the specific factors that contribute to an AI system's decisions and hold employees accountable for their actions when working with AI.

Related Patterns

Here are the related patterns of the code of RAI pattern:

- G.9. Leadership commitment for RAI: The management team is responsible for upholding and enforcing the code of RAI within the organization.
- G.13. RAI training: The code of RAI can be included in an organization's RAI training program.
- G.14. Role-level accountability contract: The code of RAI can define accountability in an organization.

Known Uses

Here are the known uses of the code of RAI pattern:

- The Association for the Advancement of Artificial Intelligence (AAAI) has issued a Code of Professional Ethics and Conduct to act as a standard for ethical conduct for all AAAI members.[38]

- Bosch set a code of ethics to establish the guidelines for the use of AI.[39]

- BMW has released a code of ethics for AI, comprising seven ethical principles for the use of AI.[40]

G.12. RAI Risk Assessment

An RAI risk assessment is conducted to measure the likelihood and consequence of the potential RAI risks associated with the development and use of AI systems.

Context

Despite the widespread adoption of various AI domains, there are many concerns that the potential failures of complex and opaque AI systems may have significant negative consequences for individuals, organizations, and society, and may cause more harm than benefit. RAI laws and regulations are still in their early stages. RAI risks can occur at any stage of the AI system's lifecycle, cross-cutting AI components, non-AI components, and data components.

Problem

How can we assess the risks associated with AI systems?

Solution

An organization needs to design an RAI risk assessment framework or extend the existing IT risk assessment framework to include ethical considerations for AI systems. The RAI risk assessment should be adaptable to effectively address domain-specific risks (such as those in the military or healthcare domains) and emerging risks in constantly evolving AI systems. The RAI risk assessment framework should be co-designed with key stakeholders, including the RAI risk committee, development teams, and prospective purchasers, in a dynamic, adaptive, and extensible manner that takes into account various context factors, such as culture, application domains, and automation levels.

---

38. https://www.aaai.org/Conferences/code-of-ethics-and-conduct.php.

39. https://www.bosch-ai.com/industrial-ai/code-of-ethics-for-ai/.

40. https://www.press.bmwgroup.com/global/article/detail/T0318411EN/seven-principles-for-ai-bmw-group-sets-out-code-of-ethics-for-the-use-of-artificial-intelligence.

The risk assessment process can be effectively guided by checklists or questions. To avoid subjective views on risk assessment outcomes, it is important to incorporate concrete risk metrics and measurements in calculating the risk assessment score.

Benefits

Here are the benefits of the RAI risk assessment pattern:

- **Enabled oversight:** Conducting an RAI risk assessment is a crucial step in the process of RAI governance to enable oversight.

- **Identification of RAI risks:** RAI risk assessment helps to identify potential RAI risks associated with the development and use of AI systems.

- **Enforced controls:** Once the RAI risks have been identified, organizations can implement controls to mitigate and manage those risks.

Drawbacks

Here are the drawbacks of the RAI risk assessment pattern:

- **Subjective view:** The assessment process may involve subjective judgment when rating the risk, particularly for principles that are difficult to quantify.

- **One-off assessment:** Currently, the RAI risk assessment is often performed as one-time events, rather than being integrated into ongoing risk management processes.

- **Overemphasis on risk assessment:** It is essential to obtain a balance between risk assessment and mitigation. While risk assessment provides valuable insights into the likelihood and consequence of potential risks, it may inadvertently get attention and resources away from proactive risk mitigation efforts.

Related Patterns

Here are the related patterns of the risk assessment pattern:

- G.10. RAI risk committee: Conducting an RAI risk assessment is an important responsibility for an RAI risk committee.

- G.16. Standardized reporting: The results of an RAI risk assessment should be reported to the RAI governors.

- G.23. Failure mode and effects analysis (FMEA): FMEA is an RAI risk assessment method that is commonly used in the development process and product design.

- P.16. Extensible, adaptive, and dynamic risk assessment: The RAI risk assessment framework within an organization can be designed in an extensible, adaptive, and dynamic way.

Known Uses

Here are the known uses of the RAI risk assessment pattern:

- The ISO/IEC JTC 1/SC 42 committee is developing ISO/IEC 23894 on Artificial Intelligence and Risk Management.[41]

- NIST released the initial draft of the AI Risk Management Framework that provides a standard process for managing risks of AI systems.[42]

- The Canadian government has released the Algorithmic Impact Assessment tool to identify the risks associated with automated decision-making systems.[43]

- The Australian NSW government is mandating all its agencies that are developing AI systems to go through the NSW AI Assurance Framework.[44]

- CSIRO has developed a question bank for AI risk assessment. The questions were extracted from five major AI risk assessment frameworks.[45]

G.13. RAI Training

RAI training is designed to improve the level of awareness and skill of employees in implementing RAI.

Context

If not developed and used responsibly, AI systems can pose significant risks. It is important that the employees of an organization think critically about the potential implications of AI on their work and make responsible choices during the development and use of AI systems. Doing so includes considering the potential RAI risks and impacts on various stakeholders and taking steps to mitigate those risks.

Problem

How can we improve organizational awareness and skill in RAI?

---

41. https://www.iso.org/standard/77304.html.

42. https://www.nist.gov/itl/ai-risk-management-framework.

43. https://www.canada.ca/en/government/system/digital-government/digital-government-innovations/responsible-use-ai/algorithmic-impact-assessment.html.

44. https://www.digital.nsw.gov.au/policy/artificial-intelligence/nsw-ai-assurance-framework.

45. https://arxiv.org/abs/2305.09300.

Solution

RAI training can be an effective way to help organizations ensure that they are adopting AI in a legally compliant, ethical, and responsible manner. Organizations can provide employees with knowledge and instructions on how to deal with RAI issues and reduce potential RAI risks when they develop or use AI systems. The training programs can be designed to meet specific needs of different roles within the organization and can cover a wide range of topics related to RAI. Topics can include governance for RAI, ethical operations of AI systems, trustworthy development processes, and RAI-by-design with case studies (e.g., ethical/unethical agents,[46] autonomous vehicles[47]).

Benefits

Here are the benefits of the RAI training pattern:

- **Increased organizational awareness:** RAI training helps provide employees with a deeper understanding and knowledge of RAI principles and best practices.

- **Increased skill:** RAI training helps sharpen the employees' skills in developing or using AI systems responsibly.

Drawbacks

Here are the drawbacks of the RAI training pattern:

- **Increased cost:** RAI training can incur additional costs for an organization. These costs may include the cost of developing and delivering the training program, as well as any expenses related to bringing in outside experts or facilitators to provide the training.

- **Limited content:** RAI involves broad knowledge and skills (e.g., laws and regulations, principles, guidelines, and methods). However, due to time constraints, RAI training may be able to cover only a subset of this content.

Related Patterns

Here are the related patterns of the RAI training pattern:

- G.3. RAI certification: Upon successful completion of an RAI training program, an employee or organization may be granted an RAI certificate as recognition of their RAI knowledge and commitment.

---

46. A. Weiss et al., "Using the Design of Adversarial Chatbots as a Means to Expose Computer Science Students to the Importance of Ethics and Responsible Design of AI Technologies," *IFIP Conference on Human-Computer Interaction*, 2021.

47. H. Furey and F. Martin, "AI Education Matters: A Modular Approach to AI Ethics Education," *AI Matters* 4, no. 4 (2019): 13–15.

- G.11. Code of ethics for RAI: The RAI training program can include a code of ethics for RAI as part of the curriculum.

- G.14. Role-level accountability contract: Organizations can provide training to ensure their employees understand their accountability and responsibility when developing AI systems.

Known Uses

Here are the known uses of the RAI training pattern:

- MIT offers a three-day course titled "Ethics of AI: Safeguarding Humanity" introducing the ethics of AI development and deployment.[48]

- The University of Sydney Technology (UTS) designed a short course titled "Ethical AI: From Principles to Practice" for business executives.[49]

- The University of Helsinki created a free online course titled "The Ethics of AI" for anyone who is interested in AI ethics.[50]

G.14. Role-Level Accountability Contract

A role-level accountability contract is a document that describes the specific roles and responsibilities of individuals or organizations involved in the various stages of the AI system lifecycle.

Context

To ensure that AI systems are developed and used responsibly, organizations need to have an appropriate approach to enabling accountability throughout the entire lifecycle of AI systems.

Problem

How can we identify the individuals who should be held accountable when an AI system misbehaves?

---

48. https://professional.mit.edu/course-catalog/ethics-ai-safeguarding-humanity.

49. https://open.uts.edu.au/uts-open/study-area/Technology/ethical-ai-from-principles-to-practice/.

50. https://ethics-of-ai.mooc.fi/.

Solution

Role-level accountability is a concept that each individual involved at any stage of the AI system lifecycle is accountable for the outcome of the AI system at their particular role.[51] To establish role-level accountability, organizations must develop clear policies and rules that outline the roles and responsibilities of individuals within the organization and to make these policies and rules accessible to development teams. Formal contracts can be used to help define the boundaries of responsibilities and to hold individuals accountable for their actions. For example, contracts can be signed between organizations and employees, or between system users, data contributors, and the project team. Diverse types of ethical quality constraints can be enforced as contracts, such as service contracts, model contracts, and data contracts.

Benefits

Here are the benefits of the role-level accountability contract pattern:

- **Increased awareness:** Developers primarily focus on the techniques of AI systems and may not be familiar with the ethical principles. Role-level accountability contracts make the developers keeps RAI in mind at every step.

- **Improved productivity:** Role-level accountability contracts help to eliminate the time and effort that employees spend on distracting activities (such as tasks unrelated to their core responsibilities) by providing clear expectations for their roles and responsibilities.

Drawbacks

Here are the drawbacks of the role-level accountability contract pattern:

- **Complexity:** Role-level accountability contracts can be complex because they may involve various parties and require detailed definitions of roles and responsibilities.

- **Reduced flexibility:** Role-level accountability contracts may result in decreased flexibility and adaptability of employees because they may feel confined to their specific roles and find it challenging to contribute beyond their prescribed responsibilities.

Related Patterns

Here are the related patterns of the role-level accountability contract pattern:

- **G.11. Code of ethics for RAI:** A code of ethics may contain ethical policies for different roles within an organization.

- **G.13. RAI training:** Organizations can provide training to help employees understand their accountability and responsibility when developing or operating an AI system.

---

51. L. Zhu et al., "AI and Ethics—Operationalising Responsible AI," arXiv preprint arXiv:2105.08867, 2021.

Known Uses

Here are the known uses of the role-level accountability contract pattern:

- Australia's National Data Commissioner created a data sharing agreement template for using Australian Government data.[52]

- The terms of service of data.ai specify the conditions and restrictions for using and accessing the services (the data.ai website and mobile app) provided by data.ai.[53]

- The end-user license agreement (EULA) of Viz.ai describes the terms and conditions for users to access the Viz.ai App.[54]

- Digital.ai's software evaluation agreement contains the terms and conditions for using certain software provided by Digital.ai.[55] The agreement serves as a legally binding contract between the customer and the software supplier that governs the customer's use of the software.

G.15. RAI Bill of Materials

An RAI bill of materials maintains a list of components used to create an AI software product, which AI solution procurers and consumers can use to check the supply chain details of each component of interest and make buying decisions.

Context

The development of AI systems often involves complex and dynamic software supply chains, because many organizations procure AI technologies and solutions from third parties to build their AI systems. These systems may be assembled using a variety of commercial or open-source AI and non-AI components from different sources. While procuring AI technologies and solutions from third parties can be cost-efficient, this approach can also raise concerns about security and integrity. According to Sonatype's 2021 report on the state of the software supply chain, software supply chain attacks increased 650 percent in 2021, while it was 430 percent in 2020.[56]

Problem

How can we build trust in AI system supply chains?

---

52. https://www.datacommissioner.gov.au/data-management/data-sharing-agreement.

53. https://www.data.ai/en/legal/terms.

54. https://www.viz.ai/eula.

55. https://digital.ai/software-evaluation-agreement.

56. https://www.sonatype.com/resources/state-of-the-software-supply-chain-2021.

Solution

An RAI bill of materials keeps a list of components used to create an AI software product. AI solution procurers and consumers can use this list to check the supply chain details of each component of interest and make buying decisions. According to *The Minimum Elements for a Software Bill of Materials* from NTIA,[57] the supply chain details should at least include component name, version, supplier, dependency relationship, author of software bill of materials data, and timestamp. This information provides traceability and transparency about the components and can allow procurers and consumers to easily check component information, such as supply chain details and context information, and to track ethical issues. By maintaining an RAI bill of materials, organizations can help build trust and confidence in their AI systems by providing detailed and transparent information about the components used in their systems.

Benefits

Here are the benefits of the RAI bill of materials pattern:

- **Reduced vulnerability:** An RAI bill of materials can enable faster vulnerability identification by providing detailed and transparent information about the third-party components used in an AI system.

- **Increased visibility:** An RAI bill of materials can make the supply chain of AI systems more visible and transparent.

Drawbacks

Here are the drawbacks of the RAI bill of materials pattern:

- **Increased cost:** An RAI bill of materials may need to be updated frequently since AI systems evolve over time. Maintaining and updating the bill of materials can incur additional management costs, because keeping the information accurate and current may require additional time and resources.

- **Lack of data integrity:** The data integrity of an RAI bill of materials is dependent on the tool that is adopted for creating and maintaining the information.

Related Patterns

Here are the related patterns of the RAI bill of materials pattern:

- D.1. RAI bill of material registry: The supply chain information of AI system components can be maintained in an AI software bill of material registry.

- D.2. Verifiable RAI credential: A verifiable RAI credential can be applied to a bill of materials to provide proof of responsibility at a specific point in the supply chain.

---

57. https://www.ntia.doc.gov/files/ntia/publications/sbom_minimum_elements_report.pdf.

Known Uses

Here are the known uses of the RAI bill of materials pattern:

- Dependency-Track is a software bill of material platform that allows organizations to track third-party components' supply chain information and identify their known vulnerabilities. [58]

- The Software Package Data Exchange (SPDX) is a software bill of material standard for exchanging software supply chain–related information, including components' basic information, security information, and IP information (such as licenses and copyrights).[59]

- CycloneDX is a standard for communicating software bill of material information for performing a software supply chain security analysis.[60]

G.16. Standardized Reporting

Organizations should establish standardized processes and templates for informing different stakeholders about the development process and product design of AI systems.

Context

AI is a high-stakes technology that requires careful oversight to manage RAI risks and build public trust in AI. Trust is a fundamental element for the widespread adoption of AI applications across various domains. Ensuring that all stakeholders are informed about the development and use of AI systems is crucial to increase trust.

Problem

How can organizations proactively accept the oversight from governments and the public?

Solution

Organizations can establish standardized processes and templates for informing stakeholders (such as RAI governors, AI users, and consumers) about the development process and product design of AI systems. RAI laws and regulations may require such reporting to ensure the transparency and explainability of AI systems. AI product providers may be required to file with the governments for impact assessment when launching new AI products and to inform users when AI is being used to interact with them and explain the purposes and design of AI systems.

---

58. https://www.nature.com/articles/s41746-021-00403-w.

59. https://spdx.dev/.

60. https://cyclonedx.org/.

Benefits

Here are the benefits of the standardized reporting pattern:

- **Consistency:** Standardized reporting ensures all the reports follow a uniform format and structure, making it easier for stakeholders to navigate and understand the information.

- **Regulatory compliance:** In some regions, standardized reporting is required to meet legal and regulatory compliance requirements.

Drawbacks

- **Cost:** Standardized reporting can be resource-intensive and may incur additional cost to meet the disclosure requirements.

- **Information overload:** If there is too much information being reported, stakeholders may have difficulty understanding and processing all the reported information.

Related Patterns

G.12. RAI risk assessment: The results of an RAI risk assessment can be an important part of standardized reporting.

Known Uses

Here are the known uses of the standardized reporting pattern:

- In 2022, the Cyberspace Administration of China published Administrative Provisions on Algorithmic Recommendations for Internet Information Services, which includes transparent disclosure requirements for online service providers.[61]

- In the EU's AI Act, AI system providers (i.e., AI technology or solution producers) are required to report and disclose the incidents of AI systems.[62]

- The European Union's General Data Protection Regulation (GDPR) requires companies to provide transparent and easily understandable information about the processing of personal data, including when AI is involved.[63]

---

61. http://www.cac.gov.cn/2022-01/04/c_1642894606364259.htm.

62. https://artificialintelligenceact.eu.

63. https://gdpr-info.eu.

Team-Level Governance Patterns

Team-level governance is primarily focused on the management of AI projects and the overall development processes. In this section, we discuss the governance patterns that development teams can use to ensure that AI projects are carried out responsibly. The target users for these patterns are the development teams, while the stakeholders who are impacted by these patterns are AI users, consumers, and those who may be affected by the use of AI.

G.17. Customized Agile Process

Agile development processes can be adapted and customized by incorporating RAI principles.

Context

Organizations have increasingly adopted Agile development to incrementally and iteratively develop software systems, including AI systems. However, the existing agile development methods mainly focus on delivering business value rather than ethical principles. RAI involves incorporating ethical principles into the development of AI systems. Failing to consider ethical principles in the development of AI systems can pose risks for stakeholders.

Problem

How can agile development methods be adapted to effectively address ethical issues in the development of AI systems?

Solution

To address ethical issues and ensure the responsible development of AI systems, it is necessary to integrate AI ethics principles into agile development methods. Various extension points can be added, including artifacts, roles, ceremonies, practices, and culture. This can be done through modifying existing artifacts (e.g., user stories) or adding new artifacts (e.g., regulatory requirements), as well as promoting RAI through existing roles (e.g., product) or new roles (e.g., ethicist). Modifying existing ceremonies (e.g., sprint planning) or introducing new ceremonies (e.g., ethics-oriented meetings) can also be helpful. Practices (e.g., user acceptance testing) and culture (e.g., hiring) are two effective ways to address ethical concerns in the agile development process.

Benefits

Here are the benefits of the customized agile process pattern:

- **Human-centric view:** The customized agile process pattern places a strong emphasis on AI ethics principles and human values.

- **Improved responsiveness:** Integrating ethics into the agile process enables the development team to respond quickly to emerging ethical concerns.

Drawbacks

Here are the drawbacks of the customized agile process pattern:

- **Incompleteness:** Some extension points may be overlooked.

- **Burden on organizations:** Customizing agile processes may place an additional burden on organizations, particularly if it requires significant changes to existing processes.

Related Patterns

G.21. Continuous documentation using templates: Specific documentation templates for AI systems could be considered as new artifacts in a customized agile process.

Known Uses

Here are the known uses of the customized agile process pattern:

- Microsoft's Azure DevOps allows the customization of inherited processes.[64]

- Atola Technology provides customized agile methodology that contains different development practices.[65]

- Apptio Targetprocess is a web-based visual tool for managing projects with flexibility at various levels.[66]

---

64. https://docs.microsoft.com/en-us/azure/devops/organizations/settings/work/inheritance-process-model?view=azure-devops&tabs=agile-process.

65. https://www.airtable.com/universe/exp4OppRObzXbhOQE/custom-agile-methodology-by-atola.

66. https://www.apptio.com/products/targetprocess/.

G.18. Tight Coupling of AI and Non-AI Development

The AI and non-AI development sprints and stand-up meetings need to be closely coordinated.

Context

In AI system development, both AI and non-AI components are rapidly iterated. This process requires more frequent integration of AI and non-AI components. The development of AI components is supported by the AI model pipeline and mostly done by data scientists and data engineers who are not familiar with software engineering. Compared with non-AI components, the development of AI components is more experimental and with less methodological support. The methodological gap between AI and non-AI development can affect the frequent integration of AI and non-AI components.

Problem

How can we ensure that the integration of AI and non-AI development goes seamlessly in a responsible manner?

Solution

To ensure a clear understanding of project deliverables and progress, it can be beneficial for the AI and non-AI development sprints and stand-up meetings to be closely coordinated. The deliverables include both AI components that produce AI models and non-AI components that utilize the outputs of the AI models for overall system functionalities. To ensure tight coupling between AI and non-AI development, including effective communication and data sharing, the two teams can share sprints and use a common co-versioning registry to manage artifacts and track progress. Stand-up meetings provide an opportunity for the AI and non-AI team to confirm the current sprint is on track to meet planned objectives, while also considering both system-level and model-level (ethical) requirements when making design decisions.

Benefits

Here are the benefits of the tight coupling of AI and non-AI development pattern:

- **Effective communication:** The close alignment of AI and non-AI development results in stronger trust among the project team and improved communication regarding both system-level and model-level ethical requirements.

- **Improved traceability:** When the development of AI and non-AI components is closely aligned, it is possible to track the progress of both teams throughout the project lifecycle.

Drawbacks

Here are the drawbacks of the tight coupling of AI and non-AI development pattern:

- **Dependent relationship:** If the non-AI team heavily relies on the AI team to provide the models, their work may be delayed due to the AI team's progress or any technical issues with the AI models. Similarly, the AI team may experience similar delays if they depend on the non-AI team for functionalities or inputs.

- **Scalability concerns:** As the project scales, managing the tightly coupled AI and non-AI development may be challenging.

Related Patterns

Here are the related patterns of the tight coupling of AI and non-AI development pattern:

- D.3. Co-versioning registry: Using a common co-versioning registry can be an effective way for the AI and non-AI teams to manage the coordination of AI and non-AI components. The teams can easily track versions of data, model, code, and configurations through a co-versioning registry.

- P.17. Multi-level co-versioning: The AI and non-AI teams can utilize a common co-versioning registry to manage and track different levels of co-versioning of AI system artifacts.

Known Uses

Here are the known uses of the tight coupling of AI and non-AI development pattern:

- The Microsoft Team Data Science Process supports continuously integrating the AI model with the rest of the software.[67]

- The Amazon SageMaker Pipelines is a continuous integration and continuous delivery (CI/CD) service for machine learning, which can help automate different steps of the ML workflow.[68]

- Azure Pipelines can be used to build the CI/CD pipelines for a machine learning project.[69]

G.19. Diverse Team

Building a diverse project team can effectively eliminate bias and promote diversity and inclusion in AI systems.

---

67. https://docs.microsoft.com/en-us/azure/architecture/data-science-process/overview.

68. https://aws.amazon.com/sagemaker/pipelines/?nc1=h_ls.

69. https://www.azuredevopslabs.com/labs/vstsextend/aml/.

Context

Humans are prone to make biased or questionable decisions. AI systems are often developed to assist or replace human decision-making to produce more impartial outcomes. However, the data used to train AI models is often generated or collected by humans. As a result, the trained models may produce results that imply bias (such as racism and sexism). Also, the code of AI systems is typically written by developers, who are primarily focused on technical aspects and may bring their own biases to the development process.

Problem

How can we ensure that AI systems are developed with consideration for a wide range of perspectives and backgrounds?

Solution

Building a diverse project team is critical to reducing bias and improving diversity and inclusion in AI systems. The diversity should include representation across various dimensions, such as gender, race, age, sexual orientation, and expertise. RAI challenges are multifaceted and complex, requiring the diverse expertise of individuals from a range of disciplines, including software engineering, machine learning, social science, human-machine interaction, and user experience. However, at the end, the final deliverable of an AI project is an AI system. Therefore, software engineering people are the key to building RAI systems, because they are responsible for implementing ethical considerations into the code of AI systems.

Benefits

Here are the benefits of the diverse team pattern:

- **Diversity and inclusion:** A diverse team is crucial in identifying biases and ensuring the decisions made by AI systems are responsible. Representation of different backgrounds leads to a more thorough examination of ethical issues and a more responsible final AI product.

- **Innovation:** Diverse teams drive creative thinking and lead to more new ideas and greater innovation in AI.

Drawbacks

Here are the drawbacks of the diverse team pattern:

- **Degraded communication:** Team members may come from different backgrounds and have different communication preferences. These differences can lead to a lack of understanding and confusion.

- **Decreased productivity:** Diverse teams may be more prone to conflicts, which could affect the productivity and motivation of the team members.

Related Patterns

G.17. Stakeholder engagement: Diverse teams are often better at communicating with stakeholders and understanding their concerns because they bring a wider range of perspectives and experiences to the table.

Known Uses

Here are the known uses of the diverse team pattern:

- Google published its 2022 Diversity Annual Report, which introduces the actions the company has taken to build a flexible and inclusive workplace.[70]

- Microsoft aims to integrate diversity and inclusion principles into its hiring, communication, innovation, and development of products and technologies.[71]

- Meta has been working on creating diverse and inclusive work communities.[72]

G.20. Stakeholder Engagement

Keeping stakeholders engaged throughout the AI project is essential to building AI systems responsibly.

Context

Stakeholders in AI projects include individuals, groups, or organizations that may influence or be impacted by the project's outcomes. These stakeholders may have various ethical concerns regarding the development and use of AI systems, such as the trustworthiness of AI systems and the potential impact of AI on humanity.

Problem

How can we manage the needs and expectations of stakeholders?

Solution

Keeping stakeholder engagement throughout the AI project is essential to building AI systems responsibly. Stakeholder engagement allows AI systems to better reflect needs and expectations of stakeholders. There are various ways to engage stakeholders, such as interviews, online and offline meetings, project planning and review, and participatory design workshops. Choosing the

---

70. https://about.google/belonging/at-work/.

71. https://careers.microsoft.com/us/en/diversityandinclusion.

72. https://www.workplace.com/diversity-and-inclusion.

most effective ways to encourage stakeholders depends on the project's scope, objectives, and the stakeholders' preferences. Possible methods to measure engagement may include the number of stakeholders involved, the frequency of their participation, and the quality of feedback received from stakeholders.

Benefits

Here are the benefits of the stakeholder engagement pattern:

- **Improved trust:** Stakeholder engagement aligns the development of AI systems with societal expectations and helps build stakeholders' trust in AI projects.

- **Reduced risk:** Stakeholders may help the project team identify and mitigate potential RAI risks before they become threats.

Drawbacks

Here are the drawbacks of the stakeholder engagement pattern:

- **Conflicting opinions:** There may be conflicting opinions from different stakeholders.

- **Increased cost:** Addressing the needs and expectations from the stakeholders may incur unexpected costs.

Related Patterns

G.16. Diverse team: Project teams need to continuously engage in communication and collaboration with stakeholders throughout the entire project lifecycle. Diverse teams can improve the communication efficiency by increasing understanding toward the needs and concerns of different stakeholders.

Known Uses

Here are the known uses of the stakeholder engagement pattern:

- The Association for Project Management (APM) has published ten key principles of stakeholder engagement.[73]

- The Australian Public Service Commission has published guidelines on effective stakeholder engagement.[74]

- Deloitte has published a report on stakeholder engagement.[75]

---

73. https://www.apm.org.uk/resources/find-a-resource/stakeholder-engagement/key-principles/.

74. https://www.apsc.gov.au/initiatives-and-programs/workforce-information/taskforce-toolkit/stakeholder-engagement.

75. https://www2.deloitte.com/content/dam/Deloitte/za/Documents/governance-risk-compliance/ZA_StakeholderEngagement_04042014.pdf.

G.21. Continuous Documentation Using Templates

Continuous documentation is important to track development activities and ensure that the continuously evolving AI systems are responsible.

Context

AI system development, particularly AI model development, is often performed in a fast-paced and experimental manner. Developers may prioritize writing code, rather than keeping detailed documentation of their work. For example, when developing AI models, developers usually use computational notebooks to combine code and notes together in a single document. It is challenging to communicate the ethical characteristics of AI systems.

Problem

How can stakeholders keep track of the development and use of AI systems and facilitate communication?

Solution

Continuous documentation is important for tracking development activities and ensuring that continuously evolving AI systems are responsible. The behavior of AI systems is determined by autonomous and potentially opaque AI models that are trained on data. Therefore, project teams need to create and continuously update documentation for the key artifacts of AI systems that may lead to ethical issues, such as data and models. There have been various types of templates for documenting data and models, such as model cards, data statements, datasheets for datasets, AI service factsheets, and data statements. Additionally, traditional software documentation needs to be extended to consider ethical aspects. For example, data requirements and ethical requirements should be explicitly specified in the requirement specification, while the results of ethical acceptance tests should be included in the testing report.

Benefits

Here are the benefits of the continuous documentation pattern:

- **Provenance:** Continuous documentation is essential for keeping track of the complete history and evolution of AI systems' artifacts, such as data and model, over time.

- **Trust:** Documentation is important in clarifying the context in which AI systems are intended to be used—for example, the situations in which they can be trusted to work well.

Drawbacks

Here are the drawbacks of the continuous document pattern:

- **Time consuming:** Continuously preparing documentation can be time consuming and may divert resources away from other important tasks, such as coding and testing.

- **Error-prone:** Documentation is often created and maintained manually, which can be error-prone. For example, the documentation may not be fully consistent with the code.

Related Patterns

G.17. Customized agile process: Project documentation is important for recording the activities of a customized agile process (e.g., user acceptance testing).

Known Uses

Here are the known uses of the continuous documentation pattern:

- Google provides model cards to enable transparent model reporting on model usage, provenance, and ethical evaluation.[76]

- Microsoft designs datasheets for datasets that allow every dataset to be accompanied with a datasheet documenting its motivation, creation, composition, intended uses, and other information to improve transparency and accountability.[77]

- IBM develops AI service factsheets to maintain the AI services' purpose, performance, safety, security, and provenance information.[78]

G.22. Verifiable Claim for AI System Artifacts

A verifiable claim is a statement that supports developers in making an AI system's ethical properties publicly verifiable and enables users to conduct the verification process.

Context

The increasing use of AI in promising applications, such as autonomous vehicles and healthcare, is having a significant impact on our lives. However, despite the potential benefits of these systems, there is skepticism about the impact of AI on humans and society. The complexity and black box

---

76. https://modelcards.withgoogle.com/about.

77. https://www.microsoft.com/en-us/research/project/datasheets-for-datasets/.

78. https://www.ibm.com/blogs/research/2018/08/factsheets-ai/.

nature of AI systems raise concerns about their reliability, fairness, privacy, and other ethical considerations. As a result, AI companies are facing challenges in gaining market acceptance, because users may lack trust in these systems. The potential users of AI systems need methods for assessing the RAI qualities of AI systems and comparing them to other systems.

Problem

How can users assess the RAI qualities of an AI system and compare it to other systems?

Solution

A verifiable claim platform can be built to support developers in making ethical properties publicly verifiable and to help users in conducting the verification process. Such platforms should consider the different perspectives of the stakeholder, because developers might focus on reliability, whereas users might be more interested in fairness. A verifiable claim is a statement about an AI system or an artifact (such as model or dataset) that is substantiated by a verification mechanism. For example, auditors could issue certificates for systems, components, or models. Issue tracking systems allow users and developers to flag issues or provide experience reports. Stakeholders could directly investigate an AI system's ethical properties and obtain insights into its decision-making process through analysis tools. The platform itself provides management capabilities such as claim creation and verification, access control, and dispute management.

Benefits

Here are the benefits of the verifiable claim for AI system artifacts pattern:

- **Trust:** By providing a transparent way to assess the ethical properties of AI systems, verifiable claims can contribute to building trust and facilitating AI adoption.

- **Verification of ethical properties:** Verifiable claims enable the verification of ethical properties of AI systems and their artifacts for AI users. This makes it possible for users to make more informed decisions on how and when to use AI.

Drawbacks

- **Increased cost:** Building verifiable claim platforms can be complex and costly.

- **Reliance on third party:** Some verifiable claims may rely on third parties for the generation and verification process, which might not be always trustworthy.

Related Patterns

G.3. RAI certification: At the organization level, third-party auditors could issue certificates for AI systems that are available for verification.

Known Uses

Here are the known uses of the verifiable claim for AI system artifacts pattern:

- W3C Verifiable Claims (now known as Verifiable Credentials) Working Group (VCWG) aims to make expressing and exchanging claims that have been verified by a third party easier and more secure on the Web.[79]

- The Open Web Application Security Project (OWASP) has published a document stating the technical details and the importance of Decentralized ID & Verifiable Claims.[80]

- Ethereum Verifiable Claims is a method for off blockchain variable claims.[81]

G.23. Failure Mode and Effects Analysis (FMEA)

FMEA involves conducting a bottom-up risk assessment to identify and analyze RAI risks.

Context

Ethical issues in AI systems are often identified through extensive simulation and testing during the later stages of development. However, this can lead to significant delays in project timelines and an increase in development cost. By identifying and addressing ethical issues early in the development process, development teams can mitigate the ethical issues and avoid costly delays.

Problem

How can we ensure the ethical quality at the beginning of the development process?

Solution

FMEA conducts AI risk assessment in a systematic and qualitative way to identify and evaluate potential RAI risks.[82] This bottom-up approach allows the development team to gain a comprehensive understanding of the potential failure modes, their causes, and the impacts of the failures on the systems and their users. FMEA can provide a clear view on the mitigation actions to reduce occurrence frequency and impact and increase detection probability. When applying FMEA, it is essential to consider not only technical failures but also ethical failures that may lead to ethical dilemmas.

---

79. https://www.w3.org/2017/vc/WG/.

80. https://owasp.org/www-pdf-archive//OWASP-Austin-Mtg-2018Jan-CryptoParty-Dave-Sanford.pdf.

81. https://eips.ethereum.org/EIPS/eip-1812#ethereum-verifiable-claims.

82. C. Ebert and M. Weyrich, "Validation of Autonomous Systems," *IEEE Software* 36, no. 5 (2019): 15–23.

Benefits

Here are the benefits of the FMEA pattern:

- **Improved ethical quality:** FMEA ensures that ethical failures are prevented from occurring in the first place by thoroughly analyzing all possible ethical risks.

- **Ease of use:** FMEA is relatively easy to use in practice.

- **Early identification:** FMEA provides early identification of ethical failures and helps to avoid delays to schedules.

Drawbacks

Here are the drawbacks of the FMEA pattern:

- **Limited by expertise:** FMEA replies on experts to apply their professional knowledge and experience to the RAI risk assessment process. Thus, the quality of the analysis is limited by the expertise of the team performing the analysis.

- **Missing failures:** FMEA is better suited for bottom-up analysis and not able to detect complex system-level ethical failures that require a holistic perspective.

Related Patterns

Here are the related patterns of the FMEA pattern:

- G.12. RAI Risk Assessment: FMEA is a method of RAI risk assessment focusing on the development process and product design.

- G.24. Fault tree analysis (FTA): FTA assesses each of the possible ethical failures, whereas FMEA focuses on root causes that may lead to failures.

Known Uses

Here are the known uses of the FMEA method:

- FMEA was originally proposed in US Armed Forces Military Procedures document MIL-P-1629 in 1949 and revised in MIL-STD-1629A in 1980.[83]

- Ford Motor Company first introduced FMEA to the automotive industry for assessing safety risk in the mid-1970s.[84]

---

83. https://web.archive.org/web/20110722222459/https://assist.daps.dla.mil/quicksearch/basic_profile.cfm?ident_number=37027.

84. https://fsp.portal.covisint.com/documents/106025/14555722/FMEA+Handbook+v4.2/4c14da5c-0842-4e60-a88b-75c18e143cf7?version=1.0.

- FMEA has been extended and adopted by Toyota's Design Review Based on Failure Modes (DRBFM) for assessing potential risk and reliability for automotive and non-automotive applications.[85]

G.24. Fault Tree Analysis (FTA)

FTA is a top-down risk assessment method that is used to analyze the root causes of potential RAI risks associated with the development and use of an AI system.

Context

Compared to traditional software systems, AI systems have a higher degree of risk due to their multi-level artifact dependency, data-dependent behaviors, and potentially opaque decision-making process. Undesired system behaviors or decisions could lead to serious consequences and even cause loss of human lives. An RAI risk assessment is a critical activity to ensure AI systems are developed and used in a trustworthy and responsible way.

Problem

How can we determine the cause of potential ethical failures and anticipate the RAI risks?

Solution

FTA is a method that describes how system-level ethical failures are led by small ethical failure events through an analytical graph, known as a fault tree.[86] The development team can easily understand how ethical failures propagate throughout the AI system by using FTA. FTA can be performed during the design or operation stage to anticipate the potential RAI risks and to recommend mitigation actions.

Benefits

Here are the benefits of the fault tree analysis (FTA) pattern:

- **Reduced RAI risk:** FTA helps analyze the RAI risks related to AI system artifacts and identify the context conditions under which an AI system is unethical.

- **Prioritized risk:** FTA prioritizes ethical issues that contribute to an RAI risk.

---

85. https://www.sae.org/standards/content/j2886_201303/.

86. Ebert and Weyrich, "Validation of Autonomous Systems," 15–23.

Drawbacks

Here are the benefits of the fault tree analysis (FTA) pattern:

- **Lack of scalability:** For larger systems, FTA can be complex and may involve many ethical events and gates.

- **Inefficiency:** Each FTA graph is designed to examine only one top event.

- **Missing factors:** Time can hardly be captured in FTA.

Related Patterns

Here are the related patterns of the fault tree analysis (FTA) pattern:

- G.12. RAI Risk Assessment: FTA is a top-down method for assessing RAI risks.

- G.23. Failure Mode and Effects Analysis (FMEA): FMEA adopts a bottom-up approach investigating what may cause ethical failures, whereas FTA is a top-down approach assessing possible ethical failures. FTA examines the relationship between different ethical events, whereas FMEA does not.

Known Uses

Here are the known uses of the fault tree analysis (FTA) pattern:

- FTA was first introduced by Bell Laboratories in 1962 to assess the safety of a missile launch control system.[87]

- Boeing started using FTA to design civil aircrafts in 1966.[88]

- FTA was included in US Army Materiel Command's Engineering Design Handbook on Design for Reliability.[89]

Summary

In this chapter, we present multi-level governance patterns that can be used to implement RAI governance. The patterns are organized into groups: industry level, organization level, and team level. The industry-level governance patterns focus on the governance of AI systems at a global or national scale and typically are driven by RAI governors, such as governments, industry associations, and international organizations. Organization-level patterns focus on the governance of RAI systems

---

87. https://www.osti.gov/servlets/purl/1315144.

88. https://apps.dtic.mil/sti/citations/AD0847015.

89. https://apps.dtic.mil/sti/pdfs/ADA026006.pdf.

within an organization, such as a company or public agency. These patterns are typically used by management teams, such as executives and managers. Team-level patterns focus on the governance of AI systems within a specific project team. It is important to note that the different governance patterns are not mutually exclusive and can complement each other. Those patterns need to be selected and recomposed based on the organization context and the specific needs of the AI project.

5

Process Patterns for Trustworthy Development Processes

Ethical concerns can arise at every stage of the AI system development process, crosscutting various components of AI systems beyond just the data and AI component. As shown in Figure 5.1, potential ethical issues can manifest during requirements, design, implementation, testing, and operation.

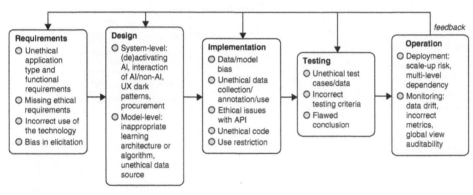

Figure 5.1
Potential ethical issues in the development process of AI systems.

At the requirements stage, there can be various ethical considerations, such as the unethical application type, missing ethical or regulatory requirements, wrong technology requirements, and bias in the requirements elicitation process. During the design stage, ethical issues can arise at both the system level and model level. At the system level, the activation of the AI component and its interaction with non-AI components can raise ethical concerns, such as the use of dark patterns in user interface and interaction (UI/UX) design. Procuring AI technologies or solutions from third parties can introduce ethical risks into the systems. At the model level, there can be inappropriate learning architecture or algorithms or unethical data sources. During the implementation stage, unwanted bias can be introduced in data collection and model training. There also can be privacy or bias issues in the data annotation and use. Although application programming interfaces (APIs) are crucial for limiting the use of AI systems and enforcing governance, ethical issues can often be associated with their design. For example, data breaches may occur through an API. At the testing stage, there can be incorrect testing criteria and flawed conclusions. Ethical checks should also be performed for test cases. When AI systems are deployed on a large scale, there can be more ethical risks. Data drift, which occurs during runtime, requires continuous monitoring and validation to ensure that the system remains responsible.

To address the responsible AI (RAI) issues that may arise during the development of AI systems, it is important to implement a set of best practices at each stage of the process. These best practices can be presented in the form of patterns that can be integrated into the development process. Figure 5.2 illustrates the process patterns that can be incorporated into the development process.

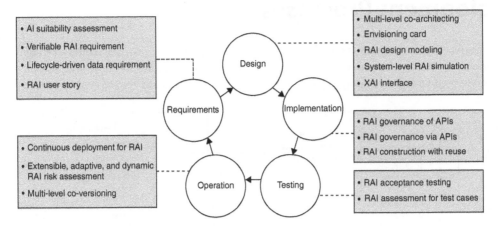

Figure 5.2
Process patterns for responsible AI.

Requirements

In practice, ethical requirements of AI systems are often neglected or only outlined as high-level project objectives. To ensure that these ethical requirements are fully captured and considered, it is important to extend and adapt existing requirements to engineering methodologies, while recognizing the unique characteristics of AI systems such as continuous learning and autonomy. The ethical principles for AI systems can be organized into two groups. The first group includes privacy protection and security; reliability and safety; fairness; human-centered values; and human, societal, and environmental well-being. These principles are similar to traditional software qualities and can be considered as nonfunctional requirements. The second group includes transparency and explainability, contestability, and accountability, which are meta-level governance issues and can be classified as functional requirements for improving users' confidence in the AI system. In this section, we introduce four process patterns that can be used in the requirements stage for RAI systems.

P.1. AI Suitability Assessment

The development team should assess the suitability of using AI in the software system they plan to build.

Context

AI technology is not always the best fit for every problem. Using AI in a software system can introduce additional complexity and risk. Thus, it is important to make sure that the benefits outweigh the potential drawbacks.

Problem

How can we determine whether to adopt AI in the design or not?

Solution

Before the development team starts to build a software system with AI, it is crucial for the team to carefully consider the suitability of using AI to solve the specific problem and to address the corresponding user needs. The team should assess whether the software system would benefit from the incorporation of AI or whether it may be negatively impacted. It is essential to ensure that the use of AI adds value to the overall system. Sometimes a heuristic-based approach may be more appropriate, because it may be easier and cheaper to develop and can provide better predictability and transparency compared to an AI-based system. To determine the suitability of using AI, developers should take into account the purpose and context of the system, whether sufficient data is available to train an AI model, how well the model is performing, the potential outcomes of the AI systems, and so on.

Benefits

Here are the benefits of the verifiable ethical requirements pattern:

- **Value of AI:** AI suitability assessment helps the development team make sure the use of AI will add value to the design and will not degrade the software system.

- **Readiness:** AI suitability assessment helps the team identify whether they have the appropriate data and infrastructure to train the AI model and support the system.

Drawbacks

Here are the drawbacks of the verifiable ethical requirements pattern:

- **Time and cost:** Conducting an AI suitability assessment can be time consuming and costly.

- **Lack of expertise:** The team may not have the necessary expertise to perform a proper assessment.

Related Patterns

D.5. AI mode switcher: The result of the AI suitability assessment may affect the design of the AI mode switcher.

Known Uses

Here are the known uses of the AI suitability assessment pattern:

- In Google PAIR Guidebook, one of the patterns is to determine whether AI adds value.[1]

- The AI Suitability Toolkit for Nonprofits provides a set of questions to consider—from whether to use AI to how to develop and maintain AI solutions.[2]

- Scott et al. propose a checklist of questions for assessing suitability of AI applications in healthcare.[3]

P.2. Verifiable RAI Requirement

RAI requirements should be expressed in a verifiable way to make the development of AI systems compliant with AI ethics principles.

Context

The development of AI systems must be guided by AI ethics principles. These principles are generally abstract and domain-agnostic. RAI requirements should be derived from the AI ethics principles to fit the specific domain and system context. By defining RAI requirements early in the AI system development process, the development team can integrate ethical considerations throughout the entire process.

---

1. https://pair.withgoogle.com/guidebook/patterns.

2. https://nethope.app.box.com/s/ot0dhatbx0ddwplux2lo924mtk1p0cew.

3. I. Scott, S. Carter, and E. Coiera, "Clinician Checklist for Assessing Suitability of Machine Learning Applications in Healthcare," *BMJ Health & Care Informatics* 28, no. 1 (2021).

Problem

How can we verify that the developed AI systems meet the RAI requirements?

Solution

Every RAI requirement included in a requirements specification document should be clearly and verifiably defined, with specific acceptance criteria. It should be possible for a person or machine to later check the AI system to confirm that it meets the RAI requirements that were derived from the AI ethics principles. The use of vague or unverifiable statements should be avoided. If it is not possible to determine whether the AI system meets a particular RAI requirement, this ethical requirement should be revised or removed from the requirements specification document.

Benefits

Here are the benefits of the verifiable RAI requirement pattern:

- **Reduced ethical risk:** When RAI requirements are considered from the beginning of the development process and RAI requirements are explicitly verified, the risk of ethical violations can be reduced.

- **Customer expectation:** By providing verifiable RAI requirements, the development team is able to ensure that the RAI aspects of the delivered AI system meet the expectation of the customer.

Drawbacks

Here are the drawbacks of the verifiable RAI requirement pattern:

- **Hard to use for some intangible RAI requirements:** Some RAI principles/requirements may not be easily quantitatively validated, such as human-centered values.

- **Additional complexity:** Creating verifiable RAI requirements can add complexity to the development process, requiring the team to define acceptance criteria.

Related Patterns

Here are the related patterns of the verifiable RAI requirement pattern:

- P.3. Lifecycle-driven data requirement: Data requirements specification could include a set of verifiable RAI requirements around data.

- P.4. RAI user story: RAI user stories can be used to elicit and document verifiable RAI requirements.

- P.5. Multi-level co-architecting: All the RAI requirements need to be considered during the architecture design.

- D.8. Continuous RAI validator: The RAI requirements need to be continuously monitored and validated at runtime.

Known Uses

Here are the known uses of the verifiable RAI requirement pattern:

- AI ethical principles can be viewed as RAI requirements for the specified functionalities offered by the AI systems or the entities providing the system.[4]

- RAI requirements should be specified explicitly as the expected system outputs and outcomes (e.g., intended benefits) in a verifiable manner.

- Qualities of machine learning can be specified as nonfunctional reliability requirements.[5]

P.3. Lifecycle-Driven Data Requirement

Data requirements must be clearly defined throughout the data lifecycle, taking into account the ethical considerations and responsibilities of all stakeholders.

Context

The effectiveness of an AI model is heavily reliant on the quality of the data used to train or evaluate it. The data lifecycle is composed of several key phases, including data collection, cleaning, preparation, validation, analysis, and termination. However, the scope of data requirements often focuses on the data analysis phase, neglecting the other key phases in the data lifecycle. This focus can result in downstream ethical concerns, such as unreliable models, lack of accountability, and unfairness. To ensure trust in AI systems, it is vital to manage the data lifecycle carefully.

Problem

How can we make sure data is responsibly used and managed?

Solution

To ensure that data is used and managed in a responsible manner, it is essential to explicitly list and specify data requirements throughout the entire data lifecycle, including collection, cleaning, preparation, validation, analysis, and termination. These requirements should take into account all relevant ethical principles and all stakeholders involved in the process, including data providers, data

---

4. L. Zhu et al., "AI and Ethics—Operationalising Responsible AI," arXiv preprint arXiv:2105.08867, 2021.

5. Q. Lu et al., "Software Engineering for Responsible AI: An Empirical Study and Operationalised Patterns," *IEEE/ACM 44th International Conference on Software Engineering: Software Engineering in Practice (ICSE-SEIP)*, 2022.

engineers, data scientists, data consumers, and data auditors. A comprehensive data requirements specification document can be created to manage and document these data requirements,[6] which can include detailed requirements on each phase of the data lifecycle (e.g., requirements about data sources and collection methods). In addition to data requirements, the specification should include basic information about the dataset, such as its vision, motivation, intended/nonintended uses, examples of data instances, and stakeholders consulted. The data requirements specification documents should have a clearly assigned owner, created date, and last updated date for traceability and accountability.

Benefits

Here are the benefits of the lifecycle-driven data requirement pattern:

- **Improved data quality:** When data requirements are specified and managed throughout the data lifecycle, the quality of the data can be improved, which in turn leads to more accurate and reliable AI models.
- **Compliance with regulations:** Having a data requirements specification can help organizations comply with RAI regulations.

Drawbacks

Here are the drawbacks of the lifecycle-driven data requirement pattern:

- **Different vocabularies:** Stakeholders may have different vocabularies about data requirements.
- **Development inefficiency:** To speed up the development and reduce the cost required, the development team may start collecting data before the data requirements specification is complete.

Related Patterns

P.2. Verifiable RAI requirement: Data requirements specification can include a set of verifiable RAI requirements around data.

Known Uses

Here are the known uses and related work of the lifecycle-driven data requirements throughout the lifecycle pattern:

- Google has created a template for dataset requirements specification,[7] which can be used to manage and track data requirements.

---

6. L. Zhu et al., "AI and Ethics—Operationalising Responsible AI," arXiv preprint arXiv:2105.08867, 2021.

7. B. Hutchinson et al., "Towards Accountability for Machine Learning Datasets: Practices from Software Engineering and Infrastructure," *Proceedings of the 2021 ACM Conference on Fairness, Accountability, and Transparency* 2021, Association for Computing Machinery: Virtual Event, Canada, 560–75.

- Requirements, including data requirements, should be regularly updated to reflect the changing needs of the users.[8]

- Data governance should be implemented and followed throughout the entire data lifecycle.[9]

P.4. RAI User Story

RAI requirements can be elicited and incorporated into the product backlog in the form of RAI user stories.

Context

Considering AI ethics from the early stages of AI system development is crucial. However, it can be challenging because AI ethics principles are often high level and abstract, providing limited guidance to the development team. Additionally, RAI requirements are often overlooked or only briefly described as project objectives. It is necessary to use specific requirements elicitation methods to collect detailed RAI requirements from relevant stakeholders.

Problem

How can RAI requirements be elicited?

Solution

In an agile development process, RAI user stories are created and added to the product backlog. These RAI user stories can be tackled by the development team during sprints. One way to facilitate the creation of RAI user stories is by using card-based toolkits, which list questions related to AI ethics principles. The answers to these questions then can be integrated into RAI user stores and included in sprint backlogs. The development team or users can write RAI user stories on cards or notes using predefined templates and assign them to different sprints based on the priority.

Benefits

Here are the benefits of the RAI user story pattern:

- **Increased traceability:** RAI user stories make RAI requirements traceable both backward and forward.

---

8. A. Vogelsang and M. Borg, "Requirements Engineering for Machine Learning: Perspectives from Data Scientists," *IEEE 27th International Requirements Engineering Conference Workshops (REW)*, 2019.

9. S. U. Lee, L. Zhu, and R. Jeffery, "A Data Governance Framework for Platform Ecosystem Process Management," *International Conference on Business Process Management*, 2018.

- **RAI requirements elicitation:** RAI user stories can help the development team elicit RAI requirements for AI systems and implement AI ethics principles from the early stage of development.

- **Ethical awareness:** RAI user stories can help to increase the RAI awareness of the development team.

Drawbacks

Here are the drawbacks of the RAI user story pattern:

- **Lack of scalability:** RAI user stories are difficult to scale for larger projects.

- **Bias:** The process of writing RAI user stories maybe influenced by the personal biases of the stakeholders involved.

- **Inability to anticipate all RAI concerns:** It is possible to miss some RAI concerns when identifying the RAI requirements.

Related Patterns

Here are the related patterns of the RAI user story pattern:

- P.2. Verifiable RAI requirements: Acceptance criteria should be included in the RAI user stories to make the ethical requirements verifiable.

- P.13. RAI acceptance testing: In the agile process, the customer can write the acceptance tests before the development team implements the RAI user story.

Known Uses

Here are the known uses and related work of the RAI user story pattern:

- The Guide for Artificial Intelligence Ethical Requirements Elicitation consists of 25 cards that the development team uses to answer questions related to ethical principles.[10] The answers are used to create RAI requirements in the form of RAI user stories, which are included in sprint backlogs.

- ECCOLA consists of 21 cards, which are divided into 8 themes and with questions to be answered by the development team.[11]

- Perera et al. assess the impacts of considering human values in requirements engineering activities, including writing user stories.[12]

---

10. https://josesiqueira.github.io/RE4AIEthicalGuide/index.html.

11. E. Halme et al., *How to Write Ethical User Stories? Impacts of the ECCOLA Method* (Springer International Publishing, 2021).

12. H. Perera et al., "The Impact of Considering Human Values During Requirements Engineering Activities," arXiv preprint arXiv:2111.15293, 2021.

Design

There has been a growing interest in incorporating ethical principles and human values into the design process of AI systems. Value-sensitive design is an approach that integrates human values throughout the entire design process. One effective way to implement value-sensitive design for responsible AI systems is through the use of participatory co-design workshops, which involve developers and stakeholders using various toolkits and methods, such as envisioning. Software design modeling methodologies should be adapted to consider ethical concerns when making design decisions. Before AI systems are deployed in the real world, it is crucial to perform system-level simulation to analyze the potential ethical impact of the AI systems' behavior. Various trust factors should be taken into consideration during the design process, including system capability, interface availability, and agent personality (such as physical representation, visual figure, and voice embodiment). There are ways to increase the level of human trust in AI systems through the use of explainable AI (XAI) user interfaces. These interfaces can incorporate features such as anthropomorphism, proactively informing users about data collection and benefits provided, informing users of the system's capabilities and limitations, and providing credentials of AI systems and operators. This section explores various process patterns that can be used in the design process from a system perspective.

P.5. Multi-Level Co-Architecting

Multi-level co-architecting is necessary to ensure the smooth integration of various components, including co-designing AI and non-AI components, as well as co-designing different components within the AI model pipeline.

Context

The architecture of AI systems is more complex than that of traditional software due to the multiple levels of integration required. On the one hand, AI models are developed by data scientists and engineers using an AI model pipeline, which typically consists of a series of automated steps such as data collection, cleaning, feature engineering, model training, and evaluation. These steps can be viewed as software components for producing AI models from a software architecture perspective. On the other hand, the resulting AI models cannot function on their own and must be integrated into software systems for deployment in the real world. The decisions made by the AI model need to be executed through actions performed by other software components. For example, after an AI model classifies a plastic bottle, a controller component must instruct a robot arm to dispose of the bottle in the appropriate waste bin.

Problem

What are the ways to ensure the seamless integration of different components in an AI system?

Solution

The architecture of an AI ecosystem is composed of three layers: the AI software supply chain, the AI system, and the operation infrastructure. The focus of the AI software supply chain layer is on the development and management of AI and non-AI components, including components of the AI model pipeline, deployment components, co-versioning components, provenance tracking components, and credential management components. The AI system layer includes AI components that incorporate AI models and non-AI components that utilize the outputs of AI components for overall system functionalities. The operation infrastructure layer primarily supports monitoring and feedback components. Ensuring the seamless integration of different components requires multi-level co-architecting, including co-designing both AI and non-AI components, as well as co-designing different components within the AI model pipeline. Both system-level and model-level (ethical) requirements must be taken into consideration when making design decisions.

Benefits

Here are the benefits of the multi-level co-architecting pattern:

- **Consideration of both system and model requirements:** Multi-level co-architecting enables the consideration of both system and model requirements in the design decision-making process.
- **Improved system-level design thinking:** Data scientists and engineers who may not have expertise in software engineering often iteratively develop and experiment with AI components. Multi-level co-architecting can enhance the system-level design thinking of the data scientists and engineers.

Drawbacks

Here are the drawbacks of the multi-level co-architecting pattern:

- **Cost:** Multi-level co-architecting may involve an increase in communication overhead.
- **Productivity:** The implementation of multi-level co-architecting may result in a slower development pace.

Related Patterns

P.2. Verifiable RAI requirements: All ethical requirements should be taken into account during the design of architecture.

Known Uses

Here are the known uses and related work of the multi-level co-architecting pattern:

- Lewis et al. propose co-architecting the AI system and the system that supports the AI model pipeline.[13]

- Lo et al. present a reference architecture of federated learning systems that includes a federated AI model pipeline and non-AI components.[14]

- Muccini and Vaidhyanathan provide an architecture of an AI-based software system that includes both AI subsystem and software subsystem.[15]

P.6. Envisioning Card

Envisioning cards are created to assist the development team in incorporating human values into the design processes of AI systems.

Context

Responsible AI refers to the development and use of AI systems that adhere to ethical principles, such as Australian AI Ethics Principles.[16] One of these principles is human-centered values. However, developers often find it challenging to implement these high-level principles in practice due to a lack of technical guidance and tools. The ethical principles do not provide concrete guidance and software engineering methods on how to design an AI system that aligns with these principles.

Problem

What are ways to ensure that human-centered values are incorporated in the design of AI systems?

Solution

Envisioning cards are designed to help the development team operationalize human values during the design processes for AI systems. The cards are based on four envisioning criteria, including

13. G. A. Lewis, I. Ozkaya, and X. Xu, "Software Architecture Challenges for ML Systems," *IEEE International Conference on Software Maintenance and Evolution (ICSME)*, 2021.

14. S. K. Lo et al., "FLRA: A Reference Architecture for Federated Learning Systems," *European Conference on Software Architecture*, 2021.

15. H. Muccini and K. Vaidhyanathan, "Software Architecture for Ml-Based Systems: What Exists and What Lies Ahead," *IEEE/ACM 1st Workshop on AI Engineering-Software Engineering for AI (WAIN)*, 2021.

16. https://www.industry.gov.au/data-and-publications/australias-artificial-intelligence-ethics-framework.

stakeholder, time, value, and pervasiveness. The stakeholder criterion helps the team consider the effects of the AI system on both direct and indirect holders. The time criterion emphasizes the long-term implication of the AI system on humans, society, and environment. The value criterion guides the team to consider the impact of the AI system on human values. The pervasiveness criterion addresses the challenges encountered if an AI system is widely adopted in terms of geography, culture, demographics, and so on.

Benefits

The benefits of using envisioning cards include

- **Low cost:** The use of envisioning cards is at a relatively low cost, in terms of both money and time.

- **Communication:** Envisioning cards provide a visual representation of ideas; the cards also make these ideas easy to understand and share with others.

Drawbacks

There are some potential drawbacks of using envisioning cards:

- **Limited scalability:** Scaling the use of envisioning cards can be challenging when working with large teams or complex AI systems.

- **Potential for biases:** Envisioning cards can be influenced by the biases of the individuals using them.

Known Uses

Here are the known uses and related work of the envisioning card pattern:

- To increase awareness of impacts on human values, the VSD Lab created envisioning cards, which can be used in the design stage based on five envisioning criteria: stakeholders, time, values, pervasiveness, and multi-lifespan.[17]

- Nathan et al. propose four envisioning criteria—stakeholders, time, values, and pervasiveness—and characterize how the criteria can be considered in interactive system design.[18]

P.7. RAI Design Modeling

RAI design modeling can be useful for capturing and analyzing ethical principles in the design process.

---

17. https://www.envisioningcards.com/.

18. L. P. Nathan et al., "Envisioning Systemic Effects on Persons and Society Throughout Interactive System Design," *Proceedings of the 7th ACM Conference on Designing Interactive Systems,* 2008.

Context

AI has been widely adopted across various domains, such as finance and HR. The widespread adoption of AI systems brings growing public interest and concerns with RAI. The autonomous and opaque decision-making of AI systems can lead to erroneous, unintended, or undesired outcomes, such as bias in hiring. To reduce these RAI risks, the development team needs to adhere to ethical principles during the design process of AI systems.

Problem

How can we ensure that ethical principles are incorporated into the design of AI systems?

Solution

Methods of design modeling can be extended and applied to support the modeling of AI components and ethical considerations. This can include using Unified Modeling Language (UML) to describe the architecture of AI systems and represent their ethical aspects, designing formal models that take into account human values, using ontology to model AI system artifacts for accountability, creating RAI knowledge bases to inform design decisions that consider ethical concerns, and using logic programming to implement ethical principles. UML can be an effective language for describing AI systems and providing the necessary information for all stakeholders to make the AI system responsible. An extension of UML could include a declarative graphic notation for AI system architecture, with additional stereotypes/metamodel elements for responsible-AI-by-design reference architecture. Use case diagrams can help define stakeholders and their purposes, which is crucial for achieving accountability. State diagrams are useful for analyzing system states and identifying states that may cause ethical failures. Design patterns, such as the AI mode switcher, can be implemented to shift the state of an AI system to a more human-controlled state. Sequence diagrams can describe human-AI interactions and ensure all necessary explanations are provided.

Benefits

The benefits of using the RAI design modeling pattern include

- **Enhanced ability to test and validate:** RAI design models can provide a complete and clear representation of an AI system's design, helping to identify RAI issues before deployment and making it easier to test and validate the system.

- **Better communication:** RAI design models can help to make the design of complex RAI systems more understandable and allow for better communication and collaboration among stakeholders.

Drawbacks

The drawbacks of the RAI design modeling pattern are

- **Time:** One disadvantage when using modeling languages is the time required to create and manage the models.
- **Complexity:** Creating accurate and comprehensive design models can be challenging because AI systems can be highly complex.

Related Patterns

D.5. AI mode switcher: An AI mode switcher can be utilized to initiate a state transition and alter the system's state to a safe state.

Known Uses

Here are the known uses and related work of the RAI design modeling pattern:

- Takeda et al. adopt SysML to represent the AI system design and describe the ethical aspects.[19]
- Fish and Stark build human values into formal models of AI systems.[20]
- Naja et al. use ontology to model the AI system artifacts for accountability.[21]

P.8. System-Level RAI Simulation

System-level RAI simulation is a cost-effective way to comprehend the characteristics and behaviors of AI systems and to assess potential RAI risks before deploying them in the real world.

Context

AI is becoming increasingly prevalent and significant in our society. Many software systems have integrated AI for identifying patterns in data and making data-driven decisions in an autonomous and potentially opaque manner. This autonomous and opaque decision-making brings a high level

---

19. M. Takeda et al., "Accountable System Design Architecture for Embodied AI: A Focus on Physical Human Support Robots," *Advanced Robotics* 33, no. 23 (2019): 1248–63.

20. B. Fish and L. Stark, "Reflexive Design for Fairness and Other Human Values in Formal Models," *Proceedings of the 2021 AAAI/ACM Conference on AI, Ethics, and Society*, 2021, Association for Computing Machinery: Virtual Event, USA. 89–99.

21. I. Naja et al., *A Semantic Framework to Support AI System Accountability and Audit* (Springer International Publishing, 2021).

of uncertainty in the behavior and can result in serious RAI risks and unintended consequences. To avoid ethical disasters and gain public trust, it is essential to have a thorough understanding of the characteristics and behaviors of AI systems.

Problem

What are ways to understand the characteristics and behaviors of AI systems to prevent severe and unnecessary consequences?

Solution

System-level RAI simulation is a cost-effective way to assess the behaviors of AI systems before deploying them in the real world. A simulation model needs to be constructed in a way that mimics the potential behaviors and decisions of the AI system and assesses the ethical impacts. The assessment results can then be shared with the development team or potential users before the AI systems are deployed in the real world.

Benefits

Here are the benefits of the system-level RAI simulation pattern:

- **Reduced ethical risks:** Simulating AI systems at the system level can uncover potential RAI risks and enhance the ethical quality of AI systems.

- **Cost efficiency:** System-level simulation can anticipate potential RAI risks and prevent severe ethical disasters before deploying AI systems in the real world.

Drawbacks

The drawbacks of the system-level RAI simulation pattern are

- **Limited accuracy:** The simulation model is based on the assumptions and data used to build the simulation model. These assumptions may not reflect real-world scenarios fully, leading to limited prediction capability.

- **Lack of scalability:** Simulation models are often designed for a specific use case; thus they may not be easily adaptable to other scenarios.

Related Patterns

D.11. RAI digital twin: An RAI digital twin performs system-level simulation in real time using live data. The assessment results are fed back to alert the system or user before unethical behavior or decisions take effect.

Known Uses

Here are the known uses of the system-level RAI simulation pattern:

- NVIDIA DRIVE Sim is an end-to-end simulation platform for self-driving vehicles.[22]

- rfPro is a software solution that provides driving simulation and digital twin capabilities for autonomous driving.[23]

- Singh et al. present a simulation-driven design approach for ensuring the safety of autonomous vehicles.[24]

P.9. XAI Interface

Explainable AI (XAI) can be viewed as a human-AI interaction problem and achieved through human-centered interface design.

Context

AI system users often lack understanding of how decisions are made by these systems and are unaware of their capabilities or limitations. The missing explainability can lead to a lack of trust in these systems, and this has been recognized as one of the most pressing challenges that need to be addressed.

Problem

How can AI users comprehend the decisions and behaviors of AI systems?

Solution

XAI can be considered as a human-AI interaction problem and achieved through human-centered interface design. One common approach to designing explainable user interfaces is using checklists or questions. These lists can assist in identifying user needs, choosing appropriate XAI techniques (such as rule-based explanations and feature attribution), and considering relevant XAI design factors.

---

22. https://developer.nvidia.com/drive/drive-sim.

23. https://rfpro.com/.

24. V. Singh et al., "Simulation Driven Design and Test for Safety of AI Based Autonomous Vehicles," *Proceedings of the IEEE/CVF Conference on Computer Vision and Pattern Recognition*, 2021.

Benefits

Here are the benefits of the XAI interface pattern:

- **Increased trust:** When clear explanations are provided to clarify how AI systems make decisions, users are better able to understand the capabilities and limitations of the AI technology and are more likely to trust and adopt the technology.

- **Reduced biases:** Explanations can help users identify and address biases in the AI systems.

Drawbacks

Here are the drawbacks of the XAI interface pattern:

- **Limited by users' background:** Users may not understand explanations with too many technical details. Explanations should be given in terms familiar to users.

- **Inefficiency:** There is no need to explain when the users are aware of the ethical risk.

Related Patterns

The related patterns of the XAI interface pattern include

- T.6. Local Explainer: Integrating local explanations into the XAI interface enhances the transparency of decision-making by providing a rationale for how and why a data instance was given a decision.

- T.7. Global Explainer: Incorporating global explanations into the interface design allows AI users with a better understanding of the global behaviors of AI systems.

- D.11. RAI digital twin: A RAI digital twin performs system-level simulation at runtime using real-time data. The simulation results are sent back to alert the system or user via XAI interfaces before the unethical behavior or decision takes effect.

Known Uses

Here are the known uses and related work of the XAI interface design pattern:

- Liao et al. provide a checklist of questions on input, output, performance (can be extended to ethical performance), how, why and why not, what if, and so on.[25]

---

25. Q. V. Liao, D. Gruen, and S. Miller, "Questioning the AI: Informing Design Practices for Explainable AI User Experiences," *Proceedings of the 2020 CHI Conference on Human Factors in Computing Systems*, 2020.

- The design of conversational interfaces can be experimented via a Wizard of Oz study,[26] in which users interact with a system that they believe to be autonomous but is actually being operated by a hidden human, called the Wizard. The conversation data is collected and analyzed to understand requirements for a self-explanatory conversational interface.

- Luxton recommends using anthropomorphism in the user interface design to improve human trust in AI systems.[27]

Implementation

Developers need to continuously maintain documentation for the implementation of both AI and non-AI components. A repository can be used to track and manage code evolution (e.g., the author of each line or change). Reusing the existing AI artifacts can speed up the development of AI systems. APIs are essential for RAI governance. On the other hand, APIs can also introduce ethical issues (e.g., data breaches). Therefore, ethical compliance checks need to be performed on APIs (e.g., through an RAI knowledge graph). This section discusses the process patterns that developers can adopt during the implementation stage.

P.10. RAI Governance of APIs

An RAI knowledge base can be built to support compliance checking for APIs.

Context

AI libraries or services offer reusable functionality APIs that developers can utilize during the development of AI systems. APIs can increase efficiency and significantly reduce the development cost and time associated with developing AI systems. However, it is important to consider potential ethical concerns, such as data privacy breaches or fairness issues, when utilizing APIs.

Problem

What are the ways to ensure that the design of APIs adheres to RAI regulations?

---

26. S. F. Jentzsch, S. Höhn, and N. Hochgeschwender, "Conversational Interfaces for Explainable AI: A Human-Centred Approach," *International Workshop on Explainable, Transparent Autonomous Agents and Multi-Agent Systems*, 2019.

27. D. D. Luxton, "Recommendations for the Ethical Use and Design of Artificial Intelligent Care Providers," *Artificial Intelligence in Medicine* 62, no. 1 (2014): 1–10.

Solution

RAI compliance checking is necessary to detect whether any potential violation exists in the design of APIs. A knowledge-driven approach can be adopted to detect ethics issues using an RAI knowledge base. The RAI knowledge base provides a structured representation of meaningful entities, concepts, and their relationships in the development of AI systems. The rich relationships between entities are made explicit and traceable across various high-level documents and AI system artifacts. The RAI knowledge base can be constructed based on ethical principles and guidelines, such as the General Data Protection Regulation (GDPR), and technical documents like API documentation to support the RAI compliance checking for APIs.

Benefits

Here are the benefits of the RAI governance of APIs pattern:

- **Compliance checking:** The RAI knowledge base, derived from the RAI regulatory documents and principles, provides structured data to support the creation of RAI compliance checking solutions for API design.

- **Reduced verification cost:** The RAI knowledge base can greatly reduce the labor cost associated with compliance checking.

Drawbacks

Here are the drawbacks of the RAI governance of APIs pattern:

- **Increased development cost:** Building an RAI knowledge base using natural language processing techniques can be time consuming and error prone.

- **Lack of expertise:** It may require expertise in RAI regulations, as well as technical knowledge of API design.

Related Patterns

D.10. RAI knowledge base: The RAI knowledge base can be built to perform compliance checking for APIs.

Known Uses

Here are the known uses and related work of the RAI governance of APIs pattern:

- Pandit et al. create a knowledge-based system for GDPR compliance checking.[28]

---

28. H. J. Pandit, D. O'Sullivan, and D. Lewis, "Towards Knowledge-Based Systems for GDPR Compliance," in *CKGSemStats@ ISWC*, 2018.

- Libal designs a tool named the NAI suite that annotates GDPR article 13 and checks the process of data collection and processing.[29]

- Hussain et al. present the effects of API security mechanisms on GDPR.[30]

P.11. RAI Governance via APIs

To restrict the way AI systems are used, developers can provide AI services in the cloud and control the interactions with these services via APIs.

Context

Some AI systems may possess high-risk capabilities, which can be used or modified to perform harmful tasks. These capabilities may include natural language processing, speech and facial recognition, and decision-making abilities. It is crucial for developers to be aware of these high-risk capabilities and implement strict access controls to prevent any suspicious activity.

Problem

How can developers limit the use of AI systems?

Solution

To prevent harmful dual use of AI systems, developers should carefully consider both the intended and unintended uses of their AI systems. This includes being aware of ways the systems may be adapted or modified. To limit the use of AI systems, developers should implement restrictions on the way AI systems are used and prevent the users from getting around restrictions by unauthorized reverse-engineering or modification of the system design. One way to do this is by providing AI services on cloud platforms and managing interactions through API controls, rather than allowing AI systems to run locally with unrestricted access.

Benefits

Here are the benefits of using the RAI governance via APIs pattern:

- **Compliance with regulations:** Providing AI services on cloud platforms and controlling interactions through API controls can help developers comply with RAI regulatory requirements.

---

29. T. Libal, "Towards Automated GDPR Compliance Checking," *International Workshop on the Foundations of Trustworthy AI Integrating Learning, Optimization and Reasoning*, 2020.

30. F. Hussain et al., "Enterprise API Security and GDPR Compliance: Design and Implementation Perspective," *IT Professional* 22, no. 5 (2020): 81–89.

- **Protection against malicious use:** By restricting access to AI systems and preventing unauthorized modifications, developers can reduce the risk of their systems being used for harmful purposes.

Drawbacks

Here are the drawbacks of the RAI governance via APIs pattern:

- **Dependence on cloud providers:** By hosting AI services on cloud platforms, developers may become dependent on the platform providers and their policies.

- **Limited access to certain users:** Some users may be prevented from accessing the AI services if they do not have much knowledge about how to use APIs.

- **Limited performance:** Offering AI services on cloud platforms may result in longer response times compared to local deployment.

Related Patterns

G.1. AI regulation: The design of APIs must be compliant with AI regulations.

Known Uses

Here are the known uses of the RAI governance via APIs pattern:

- OpenAI's language model GPT-3 can be integrated with AI systems only via APIs by authorized users.[31]

- Google Vision AI restricts its facial recognition feature to a selected number of celebrities through the use of APIs.[32]

- Amazon Rekognition provides customizable computer vision APIs for building image and video analysis capabilities.[33]

P.12. RAI Construction with Reuse

It is highly desirable and valuable to ethically reuse the AI artifacts across different applications.

---

31. https://openai.com/api/.

32. https://cloud.google.com/vision.

33. https://aws.amazon.com/cn/rekognition/.

Context

Building AI systems from scratch can be very complex and time consuming. Larger companies usually have significant investments in AI and access to large volumes of data, allowing them to compete effectively in the market. In contrast, smaller companies may have only a small team of data scientists, making it challenging for them to compete with larger companies.

Problem

How can we build AI systems cost-effectively?

Solution

It is highly desirable and valuable to reuse AI assets, including AI components and AI pipeline artifacts, across different applications. Construction with reuse refers to the development of RAI systems using existing AI assets, such as those found from an organizational repository or an open-source platform. A marketplace can be established to facilitate the trading of reusable AI assets, including component code, models, and datasets. Blockchain technology can be utilized to create an immutable and transparent marketplace, allowing the auction-based trading of AI assets and material assets, such as cloud resources.

Benefits

Here are the benefits of the RAI construction with reuse pattern:

- **Increased development efficiency:** Using existing AI assets can significantly accelerate the development process. Reusing the assets that have been previously tested can improve the overall quality of the AI system.

- **Faster time to market:** By using existing AI assets, companies can save time and bring their AI systems to market faster.

Drawbacks

Here are the drawbacks of the RAI construction with reuse pattern:

- **Limited by the quality of AI assets:** The quality of reused AI assets may not meet the ethical requirements or may have potential RAI risks.

- **Limited customization:** The reused AI assets may limit the degree of customization for a specific application, as the assets may not perfectly align with the requirements.

- **Increased communication cost:** Reusing AI assets from external sources may require additional effort and cost for communication.

Related Patterns

D.2. Verifiable RAI credential: To ensure ethical quality, RAI credentials can be linked to the AI assets or developers, which can be supported by blockchain platforms.

Known Uses

Here are the known uses and related work of the RAI construction with reuse pattern:

- pytorch2keras is a model migration tool converting PyTorch to Keras models.[34]
- Lewis and Ozkaya highlight that glue code is necessary for integrating AI components with different systems.[35]
- SAIaaS is a blockchain-based marketplace for trading AI artifacts and running AI tasks.[36]

Testing

Testing is the process of verifying whether an AI system meets the specified requirements and fulfills the intended purpose in a responsible way. RAI acceptance testing is specially designed to identify ethical flaws and verify ethical requirements. When an ethical requirement is added, the corresponding new test cases need to be designed and pass the RAI assessment. Records of testing history should be maintained, including how the RAI issues were addressed and by whom. Traditional testing techniques can be adapted for testing AI systems. Unit testing can be performed for both AI and non-AI components based on the specification (including model-level specification). The interactions between AI and non-AI components need to be verified by incremental integration testing. Usability testing is crucial in evaluating stakeholder satisfaction. In this section, we discuss the patterns used by testers during the testing stage.

P.13. RAI Acceptance Testing

RAI acceptance testing is conducted to determine whether the ethical requirements of an AI system are met.

---

34. https://github.com/gmalivenko/pytorch2keras.

35. Lewis and Ozkaya, https://insights.sei.cmu.edu/blog/software-engineering-for-machine-learning-characterizing-and-detecting-mismatch-in-machine-learning-systems/.

36. N. Six, A. Perrichon-Chrétien, and N. Herbaut, "SAIaaS: A Blockchain-Based Solution for Secure Artificial Intelligence as a Service." The International Conference on Deep Learning, Big Data and Blockchain (Dee-BDB 2021), 67–74.

Context

AI ethics principles are designed to ensure the AI systems and their development processes are trustworthy and responsible. These principles, which are very high level, need to be captured through specific ethical requirements that can be adopted by the development team. The requirements serve as a set of agreed-upon commitments that guides the development of AI systems.

Problem

How can we make sure that the ethical requirements have been met?

Solution

RAI acceptance testing, such as bias testing, is designed to detect design flaws in RAI systems and verify that ethical requirements have been met—for example, whether the data pipeline has appropriate privacy control, fairness testing for training, and validation data. In an agile development process, ethical requirements can be framed as ethical user stories and associated with corresponding acceptance tests. These tests serve as a contract between the customer and development team, and can be used to quantify the behavior of the AI system. The acceptance criteria for each ethical principle should be clearly defined in a testable way. The history of ethical acceptance testing should be recorded and tracked, including how and by whom the ethical issues were addressed. A testing leader may be appointed to lead the ethical acceptance testing for each principle. For example, if bias is detected at runtime, the monitoring reports are returned to the bias testing leader for review.

Benefits

Here are the benefits of the RAI acceptance testing pattern:

- **Measurement of ethical requirements:** RAI acceptance tests help capture the ethical requirements and measure the extent to which the AI system meets the requirements.

- **Improved users' confidence:** RAI acceptance tests ensure that the decisions and behaviors of AI systems are consistent with AI ethics principles.

Drawbacks

There are some drawbacks of the RAI acceptance testing pattern:

- **Limited maintainability:** RAI acceptance tests may require frequent updates as ethical requirements evolve over time.

- **Limited coverage:** RAI acceptance tests may not be able to cover all possible ethical concerns and scenarios.

Related Patterns

The related patterns of the RAI acceptance testing pattern include

- P.4. RAI user story: In the agile process, the customer or product owner can write acceptance tests before the development team implements the ethical user story.

- P.14. RAI assessment for test cases: The ethical quality of all the test cases designed for RAI acceptance testing should be assessed.

Known Uses

Here are the known uses and related work of the RAI acceptance testing pattern:

- Chattopadhyay et al. test the robots' functionalities to detect faults and investigate how these faults can potentially lead to nonadherence with IEEE ethics principles.[37]

- Xie and Wu propose a method of testing the fairness of machine learning models.[38]

- Aggarwal et al. present a technique for automatically generating test inputs to detect discrimination against individuals.[39]

P.14. RAI Assessment for Test Cases

All the test cases for RAI acceptance testing should pass RAI assessment.

Context

Ensuring the ethical quality assurance for AI systems relies heavily on RAI acceptance testing, which aims to identify and solve ethical concerns with the AI system. A set of test cases with expected results should be maintained to detect possible ethical failures in various extreme situations. However, it is also important to note that the test cases themselves may contain ethical issues, such as fairness or privacy issues in the test data.

---

37. A. Chattopadhyay, A. Ali, and D. Thaxton. "Assessing the Alignment of Social Robots with Trustworthy AI Design Guidelines: A Preliminary Research Study," *Proceedings of the Eleventh ACM Conference on Data and Application Security and Privacy*, 2021.

38. W. Xie and P. Wu, "Fairness Testing of Machine Learning Models Using Deep Reinforcement Learning," *IEEE 19th International Conference on Trust, Security and Privacy in Computing and Communications (TrustCom)*, 2020.

39. A. Aggarwal et al., "Black Box Fairness Testing of Machine Learning Models," *Proceedings of the 2019 27th ACM Joint Meeting on European Software Engineering Conference and Symposium on the Foundations of Software Engineering*, 2019.

Problem

How can we ensure the ethical quality of test cases?

Solution

Creating high-quality test cases is an integral part of RAI acceptance testing. A test case usually includes an ID, description, preconditions, test steps, test data, expected results, actual results, status, creator name, creation date, executor name, and execution date. All the test cases for verification and validation must pass an RAI assessment, which includes evaluating the RAI metrics of the test steps and test data. Creation and execution information is essential to track the accountability of ethical issues with test cases. The assessment process can be integrated into the design of tools used to generate test cases.

Benefits

The benefits of the RAI assessment for test cases pattern include

- **Ethical quality:** RAI assessment can help improve the overall quality of the test case by identifying and address any ethical issues in the AI systems.

- **Adherence to ethical principles:** By conducting RAI assessment, developers can ensure that the test cases align with ethical principles.

Drawbacks

Here are the drawbacks of the RAI assessment for test cases pattern:

- **Limited scalability:** New test cases need to be continually added and assessed when new ethical requirements emerge or the operational context evolves.

- **Increased cost:** Conducting an RAI assessment for test cases can introduce additional development efforts and cost.

Related Patterns

P.13. RAI acceptance testing: The ethical quality of all test cases designed for RAI acceptance testing should be assessed.

Known Uses

Here are the known uses and related work of the RAI assessment for test cases pattern:

- Salman presents an approach for generating test cases based on the specifications using natural language processing techniques.[40]

- Wang et al. propose an approach for automatically generating unit tests for machine learning libraries.[41]

- Pynguin is a tool for developers to automatically generate unit tests.[42]

Operations

Given the continual learning of AI systems based on new data and the increased uncertainty and risks associated with the autonomy of the AI systems, there is a growing need for effective deployment strategies and continuous validation of RAI requirements. The current practices for ethical risk assessment are often one-time assessments rather than continuous assessments. Previous work on continuous monitoring and validation has primarily focused on the AI system outputs, such as performance metrics like accuracy, precision, and recall, rather than assessing the outcomes—that is, whether the AI system behaves and make decisions responsibly. An AI system usually involves the co-evolution of data, model, code, and configurations. This co-evolution can also occur between AI and non-AI components. The states of AI systems should be recorded to ensure traceability and accountability. This section presents the process patterns that can be used at the operation stage.

P.15. Continuous Deployment for RAI

New versions of AI systems can be seamlessly deployed into production environments by utilizing various deployment strategies that ensure fulfillment of RAI requirements.

Context

AI systems are often required to evolve frequently due to their dependence on data. Because the ethical performance of AI models may degrade over time, they need to be retrained with new data or features, and reintegrated into the AI components. The non-AI components may also need to be upgraded. As a result, it is necessary to continuously and frequently deploy new versions of AI systems into production environments. However, the autonomy of AI systems introduces a higher

---

40. A. Salman, "Test Case Generation from Specifications Using Natural Language Processing," thesis, KTH Royal Institute of Technology, 2020.

41. S. Wang et al., "Automatic Unit Test Generation for Machine Learning Libraries: How Far Are We?" *IEEE/ACM 43rd International Conference on Software Engineering (ICSE)*, 2021.

42. https://github.com/se2p/pynguin.

degree of uncertainty and risk. To mitigate the risks, various deployment strategies that support continuous deployment are highly desirable.

Problem

How can we ensure that new versions of AI systems are seamlessly deployed to production environments?

Solution

Various deployment strategies for AI systems can be used to ensure seamless deployment to production environments. Phased deployment refers to the process of initially deploying AI systems to a sub-group of users with the goal of reducing ethical risk. The new version of AI systems is rolled out incrementally and runs alongside the old version. Phased deployment also can be used to better supervise and control automation. This deployment is usually dependent on the potential consequences of the situation and the level of trust that users may have in the automated decisions made by the AI systems. Another strategy is A/B testing deployment, which is commonly used in industry. This type of deployment involves deploying different versions of the AI model to production and comparing their performance. The model that performs best in terms of ethical performance is selected. Additionally, existing practices, such as redundancy, can also be applied to AI components in an AI system, where multiple AI models work independently to improve ethical performance.

Benefits

Here are the benefits of the continuous deployment for RAI pattern:

- **Reduced ethical risk:** When small changes are frequently deployed with various deployment strategies, it is easier to identify and address ethical risks early on, which can lead to improved ethical quality of the overall system.

- **Improved customer satisfaction:** Continuous deployment with various strategies allows for faster delivery of new models with better ethical quality, resulting in improved customer satisfaction.

Drawbacks

Here are the drawbacks of the continuous deployment for RAI pattern:

- **Increased complexity:** Frequent deployment using different deployment strategies can make it more complex to keep track of the changes made and their potential impact on the overall system.

- **Reduced monitorability:** Monitoring can be challenging, especially if the AI system is large and complex.

Related Patterns

Both D.6. multi-model decision maker and D.7. homogenous redundancy apply redundancy as deployment strategies at different levels (i.e., AI models and components, respectively).

Known Uses

Here are the known uses of the continuous deployment for RAI pattern:

- Sato et al. summarize various deployment strategies for machine learning applications.[43]
- Amazon SageMarker provides services for training and deploying machine learning models. [44]
- Microsoft Azure Machine Learning is a platform for automating the machine learning lifecycle, including deployment.[45]

P.16. Extensible, Adaptive, and Dynamic RAI Risk Assessment

It is essential to continuously perform risk assessment and mitigation for RAI systems.

Context

The current risk-based approach to implement RAI often involves a done-once-and-forget algorithm-level risk assessment and mitigation for a sub-group of ethical principles, such as privacy or fairness, at a particular development step. However, this approach is inadequate for highly uncertain and continual learning AI systems. Furthermore, the context of AI systems can vary greatly across different application domains, organizations, cultures, and regions.

Problem

How can we measure the extent to which an AI system adheres to AI ethics principles in a given context?

Solution

It is essential to continuously perform risk assessment and mitigation for RAI systems. The RAI risk assessment framework can be built with specific extension points for different contexts, such as the

---

43. https://martinfowler.com/articles/cd4ml.html.

44. https://aws.amazon.com/cn/sagemaker/.

45. https://learn.microsoft.com/en-us/azure/machine-learning/overview-what-is-azure-machine-learning.

culture context. The risk mitigation can be approached in three ways: reducing the frequency of occurrence, decreasing the size of consequences, and improving the response to consequences.

Benefits

- **Better alignment with context:** By considering various extension points (such as cultural context), the RAI risk assessment and mitigation process can be better aligned with the specific context in which the AI systems is operating.

- **Reduced legal and reputational risks:** By continuously identifying and mitigating risks, the AI system can be less likely to violate laws and avoid reputational damage.

Drawbacks

- **Limited measurability:** It is hard to measure some of the ethics principles.

Related Patterns

G.12. RAI risk assessment: An organization's RAI risk assessment framework can be designed to be extensible, adaptive, and dynamic.

Known Uses

Here are the known uses of the extensible, adaptive, and dynamic ethical assessment pattern:

- NIST is developing an AI Risk Management Framework to improve AI trustworthiness.[46]

- The ISO/IEC JTC 1/SC 42 committee is developing ISO/IEC 23894 on artificial intelligence and risk management.[47]

- The Canadian government has released the Algorithmic Impact Assessment tool to identify the risks associated with automated decision-making systems.[48]

- The Australian NSW government is mandating all its agencies that are developing AI systems to go through the NSW AI Assurance Framework.[49]

---

46. https://www.federalregister.gov/documents/2021/07/29/2021-16176/artificial-intelligence-risk-management-framework.

47. https://www.iso.org/standard/77304.html.

48. https://www.canada.ca/en/government/system/digital-government/digital-government-innovations/responsible-use-ai/algorithmic-impact-assessment.html.

49. https://www.digital.nsw.gov.au/policy/artificial-intelligence/nsw-ai-assurance-framework.

- OpenAI has introduced a range of risk measurement methods:[50] (1) various safety measures to assess the likelihood of GPT-4 generating undesired outputs; (2) predicting future capabilities of models via scaling laws and emerging properties; and (3) predicting acceleration risk by recruiting expert forecasters.

P.17. Multi-Level Co-Versioning

Multi-level co-versioning can capture the relationships and dependencies of AI system artifacts at different levels.

Context

Compared with traditional software, AI systems evolve more frequently due to their dependence on data. This evolution results in various versions of AI system artifacts at different levels. At the system level, there can be multiple versions of AI components and non-AI components. At the supply chain level, there can be different versions of data, models, code, and configurations, which can be used to produce different versions of AI components.

Problem

How can we track the co-evolution of AI artifacts at different levels?

Solution

AI systems involve two levels of relationships and dependencies across various AI artifacts, including the supply chain level and system level. At the system level, AI components that embed AI models need to be integrated into AI systems and interact with non-AI components. At the supply chain level, the retraining of AI models introduces new versions of data, code, and configuration parameters. If federated learning is adopted, for each round of training, a global model is created based on local models sent from participating clients. It is important to capture all these dependencies throughout the development process by managing and tracking versions of various artifacts.

Benefits

Here are the benefits of the multi-level co-versioning pattern:

- **Traceability:** Multi-level co-versioning provides end-to-end traceability throughout the entire lifecycle of AI systems.

---

50. https://cdn.openai.com/papers/gpt-4.pdf.

- **Accountability:** Multi-level co-versioning enables the tracking of accountable roles and liability.

Drawbacks

- **Increased cost:** The collection and documentation of co-versioning information incur additional development costs.

- **Difficulty in capturing all dependencies:** It is challenging to capture all the dependencies between different versions of AI artifacts, particularly if the system is complex and evolves frequently.

Related Patterns

Here are the related patterns of the multi-level co-versioning pattern:

- G.18. Tight coupling of AI and non-AI development: The AI team and non-AI team can use a common co-versioning registry to manage the co-versioning of AI system artifacts.

- D.3. Co-versioning registry: The co-versioning registry can be designed to capture the co-evolution of AI artifacts at different levels.

- D.4. Federated learner: Federated learning requires co-versioning of local models and global models.

Known Uses

Here are the known uses of the multi-level co-versioning pattern:

- MLflow Model Registry on Databricks is a model repository and set of APIs that enable the management of the full lifecycle of MLflow Models, including model lineage and versioning.[51]

- Amazon uses a tool for automatically tracking metadata and the provenance of AI model training and experiments.[52]

- Data Version Control (DVC) manages co-versioning of data and machine learning models.[53]

---

51. https://docs.databricks.com/applications/mlflow/model-registry.html.

52. https://www.amazon.science/publications/automatically-tracking-metadata-and-provenance-of-machine-learning-experiments.

53. https://dvc.org/.

Summary

In this chapter, we discuss the process patterns that can be used by different roles in the development team through the entire lifecycle of AI systems, rather than just focusing on the AI model pipeline. Each pattern is described using the extended structure of a software engineering pattern. These patterns have been identified from both industry tools and academic papers, which can be used in various stages of the AI system development process.

Product Patterns for Responsible-AI-by-Design

Responsible AI issues go beyond data and algorithms and are often at the system level, cross-cutting many system components and the entire software engineering lifecycle. The industry lacks tools to translate high-level principles to verifiable and actionable criteria for designing and deploying AI systems.[1] This chapter identifies one missing element as the system-level guidance—how to design the architecture of responsible AI systems. We present a collection of product patterns (i.e., architectural design patterns in software engineering) for the design of responsible AI systems. Such patterns can be embedded into the AI systems as product features or a piece of structural design that is across multiple architectural elements. We have limited the scope of this chapter to the patterns that can be *embedded* into the AI systems. The governance patterns and engineering best practices of the development process including the model training pipeline are discussed, respectively, in Chapter 4 and Chapter 5.

In software engineering, a design pattern can be used as a reusable solution to a problem that commonly occurs within a given context during software design.[2] Adopting a product pattern (i.e., design pattern) can be driven by trade-offs among quality attributes. The pattern collection provides architectural guidance for developers to build responsible AI systems. Using the patterns in an application architecture can better align it with responsible AI principles and achieve other quality attributes.

---

1. I. D. Raji et al., "Closing the AI Accountability Gap: Defining an End-to-End Framework for Internal Algorithmic Auditing," *Proceedings of the 2020 Conference on Fairness, Accountability, and Transparency,* 2020.

2. K. Beck, "Using Pattern Languages for Object-Oriented Programs," 1987, http://c2.com/doc/oopsla87.html; D. J. Meszaros and G. J. Doble, "A Pattern Language for Pattern Writing," *Proceedings of International Conference on Pattern Languages of Program Design,* 1997.

Product Pattern Collection Overview

The product pattern collection covers 14 product patterns that deal with the system-level design challenges of responsible AI systems and the relationship among the individual product patterns. The product patterns help to shape the architectural elements and their interactions in AI systems. Figure 6.1 gives an overview of these patterns and classifies them into three layers: the supply chain layer, system layer, and operation infrastructure layer. Applying the patterns to an AI system can better align it with high-level AI ethics principles and achieve other quality attributes. These product patterns can be *embedded* into AI systems or the AI model training pipeline as product features. Some of the patterns are identified from existing AI systems, whereas others are identified from broader existing software systems but are applicable to AI systems.

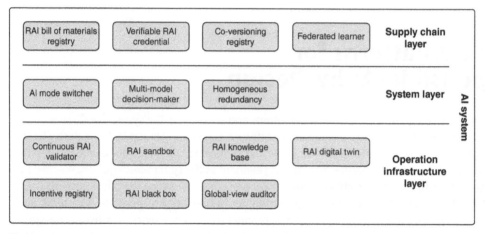

Figure 6.1
Product pattern overview.

RAI bill of materials registry and verifiable RAI credential are two patterns that are applied on the software supply chain to provide traceability and accountability of software components. Ten product patterns are applicable to the AI system. Homogeneous redundancy and multi-model decision-maker could improve the system reliability at different abstraction levels. The behaviors and the decision-making outcomes of the AI system are monitored and validated against the ethical requirements using a continuous RAI validator, and global-view auditors are used to achieve consensus if multiple components are monitored. An RAI black box could be embedded in an AI system to investigate why and how an AI system causes an accident or a near miss. An incentive registry increases motivation for ethical behaviors and decisions for the ecosystem of the AI system. The RAI knowledge base provides a basis for other components within the AI system to perform their tasks responsibly. The AI mode switcher offers users an efficient invocation and dismissal mechanism for activating or deactivating AI components when needed. A co-versioning registry tracks the co-evolution of components or AI artifacts at different levels. A federated learner is a paradigm of AI systems that preserves the data privacy by training models locally and formulating a global model on a central server based on local model updates. The last two patterns, RAI digital twin and RAI sandbox, provide simulation and emulation of the AI system.

Dealing with Trade-Offs

There are trade-offs between quality attributes and ethical principles or between some of the ethics principles. Privacy and utilities are often conflicting. For example, to fulfill privacy requirements, the datasets can be de-identified and aggregated so that individuals cannot be uniquely identified, which may lead to worse distributional properties and affect the reliability.[3] Conflicting requirements also happen between accountability and privacy. For example, when activities are not compliant to some regulations or standards, we need to find out where this noncompliance happened and whom to blame to address accountability. In this case, there might be an issue about data privacy. The richer data is, the more we can learn from it. Conversely, the smaller our data is, the more limited our checking abilities would be.

The current practice of dealing with conflicting ethics principles is usually the developers following one principle while overriding the others rather than building balanced trade-offs with stakeholders and making the ultimate value and risk call. Patterns can be used in an inclusive manner to deal with the system-level trade-offs among conflicting responsible AI principles and other quality attributes.

Supply Chain Patterns

The AI software supply chain includes both non-AI component development and AI component development, which can be viewed as a supply chain layer in the AI ecosystem. This section covers the first four product patterns that could be applied to the AI software supply chain.

D.1. RAI Bill of Materials Registry

The RAI bill of materials registry keeps a formal machine-readable record of the supply chain details of the components used in building an AI system, such as component name, version, supplier, dependency relationship, author, and timestamp.

---

3. M. K. Ahuja et al., "Opening the Software Engineering Toolbox for the Assessment of Trustworthy AI," arXiv preprint arXiv:2007.07768, 2020.

Context

From a software supply chain angle, AI product vendors often create AI systems by assembling commercial and/or open-source AI and/or non-AI components from third parties. Development of AI systems involves a complex and dynamic software supply chain.

Problem

The trust that stakeholders place in an AI system is proportional to how trustworthy and transparent the supply chain of the AI system is.[4] Bringing transparency to the AI system supply chains and enabling connections across supply chains are critical to identifying and removing the weak links in the software supply chains. How do we bring transparency to the AI system supply chain to enable the stakeholders of AI systems to track the supply chain information of the AI components?

Solution

The RAI bill of materials registry keeps a formal machine-readable record of the supply chain details of the components used in building a software system.[5] A bill of materials is essentially a nested inventory that covers the ingredients of a software component, such as component name, version, supplier, dependency relationship, author, and timestamp. In addition to supply chain details of the components, context documents (like model cards for reporting AI models,[6] and datasheets for the datasets used to train AI models[7]) can also be integrated to the bill of materials. A real-world AI system is composed of a vast and complex infrastructure, where the AI components might be a small fraction of the whole AI system. As shown in Figure 6.2, every component, either AI component or non-AI component, could be associated with an RAI bill of materials.[8]

The main purpose of the RAI bill of materials is to provide traceability and transparency into the components within AI systems so that ethical issues can be tracked and addressed. An immutable data infrastructure is needed to store the bill of materials. For example, the manufacturers of autonomous vehicles could maintain a material registry contract on blockchain to track their components' supply chain information, such as the version and supplier of the third-party navigation components.

---

4. NTIA Multistakeholder Process on Software Component Transparency Framing Working Group, *Transparency: Establishing a Common Software Bill of Material (SBOM)*, 2019.

5. United States Department of Commerce, The Minimum Elements for a Software Bill of Materials (SBOM), 2021.

6. M. Mitchell et al., "Model Cards for Model Reporting," Proceedings of the Conference on Fairness, Accountability, and Transparency, 2019.

7. T. Gebru et al., "Datasheets for Datasets," *Communications of the ACM* 64, no. 12 (2021): 86–92.

8. D. Sculley et al., "Hidden Technical Debt in Machine Learning Systems," *Advances in Neural Information Processing Systems* (2015): 28.

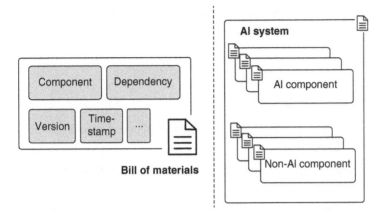

Figure 6.2
RAI bill of materials registry of software components within an AI system.

Benefits

Here are the benefits of the RAI bill of materials registry pattern:

- **Increased transparency:** Stakeholders can access the supply chain details of each component of interest in AI systems via the RAI bill of materials.

- **Increased accountability:** The supply chain details recorded in the RAI bill of materials could be used to identify the acknowledgment and responsibility for the components and decisions of interest.

- **Integrity:** The RAI bill of materials helps with continuous verification of the integrity of individual components and the overall AI system.

Drawbacks

Increased management effort: As AI systems evolve over time, the RAI bill of materials may need to be updated frequently. The cost of managing the RAI bill of materials of all the components is proportional to the complexity of the AI system.

Related Patterns

Here are the related patterns of the RAI bill of materials registry pattern:

- D.2. Verifiable RAI credential: Verifiable RAI credentials could be applied with the RAI bill of materials to provide proof of responsibility at a point of the supply chain.

- G.15. RAI bill of materials: The supply chain information of AI system components can be maintained in an RAI software bill of material registry.

Known Uses

Here are the known uses of the RAI bill of materials pattern:

- Dependency Track is widely used by practitioners to track supply chain information of components and to identify known vulnerabilities.[9]

- Software Package Data Exchange (SPDX)[10] and CycloneDX[11] are two standards for exchanging a software bill of material information for security analysis.

- OpenBOM is a data management platform for manufacturing companies.[12] OpenBOM provides solutions to support a bill of materials across networks of engineers, supply chain managers, and contract manufacturers.

- Codenotary provides digital solutions for a software bill of materials (SBOM).[13] The company provides a community attestation service for the open-source software community.

D.2. Verifiable RAI Credential

To improve human trust in AI systems, trusted authorities can issue verifiable RAI credentials, and users or AI systems can verify them. Such verifiable data offers the proof evidence of ethical compliance for (1) AI systems, components, and models; (2) developers, operators, users, and organizations; and (3) development processes.

Context

An AI system consists of AI components and non-AI components that are interconnected and work together to achieve the system's objective. Compared with traditional software, AI systems have a higher degree of uncertainty and risks associated with the autonomy of AI components. Building trust in AI systems might unlock the market and increase adoption of AI systems. The operation of AI systems is in an ecosystem with multiple stakeholders. Trust is the subjective perception of

---

9. https://dependencytrack.org/.

10. https://spdx.dev/.

11. https://cyclonedx.org/.

12. https://www.openbom.com/.

13. https://codenotary.com/.

different stakeholders where they believe using the AI systems could improve the performance of their work.[14]

Problem

Trust of different stakeholders within the ecosystem of an AI system is important to the efficient functioning of the AI system. The trust toward an AI system covers various aspects of the system, including the hardware, the execution environment, the software components, the AI models, and the operators who operate the AI system. Trust is a subjective perception where stakeholders interact with the AI system. How can we improve the perceived trust of different stakeholders when they do not have a prior trust relationship with the AI system and/or the operators operating the AI system?

Solutions

Verifiable RAI credentials can be used as evidence of ethical compliance for AI systems, components, models, developers, operators, users, organizations, and development processes of the AI systems. Verifiable credentials are data that could be cryptographically verified and be presented with strong proofs. A publicly accessible data infrastructure needs to be built to support the generation and verification of the ethical credentials on a neutral data platform.

A conceptual overview of verifiable credentials is given in Figure 6.3, which demonstrates the main roles and their relationships in credential verification. The credential holder could be a digital asset, like the AI system, or a component of an AI system, or a human, like a user or a developer. The credential is issued by a trusted authority (issuer), like a government agency or a leading company in industry. A credential is a verifiable claim that includes a piece of fact that is attested to and digitally signed by the issuer about the holder[15] (for example, the evidence that a component of an AI system complies with an AI regulation or the evidence that a person is allowed to operate an AI system). Anyone who trusts the issuer could be a verifier of the claim. A verifier requests a specific credential and verifies the validity of the credential via the issuer's signature.

In the context of AI systems, various RAI credentials are issued by different authorities. Before using AI systems, users may verify the systems' ethical credentials to check whether the systems are compliant with AI ethics principles or regulations.[16] Alternatively, the users may be required to provide the ethical credentials to use and operate the AI systems—for example, to ensure the flight safety of drones.

---

14. F. D. Davis, "Perceived Usefulness, Perceived Ease of Use, and User Acceptance of Information Technology," *MIS Quarterly* (1989): 319–40.

15. W3C, Verifiable Credentials Data Model v1.1, 2022.

16. W. Chu, "A Decentralized Approach Towards Responsible AI in Social Ecosystems," arXiv preprint arXiv:2102.06362, 2021.

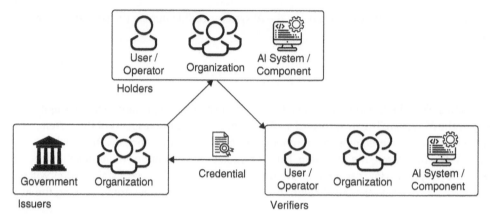

Figure 6.3
Verifiable RAI credential.

Benefits

Here are the benefits of the verifiable RAI credentials pattern:

- **Increased trust:** A verifiable credential increases user trust toward an AI system through conferring the trust that the user has with the authority that issues the credential to AI systems, the organizations that develop AI systems, and the operators that operate AI systems. Such a transitive trust relationship is critical in the efficient functioning of the AI system.

- **AI system adoption:** With an RAI credential, an AI system provides proof of compliance as an incentive for the users to use the AI system, thus increasing AI adoption.

- **Awareness of RAI issues:** Verifying ethical credentials requires an interaction between the user and the AI system, which helps to increase the awareness of AI ethical issues.

Drawbacks

Here are the drawbacks of the verifiable RAI credentials pattern:

- **Set-once-and-forget:** The verifiable RAI credential can be set-once-and-forget for organizations and processes.

- **Human in the loop:** Human interaction is needed to verify the RAI credential.

- **Interoperability:** Different authorities may use different forms or techniques for verifiable credentials. Standards could help achieve interoperability.

- **Authenticity:** RAI credentials may be forged, which makes verification of authenticity of the RAI credentials challenging.

Related Patterns

Here are the related patterns of the verifiable RAI credentials pattern:

- D.1. RAI bill of materials registry: A verifiable RAI credential could be applied with the RAI bill of materials to provide proof at every point of the software supply chain.

- G.15. RAI bill of materials: The RAI bill of materials can be provided with verifiable RAI credentials for proof of responsibility at a point in the supply chain.

- P.12. RAI construction with reuse: To ensure ethical quality, RAI credentials can be bound with the AI assets or developers, which can also be supported by blockchain platforms.

Known Uses

Here are the known uses of the verifiable RAI credentials pattern:

- Azure Active Directory Verifiable Credentials is a solution of decentralized ID management that is based on the W3C standard.[17]

- Securekey is a blockchain-based infrastructure for ID management with support of verifiable credentials.[18]

- Malta AI-ITA certification is the world's first national AI certification scheme for AI systems to be developed in a responsible manner.[19]

D.3. Co-Versioning Registry

The co-versioning registry can track the co-evolution of components or AI artifacts at different levels.

Context

Compared with traditional software systems, AI systems involve different levels of dependencies across artifacts, including datasets, AI models, AI components, and non-AI components that interact with the AI components. AI systems also, in general, evolve more frequently due to their data-dependent behaviors.

---

17. https://docs.microsoft.com/en-us/azure/active-directory/verifiable-credentials/.

18. https://securekey.com/.

19. https://mdia.gov.mt/wp-content/uploads/2019/10/AI-ITA-Guidelines-03OCT19.pdf.

Problem

How can we capture the relationships and dependencies among system components and AI artifacts of AI systems?

Solution

Compared with traditional software, AI systems involve different levels of dependencies and may evolve more frequently due to their data-dependent behaviors. From the viewpoint of the AI system, it is important to know the version of the AI component integrated into the system. From the viewpoint of the AI component, it is important to know what datasets and parameters were used to train the AI model and what data was used to evaluate the AI model.

Co-versioning of the components or AI artifacts of AI systems provides end-to-end provenance guarantees across the entire lifecycle of AI systems. As shown in Figure 6.4, a co-versioning registry can track the co-evolution of software components and/or AI artifacts. There are different levels of co-versioning: co-versioning of AI components and non-AI components, co-versioning of the artifacts within the AI components (i.e., co-versioning of data, model, code, configurations), and co-versioning of local models and global models in federated learning. Co-versioning enables effective maintenance and evolution of AI components because the deployed model or code can be traced to the exact set of artifacts, parameters, and metadata that were used to develop the model and code.

Example

A publicly accessible data infrastructure (e.g., using blockchain) can be used to store the co-versioning registry to provide a trustworthy trace for dependencies. A smart contract–based co-versioning registry can be deployed on blockchain to manage different versions of visual perception models and the corresponding training datasets.

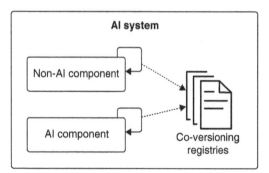

Figure 6.4
Co-versioning registry.

Benefits

Traceability and accountability: Co-versioning at different levels of AI systems, including AI artifacts and/or software components, provides end-to-end provenance across the entire lifecycle of AI systems.

Drawbacks

Complexity: Depending on the granularity of the information documented, co-versioning might largely increase the complexity of provenance data and the corresponding query function.

Related Patterns

Here are the related patterns of the co-versioning registry pattern:

- D.4. Federated learner: A co-versioning registry could be applied to the federated learner for co-versioning of local models and global models.

- G.18. Tight coupling of AI and non-AI development: The AI team and non-AI team can use a common co-versioning registry to manage the co-versioning of AI components and non-AI components. Also, the AI team can build up a co-versioning registry to track the co-versioning of AI artifacts, including data, model, code, and configurations.

- P.17. Multi-level co-versioning: A co-versioning registry can be designed to capture the co-evolution of AI artifacts at different levels.

Known Uses

Here are the known uses of the co-versioning registry pattern:

- The MLflow model registry on Databricks is a model repository and set of APIs that enable management of the full lifecycle of MLflow models, including model lineage and versioning.[20]

- Amazon uses a tool for automatically tracking metadata and provenance of AI model training and experiments.[21]

- Data Version Control (DVC) is a data and AI experiment management tool that takes advantage of the existing engineering toolset (e.g., Git, CI/CD, etc.).[22]

- Pachyderm's data lineage is an immutable record for all activities and assets in the AI lifecycle, including tracking every version of the code, models, and data.[23]

---

20. https://docs.databricks.com/applications/mlflow/model-registry.html.

21. https://www.amazon.science/publications/automatically-tracking-metadata-and-provenance-of-machine-learning-experiments.

22. https://dvc.org/.

23. https://www.pachyderm.com/features/#automated-data-versioning.

- The Verta enterprise MLOps platform supports state-of-the-art experiment tracking, model reproducibility, dataset versioning, and model metadata visualization capabilities to ensure model reproducibility and quality from experiment to production.[24]

D.4. Federated Learner

The federated learner preserves data privacy by training models locally on the client devices and formulating a global model on a central server based on the local model updates.

Context

Despite the widely deployed mobile or IoT devices generating massive amounts of data, lack of training data is still a challenge given the increasing concern in data privacy.

Problem

How can we train AI models without moving the data to a central place to protect data privacy?

Solution

As shown in Figure 6.5, federated learning is a technique that trains an AI model across multiple edge devices or servers with local data samples. The federated learner preserves the data privacy by training models locally on the client devices and formulating a global model on a central server based on the local model updates—for example, training the visual perception model locally in each vehicle. Decentralized learning is a variant of federated learning, which could use blockchain to remove the single point of failure and coordinate the learning process in a fully decentralized way.

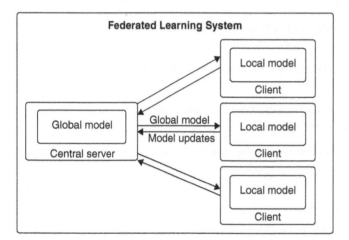

Figure 6.5
Federated learner.

24. https://docs.verta.ai/verta/.

Benefits

Here are the benefits of the federated learner pattern:

- **Privacy:** The federated learner preserves data privacy because the model is trained locally on devices without exchanging the data.

- **Increased reliability:** A distributed system like federated learning could provide better reliability compared with a fully centralized system.

Drawbacks

Here are the drawbacks of the federated learner pattern:

- **Sampling bias:** Because of the decentralized nature of federated learning, data distribution and size of the datasets are heterogeneous.

- **Performance penalty:** The federated learner trains local models on multiple devices and then aggregates the local models into a global model. This process may take longer compared with a centralized AI technique.

Related Patterns

Here are the related patterns of the federated learner pattern:

- D.3. Co-versioning registry: A co-versioning registry could be applied to federated learning for co-versioning of local models and global models.

- D.12. Incentive registry: An incentive registry could be applied to the federated learner to incentivize more devices to join the learning process.

- D.14. Global-view auditor: In a decentralized environment of federated learning, a global-view auditor could be applied.

- T.4. Secure aggregator: Secure multi-party computation is a homomorphic encryption technique that can be applied to the aggregation process in federated learning.

- T.5. Random noise data generator: Differential privacy can be applied to randomly generate noise data in the local training and aggregation process in federated learning.

- P.17. Multi-level co-versioning: Federated learning requires co-versioning of local models and global models.

Known Uses

Here are the known uses of the federated learner pattern:

- TensorFlow Federated (TFF) is an open-source framework for machine learning on decentralized data sources.[25]

- FATE is an open-source project that supports the federated AI ecosystem.[26]

- Flywheel applies federated analytics and federated learning to optimize AI development.[27]

System Patterns

An AI system includes non-AI software components and AI components. AI components are also software components; thus, some of the existing design patterns, tactics, and programming principles for conventional software development and design are also applicable to AI components. This section discusses three product patterns that could be applied on AI systems.

D.5. AI Mode Switcher

Adding an AI mode switcher to the AI system offers users efficient invocation and dismissal mechanisms for activating or deactivating the AI component when needed.

Context

Human autonomy is an individual's capacity for self-determination or self-governance, which should be supported in AI systems.

Problem

How can we enable human autonomy by allowing users to efficiently activate and deactivate the AI component when needed?

Solution

When to use AI at decision-making points can be a major architectural design decision when designing an AI system. In Figure 6.6, adding an AI mode switcher to the AI system offers users

---

25. https://www.tensorflow.org/federated.

26. https://fate.fedai.org/.

27. https://flywheel.io/.

efficient invocation and dismissal mechanisms for activating and deactivating the AI component whenever needed, thus deferring the architectural design decision to the execution time that the end user or the operator of the AI system decides. The AI mode switcher is like a *kill switch* for the AI system that could immediately shut down the AI component and thus stop its negative effects (e.g., turning off the automated driving system and disconnecting it from the internet).

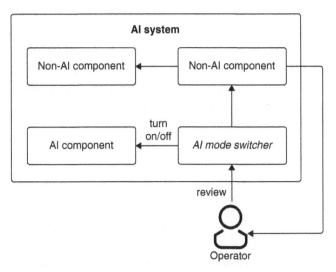

Figure 6.6
AI mode switcher.

The decisions made by the AI component can be executed automatically or reviewed by a human expert before being executed in critical situations. The purpose of the human expert is to approve or override the decisions (e.g., skipping the path generated by the navigation system). Human intervention can also happen after executing the AI decision through the fallback mechanism that reverses the system back to the state it was in before executing the AI decision. A built-in guard can be used to ensure that the AI component is activated only within the predefined conditions (such as domain of use, boundaries of competence). The end users or the operators can ask questions or report complaints/failures/near misses through a recourse channel after observing a bad decision from an AI component.

Benefits

Here are the benefits of the AI mode switcher pattern:

- **Increased trust:** An AI mode switcher gives users the choice to switch off the AI model when they do not trust the decision or recommendation provided by the AI component, thus increasing trust toward the AI system.

- **Contestability and autonomy:** The AI mode switcher enables human autonomy by allowing end users to switch off the AI component or override the decisions made by the AI component at runtime.

Drawbacks

Here are the drawbacks of the AI mode switcher pattern:

- **Efficiency:** Efficiency and performance of the decision-making points highly depend on the quality of other non-AI components involved.

- **Suitability to (near) real-time systems:** The use of an AI mode switcher in a (near) real-time system might be problematic. The performance of the system might be affected if the end user or the operator of the AI system keeps switching the AI component on and off.

Related Patterns

Here are the related patterns of the AI mode switcher pattern:

- D.9. RAI sandbox: The AI mode switcher could work with the RAI sandbox to react to a predicted RAI risk.

- D.11. RAI digital twin: The AI mode switcher could work with an RAI digital twin. When the ethical digital twin predicts a potential RAI risk, it sends an alert to the user. The user may decide to switch off the AI component using the AI mode switcher.

- P.1. AI suitability assessment: The results of the AI suitability assessment may affect the design of the AI mode switcher.

- P.7. RAI design modeling: The AI mode switcher can be applied to trigger a state transition and change the system state to a safe state.

Known Uses

Here are the known uses of the AI mode switcher pattern:

- Tesla Autopilot has multiple driver-assistance features that can be enabled or disabled during driving.[28] Users maintain control of the vehicles and can override the operation of these features at runtime.

- Waymo operates self-driving cars with an automated driving system that human safety drivers can override.[29]

---

28. https://www.tesla.com/autopilot.

29. https://waymo.com/.

- The Baidu autonomous mini-bus requires a person in the seat to supervise self-driving operations, and the bus can be switched to manual driving mode by braking.[30]

D.6. Multi-Model Decision-Maker

To improve the reliability of AI components, a multi-model decision-maker is used to employ different AI models to perform the same task or enable a single decision.

Context

It is widely recognized that the performance of an AI model may vary in different contexts given its data-dependent behavior.

Problem

How can we ensure reliability of an AI system under different contexts?

Solution

In the software reliability community, traditional architecture-based software reliability is based on software components. Existing reliability practices, like redundancy, are also applicable to AI components in an AI system. In addition, a reasonable combination of multiple AI models that normally work independently could improve the performance (e.g., accuracy) of the AI components.

As demonstrated in Figure 6.7, a multi-model decision-maker employs different models to perform the same task or enable a single decision (e.g., deploying different algorithms for visual perception). It improves the reliability by deploying different models under different contexts (e.g., different geo-location regions) and enabling fault tolerance by cross-validating ethical requirements for a single decision.[31] Different consensus protocols could be defined to make the final decision—for example, taking the majority decision. Another strategy is to accept only the same results from the employed models. In addition, the end user or the operator could step in to review the output from the multiple models and make a final decision based on human expertise.

---

30. https://apollo.auto/minibus/.

31. J. Dai et al., "More Reliable AI Solution: Breast Ultrasound Diagnosis Using Multi-AI Combination," arXiv preprint arXiv:2101.02639, 2021; M. Nafreen, S. Bhattacharya, and L. Fiondella, "Architecture-Based Software Reliability Incorporating Fault Tolerant Machine Learning," *Annual Reliability and Maintainability Symposium (RAMS)*, 2020.

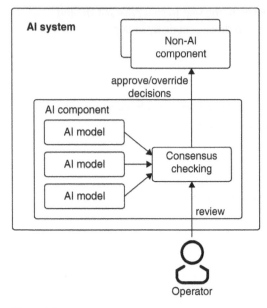

Figure 6.7
Multi-model decision-maker.

Benefits

Here are the benefits of the multi-model decision-maker pattern:

- **Increased reliability:** A multi-model decision-maker relies on the output of multiple AI models, which enables cross-validation among different AI models and fault tolerance of the AI component.

- **Fairness:** Multiple AI models could be applied to cover different contexts and make a collective and fair decision.

Drawbacks

Here are the drawbacks of the multi-model decision-maker pattern:

- **Increased development effort:** The development effort is proportional to the number of AI models used by the multi-model decision-maker. The more AI models involved, the more development effort required.

- **More required skills:** Training multiple AI models requires more skills and expertise compared with training a single AI model.

- **Decreased training efficiency:** It may take longer to train multiple AI models and reach a consensus among the AI models.

Related Patterns

Here are the related patterns of the multi-model decision-maker pattern:

- D.7. Homogeneous redundancy: Both the multi-model decision-maker and homogenous redundancy are instantiations of the widely used reliability practice for software systems. They are applications at different abstraction levels of AI systems.

- P.15. Continuous deployment for RAI: Multiple models can be deployed to make decisions.

Known Uses

Here are the known uses of the multi-model decision-maker pattern:

- Scikit-learn is a Python package that supports using multiple learning algorithms to obtain better performance through ensemble learning.[32]

- AWS fraud detection using a machine learning solution trains an unsupervised anomaly detection model, in addition to a supervised model, to augment prediction results.[33]

- IBM Watson Natural Language Understanding uses an ensemble learning framework to include predictions from multiple emotion detection models.[34]

D.7. Homogeneous Redundancy

Deploying redundant AI components (e.g., two brake control components) is a solution to deal with highly uncertain AI components that may make unethical decisions or adversary hardware components that produce malicious data or behave unethically.

Context

AI systems are highly data dependent. The reason for the uncertainty of an AI system is that the data sources at runtime are unknown at development time when the training dataset is collected. The unethical decisions or behaviors of AI systems may cause serious damage to humans or the environment.

Problem

How can we prevent the AI system from taking unethical actions?

---

32. https://github.com/scikit-learn/scikit-learn.

33. https://aws.amazon.com/solutions/implementations/fraud-detection-using-machine-learning/.

34. https://www.ibm.com/au-en/cloud/watson-natural-language-understanding.

Solution

Deploying multiple redundant and identical AI components (e.g., two brake control components) is a solution to tolerate the individual AI component with high uncertainty that may make unethical decisions or the individual adversary hardware component that produces malicious data or behaves unethically.[35] As shown in Figure 6.8, a cross-check can be conducted for the outputs provided by multiple components of a single type. The results are accepted only if there is a consensus among the redundant components.

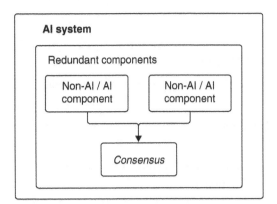

Figure 6.8
Homogeneous redundancy.

Benefits

Here are the benefits of the homogeneous redundancy pattern:

- **Fault tolerance:** The function provided by an individual AI component runs on identical redundant AI components. The results are accepted only if there is a consensus.

- **Increased safety and human control:** The end user or the operator of the AI system can further review the results that are not accepted automatically according to a consensus protocol.

Drawbacks

Here are the drawbacks of the homogeneous redundancy pattern:

- **Increased operating cost:** Running multiple identical AI components causes extra cost compared with running one single AI component.

- **Performance penalty:** The execution time of multiple AI components and the time to reach consensus create a performance penalty.

---

35. Nafreen, Bhattacharya, and Fiondella, "Architecture-Based Software Reliability Incorporating Fault Tolerant Machine Learning."

Related Patterns

Here are the related patterns of the homogeneous redundancy pattern:

- D.6. Multi-model decision-maker: Both the multi-model decision-maker and homogenous redundancy apply redundancy as a commonly used reliability practice in a traditional software system. The two redundancy patterns are applied at different levels—AI models and AI components.

- P.15. Continuous deployment for RAI: Homogenous redundancy is a deployment strategy at the component level.

Known Uses

Here are the known uses of the homogeneous redundancy pattern:

- Tesla Autopilot has two AI chips on each Tesla computer to make decisions based on a consensus of the two AI chips.[36]

- Waymo contains multiple redundant components at various levels, including redundant braking, steering, and inertial measurement systems for vehicle positioning.[37]

- The Baidu autonomous mini-bus has redundancy designs from sensors to algorithm modules to guard against hardware or software failures.[38]

Operation Infrastructure Patterns

In a real-world AI system, the required operation infrastructure is vast and complex. Due to data-dependent behavior of the AI components, the operation infrastructure requires the components for monitoring and management of the deployed AI system. Continuous model retraining, as a common practice of AI systems, is triggered by the monitoring module when data and concept shift is detected at runtime. This section includes the rest of the product patterns that are applicable to the operation infrastructure of AI software systems.

D.8. Continuous RAI Validator

A continuous RAI validator continuously monitors and validates the outcomes of AI systems (e.g., the path recommended by the navigation system) against the RAI requirements.

---

36. https://www.tesla.com/autopilot.

37. https://waymo.com/.

38. https://apollo.auto/minibus/.

Context

AI systems are complex and have dynamic data sources at execution time. Such data sources might be unknown at design time when the training data is collected for the AI components. The AI components may require continual learning based on the new data collected at execution time and thus have a high degree of risk due to the autonomy of the AI components.

Problem

How can we ensure that AI systems are compliant with AI ethics regulations and standards during the execution time of AI systems?

Solution

The AI components of an AI system often require continual learning based on new data collected during operation of the AI system. AI systems have a high degree of risk that is caused by the autonomy of the AI components. It is critical to assess the ethical risks before operating AI systems and to continuously assess the ethical risks at execution time. As shown in Figure 6.9, a continuous ethical validator deployed in an AI system continuously monitors and validates the outcomes of AI components (e.g., the path recommended by the navigation system) against the RAI requirements.

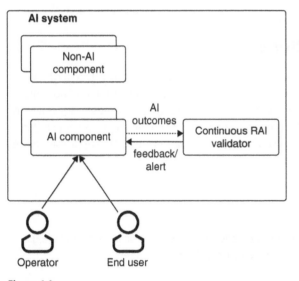

Figure 6.9
Continuous RAI validator.

The outcomes of AI systems are the consequences of decisions and behaviors of those AI systems—that is, whether the AI systems provide the intended benefits and behave appropriately given the situation. The time and frequency of validation can be configured. *Version-based feedback* and *rebuild alerts* are sent when the predefined conditions regarding the RAI requirement are met.

Benefits

Increased maintainability: At runtime, a continuous RAI validator allows *rebuilding* to be triggered if the ethical requirement is not fulfilled under a particular situation.

Drawbacks

Suitability to all RAI risks: It is difficult to validate the output of AI components against the RAI risks that are hard to quantify.

Related Patterns

Here are the related patterns of the continuous RAI validator pattern:

- D.10. RAI knowledge base: The RAI knowledge base could be the input of the continuous RAI validator.

- D.12. Incentive registry: The incentive registry can be applied with a continuous RAI validator to reward or punish the ethical or unethical behavior or decisions of AI systems.

- P.2. Verifiable RAI requirements: The RAI requirements need to be continuously monitored and validated at runtime.

Known Uses

Here are the known uses of the continuous RAI validator pattern:

- The AWS SageMaker model continuously monitors the bias drift of the AI models in production.[39]

- Qualdo is an AI monitoring solution that monitors data quality and model drift.[40]

- Azure machine learning uses the Azure Monitor to create monitoring data. The Azure Monitor is a full-stack monitoring service.[41]

- OpenAI uses ChatGPT-generated synthetic data for a close-domain hallucination at the model level.[42] Hallucination means the model makes up false information that is not based on real

---

39. https://docs.aws.amazon.com/sagemaker/latest/dg/model-monitor.html.

40. https://www.qualdo.ai/monitor-ml-model-performance-monitoring/.

41. https://docs.microsoft.com/en-us/azure/machine-learning/monitor-azure-machine-learning.

42. https://cdn.openai.com/papers/gpt-4.pdf.

data. ChatGPT itself can reliably evaluate the hallucination if the user provides the response back to it. At the system level, ChatGPT employs post-deployment monitoring, emergent feedback loops, combining with other technologies/tools (e.g., literature search), avoiding systematic risks through model diversity, testing for dangerous emergent behaviors (e.g., self-replication, power-seeking, avoiding termination, long-term planning, and working on independent goals that are not specified or trained for), testing for a capability jump caused by smart prompt engineering (e.g., chain of thoughts, few shot prompts) via usage policies (e.g., prohibiting the use of ChatGPT in the context of high-risk government decision-making).

D.9. RAI Sandbox

Given that AI is a high-stakes technology, an RAI sandbox can be applied to isolate AI components from non-AI components by running the AI components separately in a safe and isolated environment using virtual machines.

Context

Given AI systems are of high stakes, it is risky to run the entire system in the same execution environment.

Problem

How can we minimize the interference of an AI component on the rest of the AI system with other AI components and non-AI components?

Solution

The RAI sandbox can be applied to isolate an AI component from other AI components and non-AI components by running the AI component separately in a safe environment[43]—for example, sandboxing the unverified visual perception component so that the AI component can execute without affecting other components and the output of the AI system. As illustrated in Figure 6.10, an RAI sandbox is an emulated environment with no access to the rest of the AI system. An emulation environment duplicates all the hardware and software functionality of an AI system. Thus, users can run an AI component safely without affecting the operation of other components. Maximal tolerable probability of violating the RAI requirements should be defined as an ethical margin for the sandbox.

---

43. A. Lavaei et al., "Towards Trustworthy AI: Safe-Visor Architecture for Uncertified Controllers in Stochastic Cyber-Physical Systems," *Proceedings of the Workshop on Computation-Aware Algorithmic Design for Cyber-Physical Systems*, 2021.

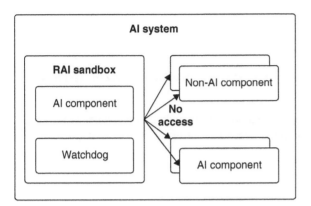

Figure 6.10

RAI sandbox.

Example

A *watchdog* can be used to limit the execution time of the AI component to reduce the RAI risk—for example, activating the visual perception component for only five minutes on the bridges built especially for autonomous vehicles.

Benefits

Here are the benefits of the RAI sandbox pattern:

- **Increased RAI quality:** The RAI sandbox enables the potential RAI risks to be detected within an isolated environment.
- **Safety:** The RAI sandbox provides a safe environment to test an AI component without affecting the rest of the AI system.

Drawbacks

Here are the drawbacks of the RAI sandbox pattern:

- **Applicability:** The RAI sandbox might be hard to use for the RAI risks that are not easy to quantify.
- **Performance penalty:** Having an emulation environment that duplicates both hardware and software of the AI system causes extra cost on the required resources or compromises performance with the same resources.

Related Patterns

Here are the related patterns of the RAI sandbox pattern:

- D.5. AI mode switcher: An AI mode switcher could work with the RAI sandbox to react to a predicted RAI risk detected by the sandbox.

- D.11. RAI digital twin: An RAI digital twin runs in a simulation environment, while the RAI sandbox is an emulation environment with both hardware and software.

Known Uses

Here are the known uses of the RAI sandbox pattern:

- Fastcase AI Sandbox provides a secure platform for users to upload a dataset and do data analysis in a safe environment.[44]

- AI Sandbox provides an AI execution and RESTful interfaces that could be used by modern programming languages.[45]

- The Norwegian Data Protection Agency introduces a regulatory sandbox that establishes a project environment for AI, where private and public companies can get free guidance on personal data protection.[46]

D.10. RAI Knowledge Base

The RAI knowledge base (e.g., the knowledge captured by a knowledge graph) makes meaningful entities and concepts, and their relationships in design, implementation, deployment, and operation of AI systems.

Context

The ecosystem of AI systems involves broad ethical knowledge, such as AI ethics principles, regulations, and guidelines. Such ethical knowledge is scattered and is usually implicit or abstract to end users or even developers and data scientists who primarily do not have a legal background and focus more on the technical aspects of AI systems.

---

44. https://cdn.openai.com/papers/gpt-4.pdf.

45. https://aisandbox.dev/.

46. https://dataethics.eu/sandbox-for-responsible-artificial-intelligence/.

Problem

The content of some regulations is not easy to understand and interpret by stakeholders who do not have a legal background. This results in negligence or ad hoc usage of relevant ethical knowledge in AI system operation. How can stakeholders apply ethical knowledge to the operation of AI systems? How can we make AI systems compliant with high-level principles and regulations?

Solution

A knowledge graph is a technology that represents entities in the real world, like objects, situations, concepts, or events, and the relationship between the entities. Knowledge graphs have been used to achieve explainable AI in different AI fields.

A knowledge graph–based RAI knowledge base makes meaningful entities and concepts and their relationships in design, implementation, deployment, and operation of AI systems. With the RAI knowledge base, the rich semantic relationships between entities are explicit and traceable across heterogeneous high-level documents on one hand and different artifacts across the AI system life-cycle on the other hand. Thus, RAI requirements of the AI system can be systematically accessed and analyzed using the RAI knowledge base.[47]

Example

There may be RAI quality issues with APIs (e.g., data privacy breaches or fairness issues). Thus, RAI compliance checking for APIs is needed to detect potential violation. RAI knowledge graphs can be built based on ethical principles and guidelines (e.g., privacy knowledge graph based on privacy act) to automatically examine whether APIs are compliant with regulations for AI ethics. A call graph might be needed for code analysis because there are interactions among different APIs.[48]

Benefits

Compliance-checking: The RAI knowledge base is extracted from the regulatory document and high-level principles. The knowledge graph provides structured data for stakeholders to employ compliance-checking solutions.

---

47. I. Naja et al., "A Semantic Framework to Support AI System Accountability and Audit," *European Semantic Web Conference*, 2021.

48. K. Sekiguchi and K. Hori, "Organic and Dynamic Tool for Use with Knowledge Base of AI Ethics for Promoting Engineers' Practice of Ethical AI Design," *AI & SOCIETY* 35, no. 1 (2020): 51–71; I. Naja et al., "A Semantic Framework to Support AI System Accountability and Audit," *European Semantic Web Conference*, 2021; I. Esnaola-Gonzalez, "An Ontology-Based Approach for Making Machine Learning Systems Accountable."

Drawbacks

Increased development effort: Building a correct and efficient knowledge base through natural language processing is time consuming and error prone.

Related Patterns

Here are the related patterns of the RAI knowledge base pattern:

- D.8. Continuous RAI validator: An RAI knowledge base could be the input of a continuous RAI validator.

- D.11. RAI digital twin: An RAI digital twin could be built based on the RAI knowledge base.

- P.10. RAI governance of APIs: RAI issues with APIs can be detected by the RAI knowledge base.

Known Uses

Here are the known uses of the RAI knowledge base pattern:

- Awesome AI Guidelines aims to provide a mapping between the ecosystem of guidelines, principles, codes of ethics, standards, and regulations around artificial intelligence.[49]

- The Responsible AI Community Portal is provided by AI Global, which is an evolving repository of reports, standards, models, government policies, datasets, and open-source software to inform and support responsible AI development.[50]

- Responsible AI Knowledge-base is a knowledge base of different areas of using and developing AI in a responsible way.[51]

D.11. RAI Digital Twin

Before running or during the operation of an AI system in the real world, an RAI digital twin could be used to perform system-level simulation to understand the behaviors of AI systems and assess potential ethical risks in a cost-effective way.

Context

The ecosystem of an AI system is complex, with multiple stakeholders and dynamic data sources. The data-dependent nature of AI systems implies a high degree of uncertainty in their behavior, which might cause harm to humans, society, and the environment.

---

49. https://github.com/EthicalML/awesome-artificial-intelligence-guidelines.

50. https://portal.ai-global.org/.

51. https://github.com/alexandrainst/responsible-ai.

Problem

What is a safe and cost-efficient way to understand the dynamic behavior of AI systems and investigate critical situations to assess the trustworthiness of AI components and AI system as a whole?

Solution

Simulation is designed to imitate a real-world situation. Before running AI systems in the real world, it is important to perform system-level simulation through an RAI digital twin running on a simulation environment to understand the behaviors of the AI system and assess RAI risks in a safe and cost-effective way, as illustrated in Figure 6.11. NASA introduced a digital twin as a digital representation of a real system used in lab-testing activities.[52] The digital twin of an AI system could be used to represent the behaviors of the AI system and forecast change impacts.

An RAI digital twin also can be used during operation of the AI system to assess the system's runtime behaviors and decisions based on the simulation model using real-time data. The assessment results can be sent back to alert the system or user before the unethical behavior or decision takes effect.[53]

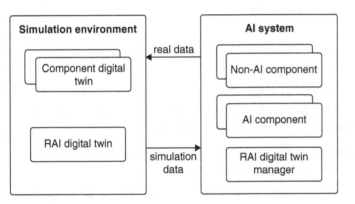

Figure 6.11
RAI digital twin.

Example

Vehicle manufacturers can use an RAI digital twin to explore the limits of autonomous vehicles based on collected real-time data.

---

52. M. Shafto et al., "Modeling, Simulation, Information Technology & Processing Roadmap," *National Aeronautics and Space Administration* 32 (2012): 1–38.

53. A. Dosovitskiy et al., "CARLA: An Open Urban Driving Simulator," *Conference on Robot Learning*, 2017.

Benefits

Here are the benefits of the RAI digital twin pattern:

- **Cost-efficiency:** An RAI digital twin is a cost-effective way to assess the RAI risks of AI systems running in the real world.

- **Increased RAI quality:** Potential RAI risks can be detected in an RAI digital twin in a simulation environment. The assessment results are sent back to the AI system in the real world before the unethical behavior or decision takes effect.

Drawbacks

Here are the drawbacks of the RAI digital twin pattern:

- **Limited by quality of the simulation model:** The RAI digital twin is a simulation of the AI system. It could not fully represent what's happening in the real world due to the dynamism of AI systems.

- **Increased cost:** Running and maintaining the RAI digital twin cause extra cost other than the operating cost of the AI system in the real world.

Related Patterns

Here are the related patterns of the RAI digital twin pattern:

- D.5. AI mode switcher: An RAI digital twin could work with an AI mode switcher to switch off the AI component in the real world if an RAI risk is detected in the RAI digital twin.

- D.9. RAI sandbox: An RAI digital twin runs in a simulation environment, while the RAI sandbox is an emulation environment with both hardware and software.

- D.10. RAI knowledge base: The RAI knowledge base could provide the basis of RAI knowledge to the RAI digital twin.

- P.8. System-level RAI simulation: An RAI digital twin performs system-level simulation at runtime using real-time data. The assessment results are sent back to alert the system or user before the unethical behavior or decision takes effect.

- P.9. XAI interface: The simulation results are sent back to alert the system or user via XAI interfaces before the unethical behavior or decision takes effect.

Known Uses

Here are the known uses of the RAI digital twin pattern:

- NVIDIA DRIVE Sim is an end-to-end simulation platform for self-driving vehicles.[54]

- rfProis a software solution that provides a driving simulation and digital twin for autonomous driving.[55]

- AirSim is a project from Microsoft AI lab, which provides a 3D version of a real environment and a simulated drone.[56]

D.12. Incentive Registry

An incentive registry records the rewards that correspond to the AI system's ethical behavior and outcome of decisions, which increases motivation for ethical behaviors and decisions for the ecosystem of the AI system, including AI components, end users, and developers of the AI system.

Context

There are serious concerns about the AI systems' ability to behave and make decisions responsibly.

Problem

How can we motivate AI systems and the stakeholders in the AI system ecosystem to perform tasks in a responsible manner?

Solution

Incentive mechanisms are effective treatments in motivating AI systems and encouraging the stakeholders involved in the AI system ecosystem to execute tasks in a responsible manner. As shown in Figure 6.12, an incentive registry records the rewards that correspond to the AI system's ethical behavior and outcome of decisions[57] (e.g., rewards for path planning without ethical risks). There are

---

54. https://developer.nvidia.com/drive/drive-sim.

55. https://www.rfpro.com/.

56. https://www.microsoft.com/en-us/ai/ai-lab-airsim-drones.

57. J. Weng et al., "Deepchain: Auditable and Privacy-Preserving Deep Learning with Blockchain-Based Incentive," *IEEE Transactions on Dependable and Secure Computing* 18, no. 5 (2019): 2438–55.

various ways to formulate the incentive mechanism, for example, using reinforcement learning, or building the incentive mechanism on a publicly accessible data infrastructure like blockchain.[58]

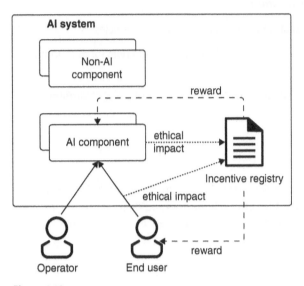

Figure 6.12
Incentive registry.

Traditional incentive mechanisms for human participants include reputation based and payment based. However, it is challenging to formulate the form of rewards in the context of responsible AI because the ethical impact of AI systems' decisions and behaviors might be hard to measure for some of the ethical principles (such as human values). Furthermore, all the stakeholders who may have different views on the ethical impact need to agree to the incentive mechanism. In addition, there may be trade-offs between different principles, which makes the design harder.

Benefits

Increased motivation for ethical behavior or decisions: An incentive mechanism provides motivation for the AI components and the stakeholders involved in the AI system's ecosystem for ethical behavior and decisions.

---

58. P. Hacker et al., "Explainable AI Under Contract and Tort Law: Legal Incentives and Technical Challenges," *Artificial Intelligence and Law* 28, no. 4 (2020): 415–39; J. Mökander and L. Floridi, "Ethics-Based Auditing to Develop Trustworthy AI," *Minds and Machines* 31, no. 2 (2021): 323–27.

Drawbacks

Here are the drawbacks of the incentive registry pattern:

- **Limitation of the incentive design:** Many stakeholders within the ecosystem of an AI system might have conflicting interests and values. Depending on the design of an incentive mechanism, it might not motivate all stakeholders for ethical behavior. Besides, an incentive mechanism provides motivation but cannot force ethical behavior or decisions.

- **Potential privacy breach risk:** There might be sensitive data stored in the incentive registry.

Related Patterns

Here are the related patterns of the incentive registry pattern:

- D.4. Federated learner: An incentive registry could be applied to the federated learner to incentivize more devices to join the learning process.

- D.8. Continuous RAI validator: An incentive registry could work with a continuous RAI validator, which validates the ethical impact of the behavior and the decisions of the AI system and the stakeholders within the ecosystem.

Known Uses

Here are the known uses of the incentive registry pattern:

- The Open Science Rewards and Incentives Registry incentivizes the development of an academic career structure that fosters outputs, practices, and behaviors to maximize contributions to a shared research knowledge system.[59]

- FLoBC is a tool for federated learning over blockchain that utilizes a reward/punishment policy to incentivize legitimate training and to punish and hinder malicious trainers.[60]

- OpenAI's GPT-4 model combines reinforcement learning with human feedback (RLHF) with rule-based reward models (RBRM) to address issues such as refusal training and inappropriate hedging.[61]

D.13. RAI Black Box

The purpose of embedding an RAI black box in an AI system is to investigate why and how an AI system caused an accident or a near miss.

---

59. https://openscienceregistry.org/.

60. https://github.com/Oschart/FLoBC.

61. https://cdn.openai.com/papers/gpt-4.pdf.

Context

AI systems may randomly fail or malfunction. If the cause of the problem cannot be tracked, these failures may reappear and cause more serious damage to humans, society, and the environment.

Problem

How can we keep track of AI systems' behaviors and decisions and explain them when accidents occur?

Solution

The black box was introduced initially for aircraft several decades ago to record critical flight data. The intention of adding a black box to aircrafts is to collect evidence of the actions of the system and the surrounding context information for analysis after near misses and failures. The near misses and failures are specific to the use cases. Although the primary usage of a black box is accident investigation, black boxes are useful for other purposes. Data collection and the analysis could support improvement of the system. The purpose of embedding an RAI black box in an AI system is to investigate why and how an AI system caused an accident or a near miss. As shown in Figure 6.13, the RAI black box continuously records sensor data, internal status data, decisions, behaviors (both system and operator), and effects.[62]

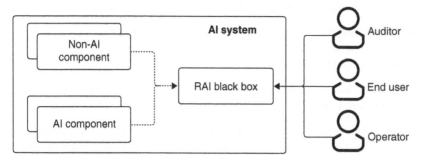

Figure 6.13
RAI black box.

For example, an RAI black box could be built into the automated driving system to record the behaviors of the system and driver and their effects.[63] All this data needs to be kept as evidence with the timestamp and location data. Designing the RAI black box is challenging because the

---

62. G. Falco and J. E. Siegel, "A Distributed Black Box Audit Trail Design Specification for Connected and Automated Vehicle Data and Software Assurance," arXiv preprint arXiv:2002.02780, 2020.

63. A. F. Winfield and M. Jirotka, "The Case for an Ethical Black Box," *Annual Conference Towards Autonomous Robotic Systems*, 2017.

ethical metrics need to be identified for data collection. Also, design decisions need to be made on what data should be recorded and where the data should be stored (e.g., using a blockchain-based immutable log or a cloud-based data storage).[64]

Benefits

Here are the benefits of the RAI black box pattern:

- **Accountability:** An RAI black box is critical to the investigation of why and how the AI system caused accidents.

- **Traceability:** An RAI black box continuously records sensor data, internal status data, decisions, behaviors (both system and operator), and effects.

Drawbacks

Privacy: The RAI black box might collect sensitive data.

Related Patterns

D.14. Global-view auditor: A global-view auditor might work with the RAI black box when the data collected by the RAI black box is analyzed.

Known Uses

Here are the known uses of the RAI black box pattern:

- RoBoTIPS aims to develop an ethical black box for social robots, to enable the explainability of their behavior.[65]

- Falco et al. proposed driving widespread assurance of highly automated systems via independent audits using a "black box."[66]

- Falco et al. proposed a "black box" audit trail for automotive software and data provenance based on distributed hash tables (DHTs).[67]

---

64. Falco and Siegel, "A Distributed Black Box Audit Trail Design Specification for Connected and Automated Vehicle Data and Software Assurance."

65. https://www.robotips.co.uk/.

66. G. Falco et al., "Governing AI Safety Through Independent Audits," *Nature Machine Intelligence* 3, no. 7 (2021): 566–71.

67. Falco and Siegel, "A Distributed Black Box Audit Trail Design Specification for Connected and Automated Vehicle Data and Software Assurance."

D.14. Global-View Auditor

A global-view auditor provides global-view accountability by finding discrepancies among the data collected from multiple AI components or AI systems and identifying liability when negative events occur.

Context

When an accident happens, more than one AI system or multiple AI components within an AI system might be involved (e.g., multiple autonomous vehicles in an accident). The data collected from each involved AI system/component might conflict with each other since the individual AI system/component may have its own perception.

Problem

How can we identify the liability when accidents occur that involve multiple AI components/systems with different perceptions?

Solution

As shown in Figure 6.14, a global-view auditor is a component that collects information from multiple AI components/systems and processes the information to identify discrepancies among the information collected. Based on the results, the global-view auditor may alert the AI component/system with a wrong perception, thus avoiding negative impacts or identifying liability when negative events occur.

This pattern can be also used to improve decision-making of an AI system by taking the knowledge from other AI components/systems. For example, an autonomous vehicle may increase its visibility by using the perceptions of others to make better decisions at runtime.[68]

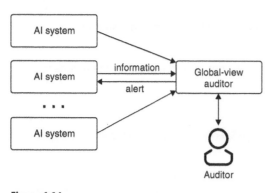

Figure 6.14
Global-view auditor.

---

68. B. S. Miguel, A. Naseer, and H. Inakoshi, "Putting Accountability of AI Systems into Practice," *Proceedings of the Twenty-Ninth International Conference on International Joint Conferences on Artificial Intelligence*, 2021.

Benefits

Here are the benefits of the global-view auditor pattern:

- **Accountability:** A global-view auditor enables accountability that covers different perceptions of AI components/systems that are involved. The global-view auditor redresses the conflicting information collected from multiple AI components/systems.

- **Traceability:** Similar to the preceding description, a global-view auditor collects information from all the AI components/systems that get involved.

Drawbacks

Performance: It takes longer to process information collected from multiple places that is potentially conflicting.

Related Patterns

Here are the related patterns of the global-view auditor pattern:

- D.4. Federated learner: In a decentralized environment of federated learning, a global-view auditor could be applied.

- D.13. RAI black box: A global-view auditor could be applied with an RAI block box of multiple AI components/systems to integrate the information collected by the RAI black boxes.

Known Uses

Here are the known uses of the global-view auditor pattern:

- FG-AI4H is an audit platform for AI models in the healthcare domain.[69]

- Seclea provides audit tools for identifying the decisions and model behaviors in AI.[70]

- NVIDIA proposes a scheme for auditing deep learning models by using semantic specifications.[71]

---

69. https://health.aiaudit.org/.

70. https://www.seclea.com/.

71. https://developer.nvidia.com/blog/nvidia-research-auditing-ai-models-for-verified-deployment-under-semantic-specifications/.

Summary

This chapter presents a collection of product patterns (i.e., design patterns in software engineering) for the design of responsible AI systems. Such patterns can be embedded into the AI systems as product features or a piece of structural design across multiple architectural elements. A product pattern defines constraints that restrict the roles of architectural elements (processing, connectors, and data) and the interaction among those elements. Adopting a product pattern causes trade-offs among quality attributes. The pattern collection provides architectural guidance for developers to build responsible AI systems.

The pattern template used in this chapter includes the name of the pattern, a short summary, the context, the problem statement, the solution, its consequences, and some examples of known real-world uses of the pattern. Consequences are identified with the corresponding quality attribute, because sometimes the solution will propose a trade-off between them.

7

Pattern-Oriented Reference Architecture for Responsible-AI-by-Design

A reference architecture serves as a software architectural template for a particular application domain.[1] It defines a standardized vocabulary for discussing the architecture's design and illustrates how various architectural components can be integrated into a cohesive and generic solution. The adoption of a reference architecture can accelerate software design while ensuring software quality through the reuse of design solutions.

Chapter 6 discussed a collection of product patterns that can be incorporated into AI systems to help achieve high-level responsible AI (RAI) principles. However, it can be hard to see how these individual product patterns should be used *together*. To help with this problem, this chapter proposes a pattern-oriented reference architecture for designing the responsible-AI-by-design architecture of an AI system. This architecture provides a comprehensive perspective on the relationships between product patterns, placed in a reusable architectural-level template. The proposed reference architecture functions as architectural design guidelines, assisting architects and developers in designing the architecture of a responsible AI system. It can be customized and instantiated based on specific requirements.

---

1. P. Clements et al., "Documenting Software Architectures: Views and Beyond," *25th International Conference on Software Engineering, 2003. Proceedings* (2003): 740–41.

Architectural Principles for Designing AI Systems

We define an AI system as a software system with one or more AI components that provide functionality for the software system. These AI components within an AI system are typically part of a larger software system. In fact, in real-world AI systems, only a small portion is the AI code.[2] Therefore, the design and implementation of an AI system need careful consideration for two different types of software components: AI components and conventional software components (non-AI components), along with their interactions.

To design high-quality architecture of AI systems, architects and developers can follow several fundamental architectural principles that guide them in making good architectural design decisions. This section discusses three such architectural principles: (1) co-architecting of AI components and non-AI components, (2) minimum complexity, and (3) design with reuse.

The most important principle is co-architecting of AI components and non-AI components. As previously discussed, an AI system comprises AI components (such as AI models) and non-AI components (for example, formatting, filtering, and validating inputs or using the outputs of an AI model elsewhere). Issues may arise when data scientists or engineers iteratively experiment with AI components without considering the non-AI components or the broader system requirements. Furthermore, combining AI and non-AI components may introduce new emergent behavior and dynamics. Simply separating the AI and non-AI concerns without careful consideration of their independency and integration may result in design failures. Thus, co-architecting of the AI components and the non-AI components enables a comprehensive architectural analysis and seamless integration of the two types of software components by design. This principle can help consider both system-level and model-level requirements (including RAI requirements) when making design decisions. Traditional scenario-based evaluation methods may need to be adapted to evaluate the architecture of AI systems with both types of software components.

The other two architectural principles are more general and applicable to conventional software architecture design. In the context of designing AI systems, software architects and developers should follow the minimum complexity principle for both the design of AI systems (e.g., software architecture, whether AI is adopted or not, and the selection of AI techniques) and the future operation of the AI systems.[3] A technology suitability assessment is needed when selecting AI techniques and algorithms. This assessment is particularly important given the increasing complexity of AI components at scale. For example, search recommendation engines or vehicle routing/arrival time prediction functions may involve dozens of AI models working together to deliver real-time predictions. These models, often continuously trained, need to work with non-AI components to ingest the latest high-quality data and then send the prediction results to other non-AI components within

---

2. D. Sculley et al., "Hidden Technical Debt in Machine Learning Systems," *Advances in Neural Information Processing Systems* (2015): 28.

3. H. Barmer et al., *Human-Centered AI* (Software Engineering Institute, 2021).

strict accuracy and timing constraints. In cases of low-confidence predictions, a human-assisted verification process becomes essential.

The final principle is design with reuse. Reuse in the context of AI systems has posed many new challenges, especially in data-driven AI systems. On the one hand, many data-driven AI components are built using unique and constantly updating datasets to tailor for the contexts, which makes reusing these components in a different context fraught with risks. On the other hand, the emergence of large language models (LLMs) and other pretrained foundation models encourages reuse directly or with minimal further customization. The inherent limitations and risks of pretrained models are often not well understood due to the opacity of complex models. Some AI components may have gone through reasonable risk assessment and certification during their original development. Even so, AI system components need to be evaluated against the requirements of a particular system and be reused as much as possible to improve productivity. An RAI bill of materials (BOM) may be a way of reusing AI components developed by a third party in a trusted manner.

Pattern-Oriented Reference Architecture

A reference architecture is a template architecture solution for a particular domain. This section presents one possible pattern-oriented reference architecture for designing responsible AI systems. Figure 7.1 informally illustrates the overall reference architecture. As a broader definition, an AI system consists of three layers, including (1) the system layer, (2) the operation infrastructure layer that provides auxiliary functions to the AI system, and (3) the supply chain layer that is responsible for generating the software components that form the AI system.

In Figure 7.1, computational software components are denoted by boxes, while passive software components (such as a database) are represented by cylinders. Components working together toward a common purpose are further grouped as modules depicted as bigger boxes. The arrows represent the flow of the information, either control flow or data flow, between different components. The gray boxes/cylinders indicate where the product patterns discussed in Chapter 6 can be applied. The white boxes/cylinders are the software components providing other essential functionalities. These are not the only patterns that could be used; the figure is illustrative of a particular reference architecture. In practice, you may wish to select a different subset of the product patterns. The product patterns illustrated in the figure follow the architectural principles for AI software systems, enabling responsible-AI-by-design.

The remainder of this chapter provides further details on each of the three layers of the reference architecture shown in Figure 7.1. We discuss the functionalities and responsibilities of each component, as well as the interactions with the rest of the AI system and its users.

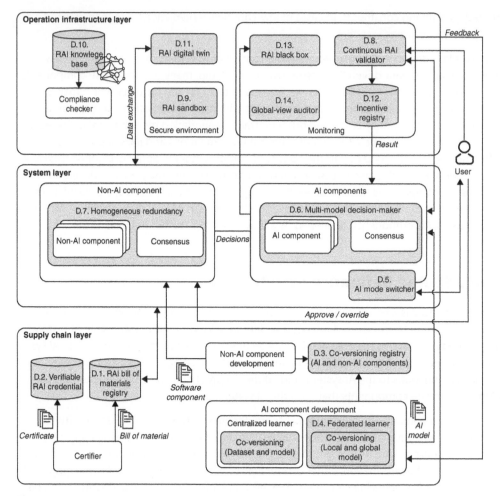

Figure 7.1
Reference architecture for designing responsible AI systems (with product patterns).

Supply Chain Layer

The supply chain layer includes all the components involved in generating the software components that compose the AI systems, including both non-AI component development and AI component development. Due to the scope of this book, Figure 7.1 omits the details of the non-AI components. The outputs of AI component development are the AI models, which are integrated into the AI components deployed within the AI system.

Within the AI component development, two components are used to create AI models: centralized learning (i.e., centralized learner) and federated learning (i.e., federated learner). The centralized learner involves moving the data from multiple data sources to a central place, where the training activity takes place. Applying the co-versioning registry pattern allows for co-versioning of the model and the datasets. Given the data-dependent behavior of an AI component, it is necessary to track the datasets and parameters used for training, the dataset used for evaluation, the evaluation results, and so on. Co-versioning various artifacts generated during the development process enables more efficient maintenance and evolution, as it facilitates tracing of the deployed AI component.

In the federated learner, data from different data sources is kept locally. Local AI models are trained on the client devices. Updates from these local models are used to form a global model at a central server. Aside from co-versioning the model and datasets at the client device, the co-versioning registry pattern can also be applied to co-version the local models and the global model. Moreover, co-versioning is desired between the development of non-AI components and AI components. From the perspective of the AI system, it is important to know which version of the AI model is used in the AI system. Following the principle of co-architecting of AI components and non-AI components, it is important to maintain synchronization of the non-AI components and AI components. Synchronization ensures that major design decisions are driven by both the system requirements and model requirements, and results in a well-aligned and integrated AI system.

During the development process, each software component, whether AI or non-AI, can be associated with a bill of materials, which keeps a machine-readable record of the software component's supply chain details—for example, Robbie's supply chain information. Following the principle of design with reuse, the AI system involves complex and dynamic software supply chains, assembling both open-source and commercial software from third parties. Consequently, attaching the RAI bill of materials to an AI component is more important compared to conventional software components. All RAI bills of materials are stored in an RAI bill of materials registry. AI systems, compared with conventional non-AI software systems, come with a higher degree of uncertainty and risk due to the autonomy of an AI component. Verifiable RAI credentials can be added to the RAI bills of materials, especially for AI components, providing evidence of responsibility at various points along the supply chain. These credentials can be maintained in a verifiable RAI credential registry.

System Layer

In a deployed AI system, two modules co-exist and interact with each other: (1) the module composed of non-AI software components and (2) the module composed of AI components with embedded AI models. It is important to note that AI components are fundamentally a subset of software components. Thus, some of the existing product patterns, tactics, and programming principles for conventional software development and design are also applicable to AI components. The existing reliability practices, like redundancy, are applicable to both non-AI components and AI components. When these practices are applied to AI components, it means a combination of more than one AI model (e.g., to decide when to let Robbie make decisions) may be needed to improve reliability of the AI component, that is, the multi-model decision-maker. The design with multiple AI models requires a consensus mechanism within the AI component to make a final decision based on different results.

Similarly, homogeneous redundancy could be applied at the component level for both AI components and non-AI components, which requires more than one redundant and identical component to be deployed in the system as a solution to tolerate the uncertainty of individual software components. In this situation, a consensus/voting mechanism across multiple components is used for the multiple components to achieve agreement.

 The AI mode switcher, attached to AI components, allows users to activate and deactivate an AI component whenever needed. Such a pattern is essential in granting users autonomy and the capability to promptly disable the AI component when negative effects emerge—for example, when Robbie no longer follows a human's instructions. Such human intervention enables the human expert to either approve or override the decisions made by the AI component. Additionally, human intervention can happen after the AI decision has been executed, achieved through a fallback loop that reverses the system to the state it was in before the AI decision was executed.

Operation Infrastructure Layer

The operation infrastructure required for a real-world AI system is vast and complex. Given the data-dependent nature of AI components, the operation infrastructure includes components designed for monitoring and management of the executing AI system. Continuous model retraining requires monitoring to be implemented. In the context of RAI, this means monitoring the deployed AI component, its interactions with the rest of the AI system, and the interaction between the AI system and users. Monitoring changes in data at runtime and their impact to the rest of the AI system and the broader ecosystem adds an extra level of complexity for both AI components and the AI system.

A continuous RAI validator monitors and validates the outcomes of AI systems against RAI requirements at runtime. The outcomes of AI systems include the result of the AI component and the impact to the users of the AI system and/or the broader ecosystem. The ethical impact of the system behavior as the output of the RAI validation is the input to the incentive registry, which records the rewards that correspond to the AI system's ethical behavior and outcome of decisions. The incentive registry provides an effective treatment in motivating the AI components, the users of the system, and other stakeholders being involved in the broader AI system ecosystem to execute tasks in a responsible way.

Apart from regular monitoring, an RAI black box can be added to the AI system to collect evidence of the system execution, decisions made by the AI components at a critical time, and the surrounding context information. The data collected by the RAI black box is used for analysis after near misses and/or failures. The RAI black box transfers the collected data to the RAI data store regularly.

A global-view auditor is necessary when deploying the AI system within a decentralized environment where multiple AI components cooperate or when multiple AI systems are working together. The global-view auditor's role involves gathering information from different AI components/systems (for example, through the RAI black box within the AI system), and subsequently processing this information to pinpoint any discrepancies.

In addition to monitoring, the operation infrastructure provides a simulation environment for AI components. An RAI sandbox is an emulated environment running in a safe and isolated virtual machine, which can separate the execution of AI components from the rest of the AI system—for example, to quarantine new features of Robbie. An RAI digital twin can perform system-level simulation to understand the behaviors of the AI system and assess potential RAI risks in a cost-effective way before running the AI system in the real world.

The RAI knowledge base captures the scattered RAI knowledge (for example, regulation) as a knowledge graph, which is the basis for other components. For example, regulatory compliance checking can be based on the structured data captured in a knowledge graph. An RAI digital twin and a continuous RAI validator may also be built using the RAI knowledge base.

Summary

Chapter 6 introduced a collection of product patterns aiming to build responsible-AI-by-design into the architecture of AI systems. These patterns can serve as a helpful guide to those designing responsible AI systems as to which key components to include. However, it can be tricky to understand how to use multiple patterns together, which is typically required in real-world cases. This chapter showed one way of using multiple product patterns together to create a reference architecture that can be reused in potentially many contexts. In practice, the reference architecture should be further customized based on the specific requirements of a particular AI system.

Principle-Specific Techniques for Responsible AI

This chapter discusses some of the principle-specific techniques to address the RAI concerns around AI models and data. Among the ethical principles, security, reliability, and safety are considered traditional software quality attributes and well studied in the dependability community. Transparency, contestability, accountability, human-centered values, and human, societal, and environmental well-being are the principles that can be addressed by the governance patterns, process patterns, and product patterns introduced in the previous chapters. This chapter mainly focuses on the techniques to deal with fairness, privacy, and explainability, which are emerging quality attributes for AI systems. Because the techniques can be embedded as product features of AI systems and viewed as product patterns, each technique is discussed in the form of a pattern. Many techniques exist for addressing fairness, privacy, and explainability. They may sometimes require adaptation for specific context. This chapter aims to provide examples to show the existence for such types of patterns, rather than providing a comprehensive list.

Fairness

As AI technology has become increasingly prevalent in data-rich domains, the issue of fairness has become a serious ethical concern that must be addressed in various types of applications, such as recruitment, criminal justice, and medical applications. It is crucial to ensure that decisions made by AI systems are not discriminatory toward certain groups or individuals.

Bias in data-driven systems is unavoidable, as differences cannot be detected without bias. In the context of fairness in AI, we focus on unwanted bias, which is a systematic error that can occur at any stage of the AI system lifecycle. To ensure fairness, we must mitigate the unwanted bias that puts privileged individuals or groups at an advantage and unprivileged individuals or groups at a disadvantage. The bias can occur within the development team and among AI users and consumers. Examples include bias in the requirements elicitation, training data collection and pre-processing, system-level or model-level design, testing cases, and monitoring metrics. Fairness metrics measure the unwanted bias in training data or AI models in a quantifiable way, while discrimination mitigation algorithms are implemented to reduce or eliminate the bias. These techniques are crucial for ensuring that AI systems are fair and unbiased toward all individuals or groups.

T.1. Fairness Assessor

Selecting appropriate metrics for measuring the fairness of AI models is crucial for detecting and mitigating fairness risk in AI systems.

Context

In the context of AI systems, unfairness refers to the situations where the outcomes of decisions and behaviors of the systems lead to discrimination against certain groups of people, such as those based on genders, races, and other protected characteristics.

Problem

How can we quantitatively measure the degree of bias for different types of fairness in AI systems?

Solution

When detecting and mitigating bias in AI models, it is critical to select the appropriate fairness metrics for measuring fairness. Some commonly used fairness metrics include

- **Demographic parity:** This metric measures the likelihood of a positive outcome (such as getting a job) across different sensitive groups (such as gender) and ensures it is the same for all groups. For example, an AI model meets the conditions of demographic parity if 10 percent of males are predicted as positive, and the same ratio applies to females. Demographic parity is used to prevent historical biases and can be achieved by modifying the training data.

- **Equalized odds:** This metric measures the equality of true positive and false positive rates between different sensitive groups (such as gender or race). For example, an AI model satisfies the conditions of equalized odds if the rate of a qualified applicant being hired and the rate of a disqualified applicant not being hired are the same for both males and females. Equalized odds should be used when a false positive outcome is costly and there is a strong need for true positive outcomes. Also, there should be a clear decision threshold for the target variable (e.g., determining fraudulent transactions).

- **Equal opportunity:** Each group of sensitive attributes should have equal true positive rates. For example, an AI model satisfies the conditions of equal opportunity if qualified loan applicants have an equal chance of getting a loan regardless of the suburb they live in. Both equalized odds and equal opportunity can be achieved through post-processing mechanisms. Equal opportunity is typically used when there is a strong need to correctly predict positive outcomes, and when introducing false positive outcomes does not have a costly impact on the users of the AI systems. Additionally, the target variable should have a clear decision threshold that is not subject to bias.

- **Fairness through awareness:** An AI model should produce similar predictions for individuals who are similar with respect to a task-specific similarity metric. This metric provides fairness guarantees at the individual level rather than at the group level. To achieve this, a distance function must be defined to measure similarity between individuals.

Benefits

The fairness assessor pattern can provide several benefits when used to detect and mitigate bias in AI systems, including

- **Quantifiable measurements and validation:** The use of fairness metrics allows for the quantification of bias, making it easier to identify and validate over time.

- **Monitorability:** Fairness metrics can be continuously monitored at runtime to detect deviation from fairness requirements.

- **Compliance:** By measuring the bias, the fairness assessor pattern can help organizations comply with laws and regulations related to fairness and discrimination.

Drawbacks

The fairness assessor pattern has some drawbacks, including

- **Limited by access to demographics:** In real-world scenarios, demographics information is often available only at a coarse level, making it challenging to accurately measure bias at a more granular level.

- **Restricted by application type:** While quantitative fairness metrics are effective for certain types of applications such as automatic recruitment, face recognition, and crime prediction, they may not be suitable for applications involving frequent human-AI interactions.

- **Reductionism:** Fairness is a complex and evolving social concept that is heavily dependent on context and can be quite subjective. Reducing fairness to metrics can oversimplify the multi-faceted nature of the concept and may mask important issues that are not captured by the metrics.

- **Conflicting metrics:** Many fairness measures are inherently in conflict with each other, making it difficult to satisfy all desirable measures of fairness simultaneously. For example, achieving demographic parity might lead to a lower true positive rate for certain groups, while achieving equalized odds might result in a lower true positive rate for other groups.

Related Patterns

T.2. Discrimination mitigator: Fairness measurement metrics can be used to measure the effectiveness of discrimination mitigation techniques.

Known Uses

Here are the known uses of the fairness assessor pattern:

- Google Fairness Gym is a simulation toolkit that analyzes the fairness of AI models with consideration for the context (e.g., temporal and environmental context).[1]
- Google Fairness Indicators is a library that enables computation of popular fairness metrics.[2]
- Facebook Fairness Flow is a fairness toolkit used by Facebook internally to identify bias in AI models.[3]

T.2. Discrimination Mitigator

Discrimination mitigation algorithms are used to address unwanted bias throughout the entire lifecycle of AI systems.

Context

In the context of AI systems, discrimination is the illegal or unfavorable treatment of an individual based on their membership in a protected group such as gender, race, or age. There are two types of discrimination that can occur in AI systems: direct discrimination happening when protected groups are explicitly used as attributes in the decision-making algorithms and indirect discrimination that occurs when protected groups are correlated with attributes in the decision-making algorithms.

Problem

How can we mitigate algorithmic discrimination in the decision-making of AI systems?

---

1. https://github.com/google/ml-fairness-gym.

2. https://github.com/tensorflow/fairness-indicators.

3. https://ai.facebook.com/blog/how-were-using-fairness-flow-to-help-build-ai-that-works-better-for-everyone/.

Solution

Algorithmic discrimination can be mitigated in three ways:

- Pre-processing techniques (such as data preprocessing techniques,[4] optimized data pre-processing techniques,[5] or data perturbation techniques for word embedding[6]) can be used to remove the underlying discrimination by removing or adjusting data points that are biased or not representative of the population the AI system will be used on.

- In-processing techniques (such as adding fairness constraints[7] or prejudice remover regularizers[8] for fair classification, or adding a minimizing adversary as one of the learning objectives[9]) can be applied during the training of the AI model to modify the learning algorithms and remove discrimination in the decision-making process, if the modification of the learning algorithms is allowed.

- Post-processing techniques (such as equalized odds or an equal opportunity predictor derived from a learned predictor,[10] removing gender associations in word embedding[11]) are used after the AI model has been trained and deployed to adjust its output and remove any unwanted bias.

Benefits

Here are the benefits of the discrimination mitigator pattern:

- **Improved model performance:** When discrimination is removed, the AI model's performance is improved and its output is more trustworthy.

- **Better balance between fairness and accuracy:** Discrimination mitigation techniques can effectively balance fairness and accuracy.

4. F. Kamiran and T. Calders, "Data Preprocessing Techniques for Classification Without Discrimination," *Knowledge and Information Systems* 33, no. 1 (2012): 1–33.

5. F. du Pin Calmon et al., "Optimized Data Pre-Processing for Discrimination Prevention," 2017, https://doi.org/10.48550/arXiv.1704.03354.

6. M.-E. Brunet et al., "Understanding the Origins of Bias in Word Embeddings," *International Conference on Machine Learning,* 2019.

7. M. B. Zafar et al., "Fairness Constraints: Mechanisms for Fair Classification," *Artificial Intelligence and Statistics,* 2017.

8. T. Kamishima et al., "Fairness-Aware Classifier with Prejudice Remover Regularizer," *Joint European Conference on Machine Learning and Knowledge Discovery in Databases,* 2012.

9. B. H. Zhang, B. Lemoine, and M. Mitchel, "Mitigating Unwanted Biases with Adversarial Learning," *Proceedings of the 2018 AAAI/ACM Conference on AI, Ethics, and Society,* 2018.

10. M. Hardt, E. Price, and N. Srebro, "Equality of Opportunity in Supervised Learning," *Advances in Neural Information Processing Systems* (2016): 29.

11. T. Bolukbasi et al., "Man Is to Computer Programmer as Woman Is to Homemaker? Debiasing Word Embeddings," *Advances in Neural Information Processing Systems* (2016): 29.

Drawbacks

Here are the drawbacks of the discrimination mitigator pattern:

- **Lack of generality:** AI models are often designed for specific tasks, which makes it difficult to extend and adapt discrimination mitigation techniques to new tasks or domains.

- **Reduced model performance:** Introducing discrimination mitigation techniques can affect the overall performance of the model.

- **Compromised accuracy:** Discrimination mitigation techniques may involve trade-offs in order to achieve fairness.

Related Patterns

T.1. Fairness assessor: Fairness measurement metrics are used as objectives of mitigation techniques.

Known Uses

Here are the known uses of the discrimination mitigator pattern:

- LinkedIn Fairness Toolkit (LiFT) is a library that is used to measure fairness and mitigate bias in large-scale AI workflows.[12] A post-processing method is used to transform scores to achieve equality of opportunity in rankings.

- Microsoft Fairlearn is a fairness toolkit that contains model assessment metrics and mitigation algorithms for AI developers to assess their AI system's fairness and mitigate the detected bias.[13]

- IBM AI Fairness 360 is a Python library that contains a comprehensive set of fairness metrics and algorithms (such as optimized processing and equalized odds post-processing) to mitigate bias in datasets and AI models.[14]

Privacy

An AI model lifecycle typically consists of four stages: data preparation, model training and evaluation, model deployment, and model serving. Data preparation involves collecting, cleaning, and pre-processing the data. Model training and evaluation use the prepared data to train and evaluate the model. Model deployment integrates the model into a software system that is deployed to a production environment. Model serving uses the model to make decisions. In the lifecycle, both

---

12. https://github.com/linkedin/LiFT.

13. https://github.com/microsoft/SEAL.

14. https://ai-fairness-360.org.

training data and models can be vulnerable to privacy attacks. To address these privacy concerns, privacy-preserving techniques can be applied in the design of AI systems in the form of product patterns, including encrypted-data-based trainer, secure aggregator, and random noise data generator.

T.3. Encrypted-Data-Based Trainer

An encrypted-data-based trainer learns AI models over encrypted data without the need for decryption, through the use of homomorphic encryption techniques.

Context

There are often privacy concerns about the training data, because it is often sensitive and should not be revealed. For example, a medical model for disease prediction is trained over the patients' private medical data, which should be protected and not disclosed to unauthorized parties.

Problem

How can we ensure the privacy of training data during the training process?

Solution

Homomorphic encryption is a privacy-preserving technique that enables computations to be performed on ciphertexts directly, resulting in the same outcome as if it were performed on the original data. For example, when the numbers 1 and 2 are encrypted and their ciphertexts are added using homomorphic encryption algorithms, the decrypted result would yield 3. This technique can be used to encrypt training data, allowing AI models to learn from the encrypted data without the need for decryption.

Benefits

Here are the benefits of the encrypted-data-based trainer pattern:

- **Data privacy:** The training data is always encrypted to reduce the risk of compromise.
- **Data usability:** There is no need to modify the features of training data to preserve the data privacy.

Drawbacks

Here are the drawbacks of the encrypted-data-based trainer pattern:

- **Training inefficiency:** Training neural networks over using data encrypted with homomorphic encryption algorithms can be challenging, because the networks become slower after the encryption is applied.

- **Lack of visibility:** After the training data is encrypted, it can be hard for data scientists to monitor the training process, such as identifying and correcting mislabeled data.

Related Patterns

T.4. Secure aggregator: The secure multi-party computation techniques used in secure aggregation are a form of homomorphic encryption techniques under a multi-party setting.

Known Uses

Here are the known uses of the encrypted-data-based trainer pattern:

- IBM HE layers enable the execution of encrypted AI workloads using homomorphic encrypted data.[15]

- Microsoft SEAL is a homomorphic encryption library that allows computation, including training, to be performed on encrypted data.[16]

- Google's Fully Homomorphic Encryption is a cryptographic technique to secure computation that does not need to share the decrypted data in order to perform operations on them.[17]

T.4. Secure Aggregator

A secure aggregator can ensure secure aggregation in federated learning through the use of multi-party computation techniques.

Context

Federated learning is a type of collaborative learning that trains models locally on client devices and aggregates the results to create a global model. While the local data remains on the client devices, the local model parameters can be inferred to reveal sensitive information.

---

15. https://ibm.github.io/helayers/.

16. https://github.com/microsoft/SEAL.

17. https://github.com/google/fully-homomorphic-encryption.

Problem

How can we ensure data privacy when aggregating local model updates in federated learning?

Solution

Secure multi-party computation can be applied in federated learning to protect the data privacy during model exchanges and aggregations. When multi-party computation is used, local model updates from individual client devices can be aggregated while keeping the privacy of the model parameters. Through the use of encryption, participating clients can securely exchange their encrypted model updates and have access only to the final aggregation result, which is performed on the secret-shared model parameter data.

Benefits

There are several benefits of using the secure aggregator pattern:

- **Data privacy and security:** Secure multi-party computation enables secure data sharing in model exchanges and aggregation. Models are protected by encryptions; this prevents them from being attacked by adversarial parties to avoid data leakage.

- **Decentralized control:** Federated learning allows for the training of models on distributed devices, which enables decentralized control of data and models.

- **Compliance with regulations:** Secure multi-party computation can help organizations comply with RAI regulations that require the protection of personal data.

Drawbacks

Here are the drawbacks of the secure aggregator pattern:

- **Aggregation inefficiency:** The efficiency of the aggregation process is affected because additional encryption steps are needed every round for each participating client device.

- **Lack of scalability:** Multi-party computation can incur significant computation and communication cost when being applied in a large-scale federated learning system.

Related Patterns

Here are the related patterns of the secure aggregator pattern:

- D.4. Federated learner: Secure multi-party computation is a homomorphic encryption technique that can be applied to the aggregation process in federated learning.

- T.3. Trainer over encrypted data: Secure multi-party computation techniques used in secure aggregation are an extension of the homomorphic encryption technique for multi-party model training.

Known Uses

Here are the known uses of the secure aggregator pattern:

- Google's SecAgg is a secure aggregation protocol that uses multi-party computation to carry out the summations of model parameter updates received from client devices in an encrypted manner.[18]

- OpenMined's PyGrid is a peer-to-peer platform that uses multi-party computation to protect the privacy of data and model parameters in federated learning.[19]

- IBM Federated Learning supports multi-party computation to enable the private aggregation of model updates.[20]

T.5. Random Noise Data Generator

Random noise data generator uses differential privacy to provide mathematically verifiable data privacy guarantees by introducing a controlled amount of random noise data in the training datasets.

Context

It is often insufficient to protect data privacy by directly removing sensitive data (such as personally identifiable information) from a dataset through data anonymization techniques (such as k-anonymity[21] and its variations). This is especially true when attackers already have some information about individuals in the dataset. Even if attackers do not have access to the full dataset, they may still be able to re-identify individuals by cross-referencing other information they have access to.

Problem

How can we prevent the private data from being leaked, especially the personally identifiable information?

Solution

Differential privacy is a privacy-preserving technique that adds a carefully tuned amount of random noise data into training datasets before using the dataset to train the model. This noise is specially calibrated to ensure the training results are not significantly impacted. In other words, the presence

---

18. https://www.tensorflow.org/federated/api_docs/python/tff/federated_secure_sum_bitwidth.

19. https://github.com/OpenMined/PyGrid/.

20. http://ibmfl.mybluemix.net.

21. L. Sweeney, "k-anonymity: A Model for Protecting Privacy," *International Journal of Uncertainty, Fuzziness and Knowledge-Based Systems* 10, no. 05 (2002): 557–70.

or absence of any single piece of data in the training dataset does not impact the results of the model training.

Benefits

Here are the benefits of the random noise data generation pattern:

- **Guaranteed data privacy:** Differential privacy can be used to reduce the risk of data leakage in AI systems by protecting the privacy of the training data. The introduction of noise in the training data makes it difficult for an attacker to infer the original data from the decisions made by the AI system.
- **Reduced risk of data memorization:** Differential privacy performs indistinguishable results on neighboring datasets, making it challenging for an attacker to memorize individual data entries.

Drawbacks

Here are the drawbacks of the random noise data generation pattern:

- **Model utility loss:** Applying differential privacy to AI systems can result in a decrease in the accuracy of the models.
- **Limited by data type:** Applying differential privacy to unstructured data, such as videos, images, and text, can be challenging.

Related Patterns

D.4. Federated Learner: Differential privacy can be used in federated learning to protect data privacy by randomly generating noise data in the local training and aggregation process.

Known Uses

Here are the known uses of the random noise data generation pattern:

- Google Differential Privacy Library is used in Google's products including Google Maps.[22]
- IBM Differential Privacy Library provides a tool suite for machine learning tasks to achieve built-in privacy guarantees. [23]
- SmartNoise is an open data differential privacy platform that is jointly developed by Microsoft and Harvard's Institute for Quantitative Social Science.[24]

---

22. https://github.com/google/differential-privacy.

23. https://github.com/IBM/differential-privacy-library.

24. https://www.microsoft.com/en-us/ai/ai-lab-differential-privacy.

Explainability

Despite the huge benefits that AI can provide to society, there is a significant challenge in understanding the decisions made by AI systems. This is particularly important in mission-critical domains such as autonomous vehicles, the military, and healthcare, where AI systems can have a direct impact on human lives. For people to trust and use these systems, they need to understand how and why the AI system arrived at a particular decision, such as the system's processes and input data for the decision outcomes. The predictions given by the AI systems are often not that useful in assisting users to make decisions unless the system explains the factors for why that decision was made. This is where explainability comes in; it is an emerging quality attribute requirement for AI systems. It can include information about the features and inputs that contributed to the decision, as well as the reasoning behind the decision.

Explainable AI (XAI) aims to make the decision-making of AI systems transparent and understandable to stakeholders. The approach provides explanations for the reasoning behind the decisions, including the strengths and weaknesses of the model. There are two types of XAI techniques in terms of the scope: local explanation techniques, which provide instance-based explanations, and global explanation techniques, which provide explanations that help to understand the general behavior of AI models.[25] Both local and global explanations can be generated using backpropagation techniques or perturbation techniques. Backpropagation techniques use a backward pass from the output prediction layer to the input layer to understand the neuronal impact and relevance of the input data on the output decisions (e.g., using saliency maps, salient relevance maps, and attribution maps). Perturbation techniques, in contrast, change the features in the input data instance (e.g., using prediction difference analysis, Randomized Input Sampling for Explanation [RISE]). XAI techniques can be either model-intrinsic or post-hoc. Rule-based models such as decision trees are model-intrinsic XAI that is inherently explainable. Post-hoc XAI techniques, such as deconvolution network and Shapley sampling methods, are model-independent and add explainability without sacrificing the model performance.

To improve human trust, explanations should take into account the background, culture, and preferences of the stakeholders. According to DARPA,[26] in addition to producing more explainable models through XAI techniques, XAI can be addressed by designing effective explanation interfaces and understanding the psychology of explanations.

T.6. Local Explainer

A local explainer provides explanations on an instance-level basis for individual input data to understand the feature importance and correlations in relation to the output predictions.

---

25. A. Das and P. Rad, "Opportunities and Challenges in Explainable Artificial Intelligence (xai): A Survey," arXiv preprint arXiv:2006.11371, 2020.

26. D. Gunning et al., "DARPA's Explainable AI (XAI) Program: A Retrospective." (Wiley Online Library, 2021), e61; D. Gunning and D. Aha, "DARPA's Explainable Artificial Intelligence (XAI) Program," *AI Magazine* 40, no. 2 (2019): 44–58.

Context

Despite the widespread adoption of AI, the models in AI systems remain opaque to users. Without trust in the AI systems, the users may be hesitant to take actions based on its recommendations.

Problem

How can a user understand a specific decision made by an AI system?

Solution

One way to understand individual decisions made by an AI system is through the use of a local explainer. A local explainer provides explanations for each input data instance, which can help users understand the feature importance and correlations that led to the specific output predictions. Two well-known local explainer algorithms are Local Interpretable Model-Agnostic Explanations (LIME) and Shapley Additive exPlanations (SHAP). LIME explains a black box model by determining the contribution of each feature to the decision output for a specific input. On the other hand, SHAP provides local explanations by comparing the decision outputs of the model when a feature is included versus excluded.

Benefits

There are several benefits to using the local explainer pattern:

- **Trust:** A local explainer provides a way to understand the reasoning behind a specific decision, making the model more transparent and easier to trust.

- **Correctness:** By providing the information about the feature importance and correlations that resulted in a decision, a local explainer can give insight into the inner workings of a model, which can help identify error or biases in the model.

Drawbacks

There are some drawbacks to using the local explainer pattern:

- **Lack of global visibility:** Local explanations do not explain the general behaviors of AI models.

- **Complexity:** A local explainer can be computationally intensive and may not scale well to complex models or large datasets.

- **Limited applicability:** Local explanations are not suitable for all types of models or use cases; for example, they work well with linear models and tabular data but may not be suitable for image or text data.

Related Patterns

Here are the related patterns of the local explainer pattern:

- T.7. Global explainer: The focus of global explanations is on the whole AI model, while local explanations consider only the individual decision.

- P.9. XAI interface: Local explanations can be integrated into the interface to explain why a data instance is given a decision.

Known Uses

Here are the known uses of the local explainer pattern:

- IBM AI Explainability 360 is a toolkit that contains five types of explainability methods, including post-doc local explanations.[27]

- Microsoft InterpretML is a Python toolkit that includes XAI techniques developed by Microsoft and third parties to explain the reasons behind the individual decisions.[28]

- Google Vertex Explainable AI provides XAI support for tabular and image data and helps users learn how each feature in the data contributed to the decision result.[29]

T.7. Global Explainer

A global explainer treats an AI model as a whole by using a set of data instances to produce explanations to understand the general behavior of the AI model.

Context

The black box nature of AI systems can be a significant challenge to their adoption and raises a number of ethical and legal concerns. One of the main reasons for this is the complexity of the models used in AI systems, particularly Deep Neural Networks (DNNs), which have a large number of parameters that can make them difficult to understand. This lack of explainability poses a barrier to widespread adoption of AI, because users may be hesitant to trust the suggestions given by AI systems.

Problem

How can we help users understand the general behavior of an AI model?

---

27. http://aix360.mybluemix.net.

28. https://interpret.ml.

29. https://cloud.google.com/vertex-ai.

Solution

A global explainer can help users understand the general behavior of an AI system by using a set of data instances to produce explanations. These explanations provide an overview of the model's behavior by visualizing the relationship between the input features and the model's output over a range of values. Global surrogate models, such as tree-based models or rule-based models, can be used to understand the complex AI models because they have inherent explainability, allowing the output decisions to be traced back to their source.

Benefits

The benefits of using the global explainer pattern include

- **Better understanding:** Global explanations simplify complex AI models by reducing them to linear counterparts, which are easier to understand.

- **Improved transparency:** Global explanations provide a general understanding of how an AI model behaves, which can help increase transparency and build trust in the AI system.

Drawbacks

The drawbacks of using the global explainer pattern include

- **Limited understandability:** Global explanations can be difficult for AI users without technical expertise to understand and provide feedback on.

- **Limited specificity:** While global explanations provide a general understanding of the model's behavior, they may lack the specificity required to understand why a specific decision was made for a particular input.

- **Lack of accuracy:** Global explanations are based on a set of data instances, which can introduce uncertainty and noise, leading to explanations that may not be entirely accurate.

Related Patterns

Here are the related patterns of the global explainer pattern:

- T.6. Local explainer: The focus of global explanations is on the whole AI model, while local explanations consider only the individual decision.

- P.9. XAI interface: Global explanations can be incorporated into the interface design to allow AI users to understand AI systems' global behaviors.

Known Uses

Here are the known uses of the global explainer pattern:

- Microsoft InterpretML provides XAI techniques that explain the AI model's overall behavior.[30]

- EthicalML-XAI provides global explanations by visualizing the behaviors of AI models in terms of input variables.[31]

- tf-explain provides insights to neural networks' global behaviors by visualizing activations of neurons.[32]

Summary

This chapter presents some of the principle-specific techniques that address the key emerging quality attributes of AI systems (i.e., fairness, privacy, and explainability). These techniques can be formed as product patterns and integrated into AI systems as product features. The details of techniques are described in the form of patterns, including a summary, the context, the problem statement, the solution, the strengths and drawbacks, related patterns, and known uses.

---

30. https://interpret.ml.

31. https://github.com/EthicalML/xai.

32. https://github.com/sicara/tf-explain.

PART III

CASE STUDIES

We introduced generic patterns for all the AI ethics principles in the previous chapters. The question remains: How can organizations effectively govern the development and use of AI systems using these patterns?

In Part III of this book, we discuss three case studies to help organizations apply the patterns in different contexts: 1) a specific company context (i.e., Telstra); 2) a specific use case context (i.e., talent acquisition); and 3) a more generic use case to select/adapt the patterns to create a coherent set of guidelines for a particular concern, namely, diversity and inclusion in AI.

Here, we briefly introduce each case study, with particular reference to which patterns in the catalogue have been applied.

Chapter 9, "Risk-Based AI Governance in Telstra," introduces a risk-based responsible AI approach adopted by Telstra, Australia's largest telecommunications company.

From the governance perspective, Telstra's approach follows three governance patterns: the leadership commitment for RAI pattern, the RAI risk committee pattern, and the RAI training pattern. Telstra has appointed an executive role for AI, known as the Executive AI Owner, within each business function. They are accountable for all the use of AI within each business function. They meet monthly, along with other corporate representatives to discuss data and AI issues. Telstra's Risk Council for AI & Data (RCAID) is responsible for assessing and approving use cases to ensure compliance with Telstra's RAI policy. The RCAID reports regularly to the Audit and Risk Committee (A&RC) of the Telstra Board, allowing AI risks to be considered in the context of other organizational risks. To support RCAID, Telstra also implements the RAI training pattern to upskill their RCAID subject matter experts (SMEs) in the special risks that arise when AI systems are used.

From the development process perspective, Telstra employs the RAI acceptance testing process pattern to routinely run fairness and explainability tests for many of the models that come to RCAID. Telstra is currently working to make the tools more automated and more deeply embedded in the development and deployment process. The evolution of these tools would be a component in an implementation of the extensible, adaptive, and dynamic RAI risk assessment process pattern.

Overall, Telstra's risk-based approach reflects several patterns presented in the Responsible AI Pattern Catalogue. It also demonstrates how governance and process patterns are linked during use across organization and team levels. The implementation of these patterns has allowed Telstra to prioritize limited skills capacity for the most significant RAI risks and use cases and integrate RAI risk management with general organizational risk management.

While Chapter 9 describes the experience of a large organization such as Telstra, Chapter 10, "Reejig: The World's First Independently Audited Ethical Talent AI," looks instead at small and medium-sized enterprises and, in particular, how a startup can tackle RAI risks. In this chapter, Reejig, a workforce intelligence platform startup company, shares their ethical talent AI approach and maps it to the patterns outlined in the Responsible AI Pattern Catalogue. The chapter explains how Reejig manages the bias issues present in datasets and algorithms through a three-stage debiasing strategy: manipulating and balancing the dataset before training, putting constraints on the model's optimization function to meet the expected criteria during training, and adding gender boost after training. This strategy reflects the fairness-related product patterns: the fairness assessor pattern and the discrimination mitigator pattern. In addition, Reejig has implemented the independent oversight pattern to assess the transparency, fairness, accountability, and privacy within the Reejig talent shortlisting algorithm independently.

Reejig's approach addresses the resource and reputation challenges faced by SMEs and startups by partnering with an independent external organization to bridge the expertise gap, enhance transparency, and boost reputation. In addition, Reejig prioritized the most important risk in applying AI to talent analytics—fairness. Reejig embeds fairness product patterns in their product by design to further reduce repetitive process-related costs while connecting to the governance pattern.

The use cases for the pattern catalogue are not limited to specific organizations that develop AI-based solutions. They can also be used to design concrete guidelines, policies, risk management profiles, and frameworks for cross-organization and cross-sector concerns. Chapter 11, "Diversity and Inclusion in Artificial Intelligence," presents such a case: guidelines on diversity and inclusion in AI (DI-AI) developed by CSIRO, Australia's national science agency. The DI-AI guideline introduces a DI-AI definition and five pillars (human, data, process, system, governance) by synthesizing existing work including patterns. Although the pillars are different from the pattern categories (governance, process, product), those working on DI-AI within an organization, project, and/or team can consider a many-to-many mapping of the guidelines and patterns that suits their specific needs. In Chapter 11, there are a few examples of how the guidelines are mapped to the patterns. This chapter is highly valuable because it sheds light on how organizations can promote diversity and inclusion in AI by leveraging the DI-AI guidelines and the Responsible AI Pattern Catalogue.

The case studies in Chapters 9 and 10 were written by industry practitioners from the respective companies. The third case study, in Chapter 11, was written by researchers from the CSIRO Diversity and Inclusion in AI team.

9

Risk-Based AI Governance in Telstra

By Stuart Powell, Telstra

Telstra is Australia's leading telecommunications and technology company, offering a full range of communications services and competing in all telecommunications markets. Through June 2022 in Australia, we provided over 18 million retail mobile services, almost 4 million retail fixed bundles and standalone data services, and just under 1 million retail fixed standalone voice services.[1] We believe it's people who give purpose to our technology. That's why our purpose is to build a connected future so everyone can thrive.

At its heart, Telstra is a customer-oriented connectivity and technology company, and we see the use of artificial intelligence as essential to our success and the future experience we offer our customers. We are also deeply conscious that this technology has the potential to cause unintended harm if not managed responsibly. So, we take very seriously our obligation to govern our use of AI with the utmost care, and we recognize that at the scale Telstra operates this is no small task. We have hundreds of teams developing software, purchasing systems, deploying, and operating solutions internally or for our customers. It is a huge job to ensure that everyone involved knows what they need to do and has the right systems and tools to do it. Even with strong commitment from the top, a long-term tools strategy, and comprehensive communication plans in place, this effort can take significant time.

While this long-term implementation is ongoing, we carry a growing risk of failing to live up to our responsible AI ambitions. As in other cases where we have long-term open risks, our aim is to focus attention on managing the highest risks first. Doing so involves identifying the highest AI risks from the top down, prioritizing tools and training for these areas, and putting tactical solutions in place

---

1. *Telstra Annual Report 2022*. Telstra Corporation Limited (2022).

to guard against potential challenges. This chapter explains the foundations for this risk-based approach to AI governance.

Policy and Awareness

Our first step toward risk-based AI governance was to create and approve a Responsible AI Policy and make people aware of it. This policy clearly set out what the expectations were and provided a mandate to require everyone to prioritize it.

Telstra Group policies consist of a short policy document and a guidance document to assist with implementation. The policy document itself is a simple, plain-English statement of what behaviors the policy mandates and is written so that all employees and contractors can understand it. Our Responsible AI Policy has a single page of eleven principles that clearly state what is expected when we deal with AI systems. For example, principle 4 says

> Appropriate due diligence must be conducted to understand both the positive and negative impacts, and possible unintended consequences, that our AI systems can have on individuals, society and on the environment. We must seek to make these impacts positive, fair, and sustainable.

Telstra was involved in the creation of the eight principles of the Federal Government's Australian AI Ethics Principles introduced in Chapter 1, and our policy draws heavily on these principles. In this original form, however, the principles require a significant amount of interpretation and, in some cases, a substantial amount of expertise to assess whether they are being applied correctly. Human-centered values, for example, require that the AI system "should respect human rights." Expecting all our AI practitioners to have sufficient expertise in human rights to be able to make this assessment could be a significant hurdle.

So, in formulating the Telstra policy, we needed to translate these principles into a statement of behavior that required no expert interpretation. In Telstra principle 4, for example, the obligation is to conduct due diligence, to understand the impact of AI systems, and to seek to make the impacts positive, and so on. These are activities that ordinary staff members can act on, relying on more expert people where required (e.g., for the due diligence investigation).

The guidance document, which runs to eleven pages, gives more background and advice on what the policy intends to accomplish and how our staff members can put this into practice. It includes, for example, two full pages on the Australian AI Ethics Principles and our support for them. It also includes practical advice on what resources and processes are available in Telstra to assist with the implementation of the policy.

Telstra's Definition of AI

In doing the policy work, we quickly found that the term *artificial intelligence* means very different things to different people. Some take a very broad view of what can be included, and others require very sophisticated algorithms to be used before it qualifies as AI.

We settled this question by adopting the following quite wide definition in our policy:

> Artificial Intelligence (AI) is a broad term used to describe a collection of technologies able to solve problems and perform tasks without explicit human guidance. These include machine learning and deep learning. Some applications of AI include natural language processing, image recognition and various robotics applications.

But we recognized that this definition had the potential to create a lot of governance work, because everything tagged as "AI" might need special review. So, in our policy we also introduced the concept of a *significant AI-informed decision*, which is defined as

> A decision where AI materially assists in the process of making the decision and the decision has significant impact, such as a legal, or similarly significant, effect for an individual or with significant legal, financial, or reputational consequences for Telstra.

While all AI systems must comply with the policy, the AI systems that are making significant AI-informed decisions need special review and governance. In doing this, our policy starts to separate our applications of AI with higher impact—those making significant AI-informed decisions—from those with less impact on stakeholders.

Awareness

To ensure that the policy was effective, we had to make people aware of its existence and the role they had to play in making it effective and sustainable.

Fortunately, we already had engagement arrangements in place for data governance to help with this task. Telstra is divided into nine separate business functions, each led by a group executive (GE), and accountability for operations flows down from these GEs. For data governance, we had established a quarterly forum for these GEs that met to discuss data issues. We were able to add AI to their agenda. Moreover, each business function had identified an executive who would take the lead on data issues for the whole of the function. We established a similar executive role for AI (the executive AI owner), who in some cases was the same person, who was accountable for all AI use within the function. These data and AI executives meet monthly, along with other corporate representatives (e.g., the chief risk officer and the chief privacy officer), to consider data and AI matters. This is our Data & AI Council.

Telstra has also identified Data and AI Risk as one of the top risks on which it reports regularly to the Audit and Risk Committee (A&RC) of the Telstra Board. Our commitment to governance of our responsible AI risk is an essential part of this report.

With the GE Forum, the Data & AI Council, and the A&RC reporting in place, it was a lot easier to inform all the relevant people about the Responsible AI Policy and to get management support to prioritize action for adherence to the policy. This approach aligns with the "leadership commitment for RAI" pattern.

Assessing Risk

Having set out the Responsible AI Policy and communicated it within the organization, we needed a method to drive compliance. In line with our top-down risk approach, we needed this method to be focused on the highest risks first.

We already had a risk assessment committee that reviewed big data projects, so we decided to expand this committee to include both AI and data to become the Risk Council for AI & Data (RCAID—pronounced "arcade"). RCAID has become a central feature of our AI governance implementation.

RCAID follows the "RAI risk committee" pattern; that is, it consists of a group of individuals who meet to assess and approve use cases to ensure their compliance with Telstra's Responsible AI Policy. The assessment is designed to be a one-off review done early in the lifecycle of a use case. Once approval is given, it is expected that the implementors of the use case will then continue to stay within the scope of the use case that they have outlined and will implement any recommendations made by the Council.

This section covers how this pattern has been implemented in Telstra and some of the learnings from practical experience.

Dimensions of Risk

Given the policy requirement to conform to the eight principles, one might think that any risk assessment would be structured around them. But, except for privacy protection and security and also reliability and safety, these are very different from the categories we normally use to assess risk. So, this assessment raised some challenges for implementation. For example, where would we find expertise to assess these risks in a way that takes into account Telstra's day-to-day operations? And what are the pathways and decision rights for escalation of these risks; would these all require new roles and other infrastructure to be put in place? If so, these principles could become very difficult and time-consuming to achieve.

Instead, we have found it much more practical to conduct risk assessments around the five dimensions shown in Table 9.1.

Table 9.1   RCAID Risk Dimensions

Risk Dimension	Description
Communications	How does the use case align with our communications to the public; how will it impact Telstra's reputation?
Cybersecurity	Does the use case align with all our cyber- and data security policies, standards, and guidelines?
Human Impact and Fairness	What effect will the use case have on our customers and other stakeholders, especially any groups that might be less able to defend their rights or are vulnerable in any way?
Legal	Is the use case consistent with our legal, regulatory, and contractual obligations?
Privacy	Does the use case treat personal information in accordance with our privacy policy and in a way that our customers and other stakeholders reasonably expect us to use it?

Four of these were existing risk management categories that we used in assessing data initiatives. Human Impact and Fairness was added to give more complete coverage of the principles. And this category also aligns with work our corporate sustainability team does.

Choosing these five risk dimensions has resulted in the following pragmatic advantages:

- We have clear precedents and/or standards that help us to understand the risks in each of these areas.

- We have pools of people with expertise in each of these categories, so we can draw on these resources to maintain the skill levels for RCAID.

- We have natural executive owners for each of these items all the way up to Group Executive (N-1) level for any escalation or conflict resolution.

Having taken this approach, we did, however, need to upskill our RCAID subject matter experts (SMEs) in the special risks that arise when AI systems are used. Upskilling involved in-depth training for our team from a local company with deep expertise in the ethics of AI. (From this initial work, we developed a 45-minute self-learning module in responsible AI that can be accessed by anyone in the company. This training contributes to our implementation of the "RAI training" pattern.)

To further equip RCAID with AI skills, we also ensure that some independent technical experts attend RCAID sessions to check that the right questions are being asked.

Levels of Risk

Telstra already has a well-developed enterprise risk management framework, including the decision-making authority and processes for handling different levels of risk. It did not take us long to determine that we should leverage this framework for the management of AI risks, rather than creating a new, independent framework that was AI-specific. The framework is well understood within the organization, and using it allows us to reuse existing risk management processes, including risk prioritization and acceptance.

The Telstra Board has also set a specific risk appetite for data and AI, and the board expects the risk to be managed using this framework.

The Telstra framework includes the risk exposure rating approach outlined in Figure 9.1. This approach includes a 5×5 matrix of risk likelihood versus risk consequence that allows each risk to be rated into four levels (low, medium, high, or critical).

The risk framework includes guidance on how to assess both likelihood and consequence ratings. We had to consider whether this guidance needed any adjustment with the introduction of AI systems.

The likelihood definitions and guidance material are straightforward and have been reused readily.

A harder question was whether AI systems changed the consequence considerations. These already have several categories for measuring the consequence of a risk (financial, customer, legal and regulatory, and so on), with good advice on what consequence rating should be applied. For example, breaches of our legal or regulatory obligations range from major to extreme, depending on the nature of the breach.

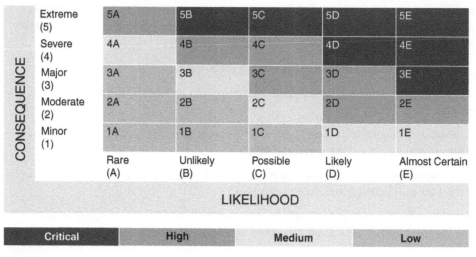

CONSEQUENCE		Rare (A)	Unlikely (B)	Possible (C)	Likely (D)	Almost Certain (E)
	Extreme (5)	5A	5B	5C	5D	5E
	Severe (4)	4A	4B	4C	4D	4E
	Major (3)	3A	3B	3C	3D	3E
	Moderate (2)	2A	2B	2C	2D	2E
	Minor (1)	1A	1B	1C	1D	1E

LIKELIHOOD

Critical	High	Medium	Low

Figure 9.1
Telstra's Risk Exposure Matrix.

After some consideration we have concluded that the existing consequence ratings work for AI systems as well. The consequences that we are concerned about, such as impact on our customers, our reputation, our regulatory obligations, or our finances, remain the same as for other risks. AI systems simply represent a different way in which these consequences can arise.

Operation of the Risk Council

With these principles in place, risk assessment by RCAID becomes straightforward. Use case sponsors from Telstra's business functions complete the RCAID use case template and present the case to a meeting of the Council. The members of RCAID then ask clarifying questions and often make recommendations for the treatment of risks that arise.

Each of the SMEs will then formally assess a use case for its impact in their area of expertise using the standard risk exposure matrix (the 5×5). This assessment involves articulating any risk, the trigger event for this risk, and the impact if the trigger event occurs. There may be several risks within each specialist area. Each risk is then rated for consequence and likelihood on the 5×5 matrix, resulting in an overall rating (low, medium, high, or critical) for that risk.

Even in AI use cases, many of the risks are not AI-specific. If data is being collected and deidentified, for example, the normal security risks apply for access control wherever the data is stored. Privacy risks consider who has access to the data at different stages in the data flow and what the reidentification risk is.

For AI-specific risks, asking the basic question "What happens if the AI algorithm fails?" goes a long way to identifying the risk. Clearly articulating the impact of false positives or false negatives on stakeholders helps to identify the consequences without needing expertise in the AI algorithm itself. The likelihood of these errors occurring may need more AI expertise (and more support from technical tools), which we can draw on for risks with higher-impact consequences.

RCAID has been given authority to approve any use case with only low or medium risks. This approval is recorded, along with any risk treatment recommendations, for later checks, including those to be made when obtaining approval to operate a system in production.

Any use case with high or critical risks in any area needs to be escalated to Telstra's Data & AI Council for approval to proceed (and further to the GE Forum, if needed). This escalation is in line with the standard risk acceptance process that Telstra uses, because high or critical risks need a higher level of executive authorization. Such authorization will always be within the risk appetite set by the Telstra Board.

An Example: Using AI to Improve Customer Service Outcomes

RCAID considered a project proposal to use information about our customers and machine learning techniques to improve customer service outcomes. Customers have a range of options for communicating with us when they have an issue. We refer to these as different "channels," and they include digital self-serve, call center, calling in via an app, and messaging via the My Telstra service app. The aim of this project is to use information about our customers to direct them to the best channel for their circumstances. For many customers the digital channels provide a better overall experience, but many are not aware of them as an option.

The proposal includes a proof-of-concept (PoC) stage followed by rollout to all customers. The project team is aware of processes to manage the experience for our most vulnerable customers, and they will be maintained and enforced while using the AI-based system.

Some of the risk assessment considerations, including their alignment with the Australian AI Ethics Principles, were as follows:

- **Overall**: The use case has social value (Human, social, and environmental well-being) if it genuinely improves the experience of customers and doesn't just cut operational expenses for Telstra. The PoC stage is committed to evaluating this value.

- **Legal/Privacy**: Regulation around privacy (Privacy protection and security) is increasingly focused on using personal information only where it is required for a useful purpose. The results of the PoC should be used to minimize the data the AI uses; if a data field doesn't make a significant contribution to the outcomes, it should be excluded.

- **Human Impact and Fairness**: There is a chance that the AI recommendations, while being appropriate for most of a cohort, might not be relevant for some individuals. To maintain fairness (Fairness), it must be easy to still access all service channels, regardless of the channels the AI recommends.

You will see that the assessment of risk was done by the SMEs in each of their disciplines, but the issues raised usually related to an AI Ethics Principle.

The use case was approved for the PoC stage.

Learnings from Practice

We have now assessed over 200 new use cases using the RCAID-based governance system. It has many strengths and has improved our confidence that we can operate in accordance with our Responsible AI Policy. But we have also had several learnings and had to adapt to make it work in practice.

The strengths of the system include

- **Company-wide application**: The assessment process works for all AI use cases, regardless of the technology platform they use or the business function that sponsors them.

- **Strong alignment with corporate structure**: By using risk categories that are owned by executives in the existing structure, we can see relatively clearly how decision escalations can be managed. And using standard corporate risk ratings makes the level of approval straightforward to determine.

- **Efficient assessment of use cases**: The "ethics committee" approach makes good use of the time of SMEs. The RCAID use case template guides use case sponsors on what information is key for the risk assessment. Because all participants have read the material before the meeting, the meeting can focus on the key points of contention and avoid a lot of detail that is not relevant to the risk assessment.

- **Clarity from multiple points of view**: On some of the more complex use cases, the discussion between the different risk SMEs, the business sponsors, and the technology team has been very helpful in clearly articulating the risks and proposing mitigations. The risks are not all independent, and having the different experts in the same conversation has been valuable in quickly finding a way forward or ruling out items that carry unacceptable risk.

Some of the key challenges and our learnings from them are covered in the following sections.

Identifying and Registering Use Cases

To adequately assess all our AI models and use cases, we first needed to find them. We also had to determine which cases needed full assessment by RCAID and which were low enough risk that this assessment was not required.

To manage this task, we created a register of all AI models used in the company. This register is a simple database that includes a basic description of the use case, the business and technical owners, and the deployment status. We initially populated it using a survey of all the business functions and all the AI platforms running models.

We then created some criteria and guidance to assess the impact of the AI models on stakeholders. Low-impact models include those that are internal, have little impact on customers or employees, and have relatively small financial implications. Higher-impact models are those that affect stakeholders more substantially, involve third parties, or have significant financial impacts for Telstra. We then worked with business model owners to assess the impact of the registered models.

Our next step was to create a backlog of in-production models that were higher impact and process them through RCAID. Lower-impact models still needed to be registered (along with the reasons for the low-impact assessment), but we did not assess them through RCAID.

For the development of new models, the impact assessment and registration happen up front. When a new model goes beyond the ideation stage, it is assessed for impact and registered. The impact rating is currently a self-assessment by the sponsoring team based on the criteria outlined previously. Higher-impact models are registered and follow the RCAID assessment process. Lower-impact models are registered and proceed to deployment. There is a periodic review of the models that have been self-assessed as low impact to check for any exceptional cases.

Support from Technology Tools

Although the "RAI risk committee" approach depends on human assessment by specialist experts, we have found it essential to support this assessment with software tools. We have developed tools, for example, to routinely run fairness and explainability tests for many of the models that come to RCAID. These tools test for model bias over several factors, including gender, age, and location, and will point out anomalies that need to be explained as part of the RCAID submission. (In doing this, these tools take the first steps in an "RAI acceptance testing" pattern.)

We have an ongoing challenge to make the output of these tools more transparent for nontechnical reviewers. At present, we rely on our more technical RCAID participants to explain the outputs to the rest of the Council, but we are exploring whether these results could be presented automatically without losing their effectiveness. This approach is not easy, as the definition of what is fair can require use-case-specific interpretation.

We also use these tools and others to test for errors (e.g., model instability and data drift) in the ongoing operation of the models in production. We are working to make these tools more automated and more deeply embedded in the development and deployment process. The evolution of these tools would be a component in an implementation of the "extensible, adaptive, and dynamic RAI risk assessment" pattern.

Governance over the Whole Lifecycle

RCAID evaluates risk at a single point in the lifecycle of an AI use case. In theory, this single assessment will hold for the whole lifetime of the case. But this is not quite how it works in practice.

One complication is that the early phases of a use case may need separate risk consideration. The risk profile for a one-off proof of concept is very different from ongoing production. It may, for example, use a much wider set of data while the designers determine what data is useful in practice. And most of the risk profiles change for a one-off trial that does not impact real stakeholders.

So, we have found that multiple assessments by RCAID may be required at different stages. In some cases the later ones are significantly easier, as the Council is already familiar with the use case.

Another issue is that the fairness and explainability tests might not be done until the model is built, which can be well after the RCAID assessment. In practice, the RCAID approval is usually given on the condition that these tests will be run, and any anomalies are reported and separately assessed.

Finally, proper governance requires some confirmation that any RCAID conditions are enforced. We have separate control points that check this enforcement when use cases get approval to operate in production. We also require ongoing monitoring by the AI model owner, and we are working to automate these checks in our operating environment.

More broadly, our ambition is to embed the responsible AI requirements as deeply as possible into the development process and foster an RAI-by-design approach that will draw on many of the patterns outlined in this book. In the work to date, we have worked closely with some of our development teams in the design of the technology tools. These tools are designed to be run with small incremental effort and to be embedded into the MLOps processes that these developers use to build and operate the models.

Scaling Up

As we develop more and more AI systems, we are very conscious that the RCAID approach could become a bottleneck in Telstra's widespread use of AI. Although we still have much more work to do on this effort, we have put some initial optimizations in place.

The first of these optimizations has already been mentioned. Low-impact use cases do not need to go to RCAID, and the criteria for these have been established. As this is based on a self-assessment by the use case creators, there is a risk that we will miss a high-impact case that was wrongly categorized. But we do periodically check all the self-rated low-risk cases and look for any that might be incorrectly rated. If any use cases look anomalous from their description, we investigate to see if the original assessment was correct.

Another simple step is to coach sponsors in the preparation of the use cases for assessment. We have updated the use case template several times to be clearer about the information required and to focus on the information that the Council really needs. Our helpful and diligent RCAID coordinator is also very good at coaching the presenting team beforehand on what to expect, what information is most relevant, and how to make the best use of the time. This coaching makes each use case easier to assess.

We have also grouped like use cases together. In some cases, we have the same people from the sponsoring business function to present the similar use cases. They will explain how the new case is similar to cases that have already been approved and highlight any new features that need special attention. We have also created "omnibus" use cases that address a range of models covering the same sort of function. These cases specify certain bounds (e.g., the diversity of use cases that will be covered, the price or discount limits for customers, and a range of approved treatments) for any model wanting to claim this use case for approval. These models are registered against the approved use case for traceability. This approach starts to implement the "extensible, adaptive, and dynamic risk assessment" pattern.

Even with these optimizations, scalability of our AI governance model remains one of our prime concerns.

Future Work

As explained at the start of the chapter, the driving need for a risk-based approach to AI governance is necessary because of the length of time required to embed responsible practices for development and use of all AI within the company. Using RCAID, as an implementation of the "RAI risk committee" pattern, has allowed us to put AI governance in place quickly, to target the highest-risk items first, and to apply our limited skilled resources to the cases with the highest governance needs.

But we recognize the need to evolve our practice as the scale of our AI deployment grows. As currently implemented, the RCAID-based approach can deal with a handful of new higher-impact use cases per month. Through the optimizations outlined in the previous section, we may be able to scale this by an order of magnitude to approve tens of new AI models per month. Our intention, however, is to have AI models driving improvements across the entire business, and the current mechanisms will be a bottleneck for this effort.

To achieve scale, we expect to adopt an ethics-by-design approach, where the ethical requirements and compliance mechanisms are widely understood and built into the AI lifecycle. Many of the patterns covered in this book will be useful for this task. We will also enhance our development and monitoring tools and environments to support responsible AI more inherently.

Even at scale, however, we expect RCAID (or some "RAI risk committee" pattern) to continue to play a role. Its agenda might include

- Providing oversight of the embedded processes and tools for managing risk through the AI lifecycle, including a check that these are remaining effective and further reviews as use cases evolve;

- Considering application of known risks in new areas of business—for example, as we create new product offerings or partner with new industry verticals; and

- Determining how to treat new risks that arise from the scaling of our AI deployments—for example, considering how risk changes as AI systems not only interact with humans but also interact with each other.

The need for human experts to come together, discuss AI risks, and determine the best way to deal with them in the context of our business will continue to be an essential part of Telstra's ongoing commitment to responsible AI.

10

Reejig: The World's First Independently Audited Ethical Talent AI

by Reejig

Reejig is an award-winning workforce intelligence platform that enables large-scale organizations to find, retain, mobilize, and upskill talent at scale.

In partnership with the University of Technology Sydney (UTS), Reejig developed the world's first independently audited Ethical Talent AI certification, setting a new benchmark in trust and ethics for industry. Reejig was recognized by the World Economic Forum as Technology Pioneer in 2022 for this leading innovation.

This chapter details how organizations across the world are using ethical talent AI to transform talent management through aggregating siloed data, placing skills first, and providing inclusive decision-making support. We cover how bias can permeate these decisions without AI that is built to specifically reduce bias.

This chapter unpacks what ethical AI is, the calls for increased regulation and laws around creating ethical AI, and the specific process Reejig undertook to develop the world's first independently audited ethical talent AI.

In this chapter we refer to *ethical AI* instead of *responsible AI,* consistent with Reejig terminology. Ethical AI refers to the same practice of developing and maintaining AI that reduces bias and supports decision-making through making good and fair recommendations.

How Is AI Being Used in Talent?

Artificial intelligence is having a transformational impact on our daily lives in the modern world. Both investment in, and adoption of, AI technology is rapidly accelerating, with market researchers at IDC predicting that investment in AI will more than double to $204 billion during the next four years.

Indeed, the impact it's having on how we both live and work cannot be understated. Google's CEO, Sundar Pichai, has suggested that AI's impact on society will be greater than fire or electricity.

The potential and influence AI has today alone underscore how high the stakes are for the decisions AI makes for us or the decisions it influences. That means ensuring those decisions and influences are ethical from the outset is mission-critical. So, what is AI in its simplest form?

Artificial intelligence refers to the ability of a machine to perform cognitive functions we associate with human minds, such as sensing, reasoning, learning, problem-solving, and acting.

AI can process large amounts of data in ways that humans cannot. It aims to support human actions by recognizing patterns, providing decision-making support, and making data-driven judgments at a scale we never used to believe possible.

In talent and workforce management specifically, AI plays a unique role in helping organizations understand how skills relate to jobs, people, training, and each other. It finds patterns and opportunities that are unseen or overlooked by individuals. It helps organizations match talent with opportunity at a scale and speed that were previously not possible.

AI has the power to do good—to transform our professional workforces, inform business decision-making, and unlock individual opportunity—but without deliberate focus, it's subject to bias in the historic data or algorithms. If datasets are demographically biased, gender skewed, or imbalanced across other factors, then the outcomes will naturally become similarly biased.

This is where ethical AI comes in.

Before we discuss what ethical AI is, it's important to know how organizations have come to use AI and depend on it for talent decisions. These use cases show why ethical requirements are so necessary, because we're talking about decisions that are made about human beings.

The following sections describe the three key areas where AI has changed how organizations have made talent and employment decisions in the modern world.

Aggregating Siloed Data Across Multiple Sources

Talent ecosystems commonly sit across multiple data sources, both internal and external.

These data sources often include an organization's Applicant Tracking Software (ATS), Candidate Relationship Management (CRM), Human Resource Information Systems (HRIS), and Learning Management Systems (LMS), which hold data about current employees, previous applicants, contingent workers, interns, and alumni, as well as other public sources such as LinkedIn.

Teams can check through each of these data sources, searching for all the information they have on any one person, but the reality of time constraints means most data goes unutilized.

AI has the power to accurately aggregate all the available data, giving organizations a streamlined way to access an individual's complete profile, their current skills, and if the AI is powerful enough, their future potential, without having to dig for it.

Example

An example of this capability is Reejig's Ethical Talent AI, which aggregates data from all possible sources, including ATS, CRM, HRIS, and LMS; enriches it with trusted public professional data; and uses it to create a live skills ecosystem for an entire workforce that doesn't rely on manual updates.

Providing Decision-Making Support at Scale

AI has several benefits for workforce strategies, but one of the most attractive for teams and organizations is its ability to provide data-driven decision-making support at scale. AI-driven decision-making support can look like

- Matching candidates to roles based on current skill sets and future predicted skills;

- Providing explainable insights as to why a candidate is well suited to a role; or

- Predicting critical moments in a person's career, whether it's that they're about to leave or that they're a perfect match for an existing opportunity.

It's important to note that AI technology doesn't—and shouldn't—make final decisions on who should get the job but instead provides decision-making support based on all available data to identify the best candidates.

When you give your talent teams this level of insight, they can be confident they have the data to make the right decision, leaving less room for guesses, gut feelings, or unconscious bias that comes with undertaking completely independent research. With relevant information at their fingertips, decision-makers are better placed to do their job effectively and efficiently.

Reducing Unconscious Bias

If the historic datasets that AI aggregates and uses are biased or skewed unfairly, then the outcomes will, of course, become similarly biased. There are numerous examples of AI recruitment tools that analyze applications and are trained by observing patterns in the (mostly male) resumes that have been submitted to the company over the years.

Unsurprisingly, these tools started preferencing male over female candidates and even started penalizing resumes that included words that are indicative of a female candidate, such as educational institution names and sports roles.

This is where ethical AI plays an incredibly important role in how we ensure bias, preferences, and penalties do not occur. Ethical AI is the outcome of successfully identifying, reducing, or eliminating bias from the data, the models, and the development of AI but relies on an AI vendor building their processes to specifically identify, reduce, or eliminate bias.

What Does Bias in Talent AI Look Like?

Bias within talent AI is usually unintentionally introduced and rarely obvious, as it generally stems from problems introduced by the *data* that is being used to train the AI and the *humans* who design and/or train those AI systems. Both data and human bias can have a detrimental effect on the decision-making support AI provides, and the decisions that go on to be made, so it's important to be aware of these kinds of bias.

Data Bias

It's safe to say all real-world data is biased to a certain extent; in most scenarios, raw data can't provide an accurate representation of the entire population. Why? The reason is strongly tied to the data quality measurements that are being undertaken, such as

- **Accuracy:** If the data values are correct or not
- **Completeness:** If the data is complete and not missing attributes
- **Consistency:** If the data is consistent across different data sources
- **Validity:** If the data value is valid given the type of data
- **Timeliness:** If the data is recent and up to date
- **Uniqueness:** If the data is duplicated

There's a saying in data industries: "Garbage in, garbage out." If the data quality is not satisfied, the results from the AI system that consumes such poor data can become skewed. And when the data contributes to the model decisions, bias can only be amplified.

Human Bias

Who introduces bias in data? Humans. Humans are involved at many touchpoints, such as collecting, preparing, and interpreting data. These points may introduce conscious or unconscious biases that could drive AI to reflect decisions based on this mindset. Humans are, after all, already conditioned to expect that certain information is correlated with other information for various reasons:

- **Stereotyping:** An individual's view or representation as a stereotype
- **Bandwagon effect:** Cognitive bias because everyone else is doing it or thinks so

- **Priming effect:** Cognitive bias that makes decision-making faster
- **Selection bias:** Human-picked data that is a nonrandom sample of a population
- **Confirmation bias:** Human tendency to favor the information that reinforces the things they already believe

As a human, you cannot avoid bias, so it's not surprising that AI systems have bias. After all, it's all about mimicking how humans make decisions. Unchecked data and algorithms can easily begin to produce bias.

For example, if an AI system is provided with biased training data, such as a small proportion of female applicants for technical roles, and the number of successful applications is even fewer then female applicants can be eliminated or ranked low by the AI system. In turn, unbiased talent AI can enable businesses to better compete for talent and can also help them create a more diverse and inclusive workforce and organizational culture.

There is growing interest and need for new ways of reducing bias or improving diversity in AI hiring tools. A lot of this interest has resulted in calls for regulations and legislation regarding how AI is used and audited for bias.

Regulating Talent AI Is a Global Issue

Until very recently, there have been no consistent and universally applicable standards for ethical AI. That means vendors across all industries can call their technology "ethical" based on a self-assessment, without the input of legal, ethical, or global regulatory experts.

But the growing examination of the impacts of AI—how machine learning processes are built and what algorithms they learn on—has led many governments and lawmakers to call for official regulations to be put in place. These regulations will ensure HR AI vendors are independently audited and held accountable, giving you confidence in your talent decision-making support.

US Legislation Being Introduced

An example of early regulation in this area is NYC Local Law 144.[1] Under Local Law 144, after January 1, 2023, for employment or promotion decisions relating to individuals in New York City, employers may only use AI decision-making tools that have been subject to an independent bias audit within the last 12 months prior to use.

AI must be audited for bias against race, ethnicity, and gender at a minimum, but many other factors need to be accounted for, such as age, disability, and socioeconomic status.

---

1. New York City Council, *File #, Int 1894-2020* (Legislative Research Center, 2022).

In addition to Local Law 144, the Blueprint for an AI Bill of Rights[2] was recently introduced, along with multiple privacy acts across California, Colorado, Virginia, and Connecticut that determine how automated decision-making tools can be used and the ability for individuals to "opt out" of being included in datasets.

European Legislation Being Introduced

The EU Commission has proposed multiple regulations, including the EU AI Act,[3] around how AI systems can be used and who has the burden of proof on how they are used.

Reejig's Approach to Ethical Talent AI

Ethical AI is a system of moral principles and techniques intended to reduce risks and inform the development and responsible use of artificial intelligence technology.

The first step to managing risk is to address bias issues in datasets and algorithms that are used in the design of AI systems through a series of **debiasing strategies**.

Debiasing Strategies

At Reejig, we use a three-stage debiasing strategy (this strategy aligns well with the fairness principle, with specific technique patterns being the "fairness assessor" pattern and the "discrimination mitigator" pattern):

- **Before training:** Training dataset manipulation and balancing
- **Training:** Putting constraints on the model's optimization function for meeting expected criteria
- **After training:** Gender boost (to introduce known "bias" to cancel other bias)

Gender debiasing, as an example, describes how we reduce bias in the data and processes.

With the before training model, we focus on dataset manipulation, aimed at reducing or neutralizing bias in the dataset. Gender swapping is a straightforward approach to this, and it can be done in two ways:

- Create an augmented dataset identical to the original dataset but biased toward the opposite gender via swapping gender keywords and training on the union of the original and data-swapped sets.

2. The White House, Blueprint for an AI Bill of Rights (Office of Science and Technology Policy, 2022), https://www.whitehouse.gov/ostp/ai-bill-of-rights/.

3. Artificial Intelligence Act, 2022, https://www.europarl.europa.eu/RegData/etudes/BRIE/2021/698792/EPRS_BRI(2021)698792_EN.pdf.

- Swap gender keywords in text (*he* to *she*, *his* to *her*, *woman* to *man*, and so on), and anonymize names (e.g., replace the name entity with a meaningless tag such as E1).

Embeddings are popularly used in natural language processing for the representation of words, converting text into a numeric vector that encodes the meaning of the words, so that machines can read and understand.

We build gender-neutral embeddings for our ethical talent AI, using word embeddings in our AI system to represent text data, such as resumes from individuals. Detecting, removing, or neutralizing bias in embeddings is crucial for ensuring that there are no stereotypes in representations for machine learning to learn.

After inspecting how much gender bias exists in embeddings for different types of data, we found that the one for job descriptions and resumes has the highest level of gender bias by default. Our strategy is to target the gender bias in the embeddings, then neutralize, equalize, and soften them. This is done in two steps:

- Define gender keywords and compute the distance between gender keywords and the target words.

- Apply hard and soft debiasing so that the distance between gender-neutral words (e.g., *nurse, engineer*) and gender pairs (e.g., *woman* vs. *man*, *girl* vs. *boy*, *female* vs. *male*) is equalized, while the original properties are preserved in the word embedding; for example, different roles are still distinguishable.

In addition, we also apply dataset balancing techniques to ensure that the distribution of different classes for training is not imbalanced.

While training the model, we use a train-valid-test split to prevent the model from being overfitted or biased toward one class. The training dataset is built from the ecosystem of talent profiles and job profiles. Separated from the training set, the validation set is used to validate the model performance during training. The test set is then built for generalization performance evaluation, used after completing the training. The best model is selected based on the best performance on the validation set. We also apply constraints in the model's optimization function to keep the results in control; this includes regularization strategies so that the learning can benefit from discriminatory features and information fed into the model is balanced.

After training, we build a long list of talent for a given job using the trained model and apply filtering to generate a short list of talent. The filtering process is to filter out the talent that doesn't satisfy the specific requirements in the job description—for example, location, job level, and accreditation. Part of the filtering is what we call "Diversity Boost," where we consider known protected attributes and introduce intentional "bias" to cancel other biases with a goal to balance the results and boost minority groups' participation.

How Ethical AI Evaluation Is Done: A Case Study in Reejig's World-First Independently Audited Ethical Talent AI

Overview

Reejig has an unwavering stance on the ethical development and deployment of our AI. As an artificial intelligence system drawing on large volumes of human data to provide automated decision-making support, we acknowledge the potential risk of facing ethical issues related to transparency, data privacy, gender bias, and/or unclear accountability for our customers and their workforces.

When developing and deploying AI, every potential application should consider how the technology will be used and who will be responsible for it. Ethical risks like bias, privacy, and transparency must be factored in from the start. This issue is complex and, if you don't have a background in ethics and data, it can be difficult to feel confident that you're using AI for good.

When we think about ethical AI, it isn't just one discrete area of the data, the algorithm, or the model itself. The ethical deployment of AI considers the end-to-end approach, inclusive of the data, the process, and the people involved.

For this reason, Reejig partnered with the University of Technology Sydney—leveraging cross-faculty collaboration, including business governance, social justice, legal compliance, and data science—to define and apply a framework for the independent assessment of transparency, fairness, accountability, and privacy within the Reejig talent shortlisting algorithm (the Reejig algorithm). This approach aligns with the "Independent Oversight" pattern.

The Reejig algorithm is a talent shortlisting system that aims to help organizations discover and connect with talent in their organizational ecosystems (including previous applicants, employees, alumni, gig workers, and contingent workers). The goal here is to ensure fairness and transparency in the application of AI to career decision-making.

The Independent Audit Approach

Reejig's independent audit was completed by the University of Technology Sydney and led by distinguished Professor Fang Chen, along with project partners KPMG, Salesforce, and Citi.

The approach taken with UTS included a combination of qualitative assessment with quantitative measurement, consistent with industry standard approaches for ethical review and based on those adopted in human ethics committees considering ethical implications of processes in health and medicine. The initial findings were complemented with a data-driven review of algorithm behavior, particularly in the context of bias and explainability based on performance against real-world data.

A Summary of the Results

- The independent validation procedure is based on alignment of design, process, and operation against the key ethical principles of transparency, fairness, accountability, and privacy in the context of gender bias.

- The combination of qualitative assessment with quantitative measurement is consistent with industry standard approaches for ethical review, and based on those adopted in human ethics committees considering ethical implications of processes in health and medicine.

- In addition to an ethical validation of their AI, Reejig successfully performed a functional validation with industry partners, including Salesforce, demonstrating that the shortlisted candidates were "fit for purpose" and represented a strong short list well aligned with the role requirements.

- The results: 97.4 percent of shortlisted candidates exceeded the benchmark acceptance score of 65 percent, with the average candidate scoring 95.1 percent.

Based on the extensive qualitative and quantitative assessment of the Reejig algorithm and surrounding processes, UTS concluded that the development and operation of the algorithm is aligned with transparency, fairness in the context of gender diversity, accountability, and privacy objectives.

This achievement represents the world's first independently audited ethical talent AI.

Recognition and Impact

In recognition of the importance of this groundbreaking research with UTS, the methodology and outcome were included in the proceedings for the 2020 IEEE Symposium on Computational Intelligence, and received the 2021 Research Impact award in recognition of the impact this research has already had in shifting understanding of what is possible in assuring ethical AI.

As mentioned previously, Reejig was recognized by the World Economic Forum as a 2022 Technology Pioneer for our innovation in developing the world's first independently audited ethical talent AI.

> A key barrier to the adoption of AI, and thus its potential to do good, has been lifted. This is significant for organizations who want to do the right thing and minimize risk to their customers, their stakeholders, and their reputation.
>
> —Mark Caine, AI and Machine Learning Lead, World Economic Forum

Project Overview

About the Reejig Algorithm

The nonbiased talent shortlisting algorithm (the Reejig algorithm) is a talent shortlisting system developed by Reejig Pty Limited (Reejig) that aims to help organizations discover and connect with talent in their organizational ecosystems. Drawing on employment and management data held within the client organization as well as potentially public data, the Reejig algorithm is focused on the automated matching of potential candidates to roles in a way that aims to minimize negative unconscious bias.

The Objectives of the Project

The objectives of the project are to independently assess the algorithm's adherence to core ethical principles of transparency, fairness, accountability, and privacy to ensure the AI was proactively addressing potential risks.

The Approach

Drawing on data analytic techniques and emerging ethical guidelines and principles, the assessment process was grounded in iterative independent qualitative and quantitative reviews of the data and modeling, algorithm behavior, and performance against two representative real-world client datasets. The approach was consistent with industry standard approaches for ethical review and based on those adopted in human ethics committees considering ethical implications of processes in health and medicine.

A core element of the framework is its iterative nature, surveying about and subsequent discussion of ethical processes, practices, and algorithm design. The UTS team conducted a detailed review in this context, examining Reejig's alignment with key ethical principles of transparency; fairness on gender; accountability; and privacy in the design, delivery, and operation of their talent shortlisting algorithm. Initial findings were complemented with a data-driven review of algorithm behavior, particularly in the context of bias and explainability based on performance against real-world data.

The project commenced in August 2019. The UTS team completed the following research activities in this project:

- Desktop, Literature, and Industry Review
- Framework development
- Framework test: Industry Partner 1 (KPMG)
- Framework test: Industry Partner 2 (Salesforce)

The Ethical AI Framework Used for the Audit

Ethical Principles

The design and deployment of the Reejig AI talent-matching algorithm were assessed by UTS against four key ethical principles of AI that their previous literature study identified as most critical (see Figure 10.1).

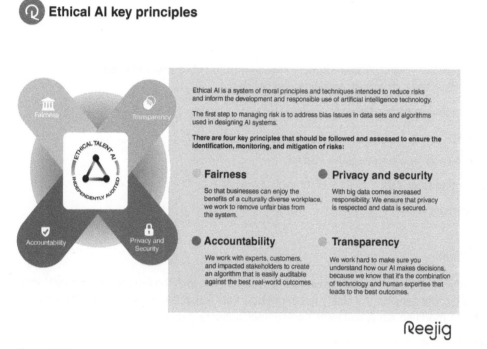

Figure 10.1
Ethical AI key principles.

Fairness

Fairness reflects an absence of prejudice or favoritism toward an individual or a group based on their inherent or acquired characteristics. Simply put, fairness means not to bias outcomes for or against particular groups of people based primarily on their membership in one of those groups.

Three principal segments of fairness were assessed:

- Bias avoidance
- Accessibility and universal design (AI systems should be user-centric and designed in a way that allows all users to employ AI systems)
- Stakeholder participation

Transparency

Transparency refers to the need to describe, inspect, and reproduce the mechanisms through which an AI system makes decisions and learns to adapt to its environment. In the context of artificial intelligence, transparency is critical, given the "black box" or hidden nature of complex contemporary algorithms that are typically deployed. In these instances, users may not understand how the data is processed and why or how an output from the algorithm is obtained. For reasons of auditability and appropriate use, it is therefore critical to develop systems or processes that aid in the explanation, traceability, and risks of algorithmic decision-making.

Accountability

Accountability is about a clear acknowledgment and assumption of responsibility and "answerability" for actions, decisions, products, and policies.

Four principal segments were reviewed:

- Auditability
- Minimizing and reporting negative impact
- Documenting trade-offs
- Ability to redress

Privacy and Security

Given the automation of learning and access to big data that provides the foundation for functional AI, *privacy and security* demand the ability to control how data (especially personal data) is being collected, stored, modified, used, and exchanged between different parties.

Three principal segments were reviewed:

- Respect for privacy and data protection
- Quality and integrity of data
- Access to data

Ethical Validation

In developing and refining the validation framework used within this project, UTS conducted both quantitative and qualitative assessments of Reejig algorithm design and deployment in the context of gender bias management:

- UTS developed and deployed new computational techniques and quantitative metrics for the validation of gender fairness and decision explainability. Representative real-world industry data was used to measure and assess algorithmic performance against these two ethical objectives. Assessments were reported to Reejig, and advice provided on subsequent action, where necessary or recommended.

- UTS developed and deployed qualitative assessments that covered each stage of the design, implementation, testing, and deployment of the Reejig algorithm. The broader UTS team performed this review, including an assessment against key ethical guidelines in the areas of transparency, fairness, accountability, and privacy.

Based on quantitative testing against representative real-world data, UTS confirmed

- An active strategy has been adopted that successfully reduces gender bias in input data.

- Outputs from the application of the algorithm do not exacerbate or reinforce gender biases.

- Reejig provides faithful explanations of why the algorithm made decisions, though these are complex and will require simplification to be optimally meaningful for end users.

Based on the final set of qualitative assessments, UTS confirmed

- The algorithm was developed with traceability in mind and includes documentation describing input data and training and testing methodology, all of which is accessible on request.

- Reejig provides a mechanism to review historical outcomes and decisions.

- Data is security managed, including auditable, authorized, and authenticated access to private data, data encryption at rest and in transit, data separation, logging of data access, application of mechanisms for notice, and control of personal data.

- Reejig has set up an adequate set of mechanisms to redress cases of harm or adverse impact produced by the Reejig algorithm.

- The characteristics, limitations, risk, and potential shortcomings of the algorithm have been communicated to end users and have been documented.

- Reejig consulted with HR professionals and end users during design and development; the developers of the solution included HR domain specialists and artificial intelligence specialists.

Based on the preceding assessments, UTS concluded that the development and operation of the algorithm are aligned with transparency, fairness in the context of gender diversity, accountability, and privacy objectives.

Functional Validation

This process engaged a select team from Salesforce's Australian Talent Acquisition function. After successful completion of the independent validation of the ethical performance of Reejig's matching AI, the intent of this functional validation was to ensure that the outcome delivered on the business outcomes of automatically surfacing a ranked short list of candidates who are suitable for the role.

As inputs, matches were made against sample roles that were business-critical for Salesforce in the region, using the public job descriptions on the Salesforce Careers site.

The critical roles nominated by the Salesforce Australia Recruitment Team were

- Account Executive – Enterprise Level – Sales

- Account Executive – Commercial – Sales

- Business Development Representative – Sales Development

- Application Security Engineer – Tech

Summary Results

- Against a benchmark score for suitability of 65 percent, the average score for shortlisted candidates across the four sample roles was 95.1 percent.

- Overall, 97.4 percent of candidates exceeded the suitability benchmark score.

- The shortlisted candidates were found to be strongly aligned with Salesforce's requirements for the sample roles.

The Benefits of Ethical Talent AI

There are multiple benefits to ethical AI, especially in the realm of talent decisions and the HR industry, where bias reduction and risk mitigation are paramount to providing an inclusive experience for applicants and internal employees alike.

Building Stronger and More Diverse Teams by Removing Bias

Bias—and especially unconscious bias—is everywhere. It permeates through every decision we make and can have a significant impact on the people we bring into teams and departments. With an ethical framework, AI can be used in a way that removes this unconscious bias from the process, allowing organizations to objectively build diversity and strengthen teams.

While AI models have been used in the past to spearhead talent drives, they often run on old company data and processes, which risk reinforcing previous biases. That means it's easy to build a "status quo" back into teams, recruiting or promoting people with exactly the same background, learnings, and skills, which removes diversity from the current organizational structure and future talent decisions.

This approach makes teams weaker, making way for the loss of a wide range of perspectives, skills, and expertise, and limiting an organization's capacity to explore new and exciting avenues for growth. Teams with increased diversity have been shown to be more profitable, more innovative, and more successful.

Maintaining Privacy and Security

AI is data hungry. So when personal data of candidates and employees is being imported and used for talent decisions, it can quickly become challenging to assess whether those decisions are ethical.

It's vital to understand whether the collection of data raises reputation or legal risks and how to mitigate them. Infusing AI algorithms with a transparent and accountable framework provides more certainty over how data is being sourced, stored, used, and retained.

Executives should work closely with their privacy, risk and security teams, and talent partners to build or assess ethical frameworks, making sure that everyone is part of the conversation (including the individual) and that the approach has transparency front of mind.

This approach will maintain ethical standards and help keep organizations compliant as circumstances change.

Demonstrating Leadership Against Competitors

Ethical AI is still an emerging field, with the World Economic Forum leading the way in helping organizations consider responsible use of the technology to reduce corporate risk. Its application within talent presents an enormous opportunity for organizations to become part of what will be a critical pillar of AI use.

By partnering with vendors that take AI ethics seriously, organizations can stay one step ahead of competitors who put ethics on the backburner. This approach creates a sustainable and ethical way for businesses to dramatically shorten and simplify talent processes in the long term.

Debiasing strategies and benefits aside, we believe that, for AI to be deemed truly "ethical," assessors must undertake a completely independent audit to determine whether its development and deployment are transparent, fair, accountable, and in line with privacy laws and regulations.

Reejig's Outlook on the Future of Ethical Talent AI

Reejig Has Led the Way in AI Ethics from Day One

Reejig has proudly pioneered the way for independent audits and ethical decision-making support. We have always taken an unwavering stance on the ethical development and deployment of our AI, which is exactly why we engaged the University of Technology Sydney to conduct an independent audit on our Talent AI.

This audit not only meant Reejig now has the world's first independently audited ethical talent AI, but also it set a new benchmark in trust and ethics for our industry. This sentiment is reflected by Reejig being named as a Technology Pioneer by the Word Economic Forum for our innovation in developing the world's first independently audited ethical talent AI and our mission toward Zero Wasted Potential.

This audit alone included cross-faculty collaboration with assessments from data science, business, law, and social justice departments, reflecting that ethics in AI is no longer just a data science issue.

A New Independent Audit of Reejig Is Already Underway

Reejig partnered with the University of Technology Sydney to conduct a second independent audit in 2022, leveraging the framework and learnings from our previous audit and acting in compliance with the new NYC legislation, to remain a pioneer in the ethical AI space.

To ensure that this audit passed international standards and was aligned with global trends, UTS engaged an ethical advisory board made up of international experts on privacy and AI from top-tier institutions and across multiple jurisdictions including the US, UK, Australia, and Europe.

Reejig proudly continues to lead the way in helping organizations achieve compliance in relation to global regulations and laws as well as providing decision-making support that is grounded in fairness, transparency, accountability, privacy, and security.

Now is the time for us to go beyond current recommendations to remove a key barrier to AI adoption. We need governments to provide firm guidance on how best to address ethical issues, but businesses and the academic community must also play a part. An ethical approach to AI should be central to business operations, from workflow and customer feedback to building models and process engineering.

Ethical AI offers a huge opportunity to get ahead of the competition. Bias sneaks into decision-making when there isn't enough data to make a fully informed decision. Taking AI ethics seriously leaves no room for bias, ensuring a stronger, more diverse workforce.

The Future of Workforce AI Will Unlock Zero Wasted Potential

There's a global movement by regulators to demand more accountability and more explainability from AI-based tools, especially those operating in areas that come with a higher risk of bias like human resources.

New legislation is just the start of a growing number of regulations that give organizations the opportunity to review the HR AI vendors they're using and their efforts to eliminate bias in employment decisions.

This effort is no longer an "ideal"; it's a must that comes with real consequences for organizations that do not have independently audited vendors on board.

Reejig is committed to using artificial intelligence for good. Our algorithms are compliant with global regulations on equal opportunity, anti-discrimination, and human rights, so you can trust you're making good and fair decisions for your people.

Our goal is to ensure that talent teams and leaders are equipped with the knowledge, data, and insights to make good and fair decisions that result in meaningful careers for individuals, optimized workforces, and better outcomes for society—something the team at Reejig call *Zero Wasted Potential*.

11

Diversity and Inclusion in Artificial Intelligence

By Didar Zowghi and Francesca da Rimini

To date, there has been little concrete practical advice about how to ensure that diversity and inclusion considerations should be embedded within both specific artificial intelligence systems and the larger global AI ecosystem. In this chapter, we present a clear definition of diversity and inclusion in AI, one that positions this concept within an evolving and holistic ecosystem. We use this definition and conceptual framing to present a set of practical guidelines primarily aimed at AI technologists, data scientists, and project leaders.

Our focus is socio-technological rather than relying on purely technical or human factors. In this chapter, we use the term *socio-technical* to cover "how humans interact with technology within the broader societal context."[1] A socio-technical perspective on diversity and inclusion in AI and the underlying issues of bias requires processes and procedures that involve stakeholders and end users; examine cultural dynamics and norms; and evaluate, monitor, and respond to societal impacts.

We do not claim completeness or that the identified challenges and proposed guidelines are exhaustive. Instead, we have distilled relevant information from key reports, systematic literature reviews, gray literature findings, and informal communication with specialists to suggest representative or indicative guidelines.

---

1. R. Schwartz et al., NIST Special Publication 1270: Towards a Standard for Identifying and Managing Bias in Artificial Intelligence, March 2022, https://nvlpubs.nist.gov/nistpubs/SpecialPublications/NIST.SP.1270.pdf.

CSIRO Data61's multidisciplinary and diverse team researched the topic of diversity and inclusion in artificial intelligence (DI-AI) in 2022. Our iterative approach examined the findings from both our own systematic literature review on DI-AI and others on related topics including fairness, trust, risk, and ethics, and an open-ended gray literature search on bias, diversity, and inclusion in AI. We noted recent work by small prominent organizations, groups, networks, and thought leaders in the DI-AI space. We have presented our draft definition and framework to Australia's National Artificial Intelligence Centre's Think Tank on Diversity and Inclusion in AI and incorporated their feedback.

A lodestone was the World Economic Forum's 2022 report *A Blueprint for Equity and Inclusion in Artificial Intelligence*.[2] It takes a comprehensive holistic and practical approach to how equity and inclusion should be considered both at the governance and development levels throughout and beyond the development lifecycle, applying core principles and methods from the inclusive design and human-centered design fields to the AI ecosystem. Also important was the National Institute of Standards and Technology's report *Towards a Standard for Identifying and Managing Bias in Artificial Intelligence*.[3] It integrates findings from an extensive literature review; opinions from experts in AI bias, AI fairness, and socio-technical systems; workshop outcomes; and public commentary on the draft.

The socio-technical theory posits that the design and performance of all organizational systems are understood and improved only if both social and technical facets are considered interdependent parts of the complex system in the context of use. The socio-technical system refers to those systems that exhibit a complex interaction between humans, systems, and the environment where the system is situated and used. AI systems as socio-technical systems are built through a complex process beyond their mathematical and algorithmic constructs. It is well understood that computational models and algorithms cannot adequately represent and describe all the societal impacts of AI. It is the values and behaviors of humans, teams, organizations, and society that inform the design, development, and deployment of AI systems in the context of their use.

When the field of artificial intelligence was first established at the Dartmouth Workshop, even though it was largely hosted by mathematicians, the participants included multiple psychologists, cognitive scientists, economists, and political scientists. This signifies the multi-disciplinary nature of AI as a field of research at the outset. Likewise, in modern-day AI systems, the need for the commitment of all stakeholders and the active participation of society is well understood. It is imperative for AI researchers and practitioners to acquire sufficient knowledge of the societal and individual implications of AI systems and understand how different humans use and live with AI systems across cultures.

The overall aims of this chapter are

- To understand the holistic, socio-technical, and evolving nature of artificial intelligence;

- To have a clear and concise definition of diversity and inclusion in AI that can be adapted and used to suit the different projects, stakeholders, and use contexts; and

---

2. World Economic Forum, *A Blueprint for Equity and Inclusion in Artificial Intelligence*, June 29, 2022, https://www.weforum.org/whitepapers/a-blueprint-for-equity-and-inclusion-in-artificial-intelligence.

3. Schwartz et al., NIST Special Publication 1270.

- To have adaptable and customizable DI-AI guidelines that indicate how, when, by whom, and where diversity and inclusion issues should be considered.

This chapter is organized into several sections. In the next section, we describe the importance of DI-AI and the potential consequences if it is neglected. We then provide the definition of DI-AI followed by the specific guidelines organized into sections in accordance with the pillars of the definition. We complete the chapter with a conclusion.

Importance of Diversity and Inclusion in AI

AI system stakeholders have begun paying more attention to diversity and inclusion in AI concerns. There are a few reasons for this—first, the expanding body of high-level frameworks and principles emanating from government, inter- and intra-governmental agencies, businesses, not-for-profit institutions, and academia.[4] These governance resources are often produced by collaborative and consultative teams, networks, and processes, encompassing a diversity of knowledge, disciplines, and perspectives. Second, some countries and states have passed, or are in the process of drafting, legislation to monitor and control the development and deployment of specific AI applications such as predictive policing and facial recognition technology. Such legislation is driven by privacy concerns; human rights issues; and diversity, inclusion, and equity concerns.[5] Third, there is growing public awareness arising from mainstream media and social media coverage of the prevalence of AI systems throughout society. Problems and failures of such systems that lead to unfair, unjust, or adverse outcomes have been exposed, helping to create general perceptions that people impacted directly or indirectly by AI systems may experience a lack of agency.

However, the literature reveals that AI projects do not consistently or adequately address concerns about bias, equity, diversity, and inclusion. The reasons are varied. First, there is the lack of practical and customizable tools operationalizing high-level principles and guidelines such as checklists, definitions, design pattern templates, questionnaires, and requirements guidelines. Second, confusion or ambiguity exists about who is responsible for diversity and inclusion in the AI development process. This includes both overall responsibility and oversight of diversity and inclusion considerations in an AI project and responsibility for specific measurable objectives in discrete project stages.

---

4. Australian Government, "Australia's Artificial Intelligence Ethics Framework," 2019, https://www.industry.gov.au/publications/australias-artificial-intelligence-ethics-framework.

5. J. Brookes, "Model Facial Recognition Law Would Ban High-Risk Use in Australia," September 22, 2022, https://www.innovationaus.com/model-facial-recognition-law-would-ban-high-risk-use-in-australia/; J. Stoyanovich and B. Howe, "Follow the Data! Algorithmic Transparency Starts with Data Transparency," *The Ethical Machine*, November 27, 2018, https://ai.shorensteincenter.org/ideas/2018/11/26/follow-the-data-algorithmic-transparency-starts-with-data-transparency; A. Kak (ed.), *Regulating Biometrics: Global Approaches and Urgent Questions* (AI Now Institute, 2020), https://ainowinstitute.org/regulatingbiometrics.html; E. M. Adams, "Bias and AI: Ensuring Inclusive Tech," *Practical Law*, Winter 2022, https://media-exp1.licdn.com/dms/document/C561FAQEpU0gdxRmJHg/feedshare-document-pdf-analyzed/0/1668819656532?e=1669852800&v=beta&t=ODBqJGBFkuj0jFzFo4nDp_tXDfyWtvee8AAVLu9g7gs.

If diversity and inclusion in AI are neglected, this can cause negative impacts on the AI ecosystem and slow down the adoption of AI. The most serious impacts include material harm to users of those systems, whether this is unjustified bad credit ratings, diminished education and employment opportunities, inaccurate medical diagnoses, or unwarranted criminal arrests. By understanding why diversity and inclusion in AI are critically important, project teams and stakeholders are better equipped to identify, monitor, and mitigate risks, barriers, obstacles, and challenges. Likewise, more informed and AI-literate citizens can better express their agency in individual and collective decision-making about their use of and participation in AI systems whether these be in domestic contexts (e.g., voice recognition systems), industry/corporate (e.g., social media recommendation systems), or government (e.g., laws constraining the use of open-street recognition technologies).

Definition of Diversity and Inclusion in Artificial Intelligence

Diversity and inclusion in artificial intelligence (AI) refers to the "inclusion" of humans with "diverse" attributes and perspectives in the data, process, system, and governance of the AI ecosystem.

Diversity refers to the representation of the differences in attributes of humans in a group or society. Attributes are known facets of diversity, including but not limited to Indigenous peoples, race, gender, age, sexual identities, cultural identities, spiritual identities, language and linguistic identities, appearance, socio-economic status, different cognitive and physical abilities, neurodiversity, and intersections of these attributes.

Inclusion is the process of proactively involving and representing the most relevant humans with diverse attributes who are impacted by, and have an impact on, the AI ecosystem context.

This definition captures the essential five pillars (components) of AI systems, and their development and deployment in a particular environment (application or business domain) within the AI ecosystem. We advocate that diversity and inclusion principles should be at the center of the AI ecosystem and must be embedded in all pillars for the specific context of AI use. Next, we provide a short description of each pillar.

AI Ecosystem

AI ecosystem in this definition refers to the collection of the five pillars (humans, data, process, system, and governance), plus the environment (application or business domain) within which the AI system will be deployed and used; see Figure 11.1.

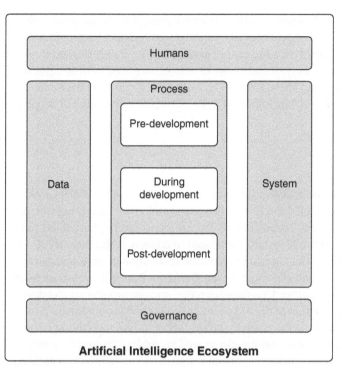

Figure 11.1
Pillars of Diversity and Inclusion in AI Ecosystem.

Humans

Humans are considered the core pillar of the AI ecosystem. Human-centeredness is achieved not only through the meaningful inclusion of relevant humans with diverse attributes in the building, using, monitoring, and evolution of AI systems, but also through their active participation and contribution in all the decision-making points of the AI system lifecycle. Two broad groups have been identified in the AI system lifecycle: those who will receive and use the AI system and those who will design, develop, and deploy AI systems to satisfy specific stakeholder needs. Those humans whose knowledge, lived experiences, and insights are essential need to be carefully identified, contacted, and engaged within all the relevant parts of the process. Integrating diversity and inclusion principles and practices throughout the AI system lifecycle has an important role to play in achieving equity for all humans.

Data

Data plays an essential role in AI systems since it is typically through very large historical datasets that AI algorithms learn and find patterns to deliver predictions and automate decisions. What, how, why, by whom, and for whom data is collected, labeled, modeled, stored, and applied has many diversity and inclusion implications. Positive and negative biases are present in the large datasets and algorithmic processes used in the development of AI models. Unwanted data biases often arise when algorithms are trained on one type of data and cannot extrapolate accurately beyond those data. In other types of AI systems (known as symbolic AI), small datasets are used both as input and validation points in building and improving knowledge-based systems. It is critical to have a fair and inclusive representation of everyone who will be impacted by AI without any unwanted or negative bias that leads to discrimination and harm.

Process

The development *process* describes all the activities and tasks that are carried out to deliver an AI system for a specific context of use. This definition divides the process into three sub-processes: pre-development, during development, and post-development. The *pre-development* phase refers to the ideation of a use case or a problem that the AI system is intended to address. It also includes clearly defining the use case or the problem and the rationale behind the application of an AI solution as well as identifying relevant stakeholders and eliciting their requirements. During *development* refers to the team partnering with stakeholders to work on data collection and preparation, model design and development, and testing and evaluation of the AI system iteratively and incrementally. *Post-development* refers to the deployment of the AI system in the context of its use, monitoring its performance, safety, reliability, and trustworthiness during use, as well as making changes as necessary during the AI system lifecycle. Diversity and inclusion principles should be carefully considered and embedded throughout the entire AI system development process.

System

An AI *system* is a computer-based system that, for a given set of human-defined objectives, typically uses large historical datasets to make predictions, recommendations, or decisions for human consumption that may have an influence in real or virtual environments. There are many techniques and methods for verifying, validating, and monitoring AI systems (e.g., testing, algorithmic analysis of models) against diversity and inclusion in AI principles. AI systems must be evaluated, tested, and monitored in the context of their use to ensure noninclusive behaviors are identified and fixed during AI system evolution. Nonadherence to practices of diversity and inclusion in the building, deployment, and use of AI systems has been shown to cause digital redlining, discrimination, and algorithmic oppression, leading to AI systems being perceived as untrustworthy and unfair.

Governance

AI *governance* is defined as a collection of structures, processes, and regulatory and risk management frameworks that are utilized to ensure the development and deployment of AI systems are compliant with laws and regulations and conform with standards, policies, and AI ethics principles. This definition focuses on AI governance specifically for conformance with diversity and inclusion principles. The governance component can be structured at the team, organization, and industry levels. Legal and risk frameworks should be developed and applied to guide inclusive practices in the AI ecosystems. Governance structures must be human-centered to ensure the delivery of inclusive, reliable, safe, secure, and trustworthy AI systems.

Guidelines for Diversity and Inclusion in Artificial Intelligence

Few guidelines exist to help AI practitioners ensure that diversity and inclusion considerations are embedded throughout the AI lifecycle (AI-LC) and after deployment. Both the AI ecosystem and the AI-LC are continually evolving. Technology, governance structures, legislation, impacts, knowledge, and community expectations are never static. Accordingly, we present a series of guidelines by taking a holistic and systematic approach and mapping them to the five pillars of diversity and inclusion in the artificial intelligence ecosystem as in our previous definition.

In some cases, regarding diversity and inclusion, literature also refers to *equity*, but for the purposes of this chapter, we exclude this term. For simplicity, we focus strictly on diversity and inclusion in AI and exclude related well-documented topics such as responsible AI, AI fairness, explainable AI, AI transparency, and AI ethics. Moreover, although research on bias in AI has informed our guidelines to some extent, we deemed it to be out of scope because this field has produced a plethora of detailed guidelines to counter different types of bias in different AI systems. For better referencing, we number the concrete guidelines with the first letter of the AI ecosystem pillar followed by a number; that is, the first guideline under Human will be [H1].

Humans

In this section, we cover guidelines for all the elements that are related to (1) enablers for humans to engage with AI, and (2) all the impacts humans have on the AI ecosystem. We refer to stakeholders as including, but not limited to, AI users, AI project team members, employers, commissioning organizations, government regulatory bodies, legislators, civil society organizations monitoring AI impact and advocating for users' rights, community organizations, industry, and people affected by AI systems.

[H1]   Integrate diversity and inclusion principles and practice throughout the AI lifecycle

Integrating diversity and inclusion principles and practices throughout the lifecycle of AI has an important role in achieving equity for all stakeholders. In particular, the integration of diversity and inclusion principles and practices through the engagement of diverse stakeholders is important. The composition of different levels of stakeholder cohorts should maintain diversity along social lines (race, gender identification, age, ability, and viewpoints) where bias is a concern. End users, AI practitioners, subject matter experts, and interdisciplinary professionals including those from the law, social sciences, and community development should be involved to identify downstream impacts comprehensively.

[H2]   Identify stakeholder knowledge and needs

Stakeholders generally hold specific knowledge, expertise, concerns, and objectives that can contribute to effective AI system design. Stakeholder expectations, needs, and feedback throughout the AI-LC should be considered. Cohorts include government regulatory bodies and civil society organizations monitoring AI impact and advocating users' rights, industry, and people affected by AI systems. There are groups whose knowledge or expertise is valuable for AI system design, but they do not necessarily have needs or requirements for the system because they will not be users or consumers. Both groups need to be involved.

[H3]   Reflect collectively on key questions—why, for whom, and by whom?

Key questions about why an AI project should happen, whom is the project for, and by whom it should be developed should be asked, answered, and revisited collectively using a diversity and inclusion lens during the AI-LC. Views from stakeholders and representatives of impacted communities should be sought. Although it might be advantageous that some AI design team members are themselves representative of impacted stakeholders and thus well placed to recognize and address potential inclusion-related harms, diverse team members should not be expected to stand in for impacted cohorts (who themselves would hold a diversity of perspectives, expectations, and experiences).

[H4]   Implement inclusive and transparent feedback mechanisms for stakeholders

Users should have accessible mechanisms to identify and report harmful or concerning AI system incidents and impacts, with such warnings shareable among relevant stakeholders. Feedback should be continuously incorporated into system updates and communicated to relevant stakeholders.

[H5]   Identify changes in the operating context

Processes to identify and respond to changes in the operating context, including the potential appearance of new groups of users who may be treated differently by the AI system, should be established. For example, a computational medical system trained in large metropolitan hospitals may not work as intended when used in small rural hospitals due to various factors including training of local healthcare personnel, quality of clinical data entered into the system, or behavioral factors affecting human interaction with AI.[6]

[H6]   Employ a socio-technical approach to human-centered AI

An approach to human in the loop that considers a broad set of socio-technical factors should be adopted. Relevant fields of expertise include human factors, psychology, organizational behavior, and human-AI interaction. However, researchers from Stanford University argue that "practitioners

---

6. World Economic Forum, A Blueprint for Equity and Inclusion in Artificial Intelligence.

should focus on AI in the loop," with humans remaining in control. They advise that "all AI systems should be designed for augmenting and assisting humans—and with human impacts at the forefront." So they advocate the idea of "human in charge" rather than human in the loop.[7]

[H7] Establish inclusive AI infrastructure

An inclusive AI ecosystem involving the broadest range of community members requires equitable access to technical infrastructure (computing, storage, networking) to facilitate the upskilling of new AI practitioners and offers opportunities for citizens' development of AI systems. Governments should invest in computing facilities and education programs, and work with civil society organizations to support national and global networks.

[H8] Develop AI literacy and education programs

An "AI-ready" person is someone who knows enough to decide how, when, and if they want to engage with AI. Critical AI literacy is the pathway to such agency. Consequently, governments should drive the equitable development of AI-related skills to everyone from the earliest years via formal, informal, and extracurricular education programs covering technical and soft skills, along with awareness of digital safety and privacy issues. Governments and civil society organizations should create, and fund grant schemes aimed at enhancing the enrollment of women in AI education. Organizations also can play a critical role via paid internships and promoting community visits, talks, workshops, and engagement with AI practitioners. To harness the potential of increasing diversity and inclusion in the global AI ecosystem, such opportunities should prioritize participation (as facilitators and participants) of people with diverse attributes (including cultural, ethnic, age, gender identification, cognitive, and professional).

[H9] Prioritize equitable hiring practices and career-building opportunities

Data science teams should be as diverse as the populations that the built AI systems will affect. Product teams leading and working on AI projects should be diverse and representative of impacted user cohorts. Diversity, equity, and inclusion in the composition of teams training, testing, and deploying AI systems should be prioritized as the diversity of experience, expertise, and backgrounds is both a critical risk mitigant and a method of broadening AI system designers' and engineers' perspectives. For example, female-identifying role models should be fostered in AI projects.[8] Diversity and inclusion employment targets and strategies should be regularly monitored and adjusted if necessary.

---

7. S. Lynch, "AI in the Loop: Humans Must Remain in Charge," October 17, 2022, https://hai.stanford.edu/news/ai-loop-humans-must-remain-charge.

8. M. Roopaei et al., "Women in AI: Barriers and Solutions," presented at the 2021 IEEE World AI IoT Congress (AIIoT), 2021.

The WEF Blueprint recommends four levers.[9] First is widening career paths by employing people from nontraditional AI backgrounds, embedding this goal in strategic workplace planning. For instance, backgrounds in marketing, social media marketing, social work, education, public health, and journalism can contribute fresh perspectives and expertise. Second, diversity and inclusion should be covered in training and development programs via mentorships, job shadowing, simulation exercises, and contact with diverse end-user panels. Third, partnerships with academic, civil society, and public sector institutions should be established to contribute to holistic and pan-disciplinary reviews of AI systems, diversity and inclusion audits, and assessment of social impacts. Fourth, a workplace culture of belonging should be created and periodically assessed via both open and confidential feedback mechanisms that include diversity markers.

[H10]   Operationalize inclusive and substantive community engagement

A vast body of knowledge about community engagement praxis exists. Guidelines and frameworks are updated and operationalized by practitioners from many disciplines, including community cultural development, community arts, social work, social sciences, architecture, and public health. However, this vital element is largely neglected in the AI ecosystem although many AI projects would benefit from considered attention to community engagement. For instance, in the health sector, AI and advanced analytics implementation in primary care should be a collaborative effort that involves patients and communities from diverse social, cultural, and economic backgrounds in an intentional and meaningful manner.[10]

A community engagement manager role could be introduced who would work with impacted communities throughout the AI-LC and for a fixed period post-deployment. Reciprocal and respectful relationships with impacted communities should be nurtured, and community expectations about both the engagement and the AI system should be defined and attended to. If impacted communities contain diverse language, ethnic, and cultural cohorts, a community engagement team from minority groups would be more appropriate. One role would be to develop tailored critical AI literacy programs, for example. Organizations must put "the voices and experiences of those most marginalized at the [center]" when implementing community engagement outcomes in an AI project.[11]

Data

Data is at the heart of artificial intelligence. What, how, why, by whom, and for whom data is collected, labeled, modeled, stored, and applied have many implications for diversity and inclusion, and increasingly so in the era of big data and machine learning. In this section, we suggest some general guidelines that can be adapted to suit the specific context of an AI project.

---

9. World Economic Forum, A Blueprint for Equity and Inclusion in Artificial Intelligence.

10. C. R. Clark et al., "Health Care Equity in the Use of Advanced Analytics and Artificial Intelligence Technologies in Primary Care," *Journal of General Internal Medicine* 36, no. 10 (October 2021), doi: 0.1007/s11606-021-06846-x.

11. World Economic Forum, A Blueprint for Equity and Inclusion in Artificial Intelligence.

[D1]   Establish a clear rationale for data collection

For data collection involving human subjects, why, how, and by whom data is being collected should be established in the pre-design stage. Potential data challenges or data bias issues that have implications for diversity and inclusion should be identified by key stakeholders and data scientists. For example, in the health application domain, diverse data sources ensuring equitable AI should be identified and collected. Data sources used in primary care decision-making must not only reflect clinical data but also incorporate social determinants of health (that is, where patients are born, grow, work, live, and age). Project teams should develop mitigation and monitoring strategies to counter data issues. All such information should be captured systematically and reviewed regularly.

[D2]   Involve stakeholders and nonexperts in the selection, collection, and analysis of demographically representative qualitative data

Representatives of impacted stakeholders should be identified and partnered with on data collection methods. This is particularly important when identifying new or nontraditional data-gathering resources and methods. To increase representativeness and responsible interpretation, when collecting and analyzing specific datasets, include diverse viewpoints and not only those of experts. Technology or datasets deemed nonproblematic by one group may be predicted to be disastrous by others. Training datasets should be demographically representative of the cohorts or communities on whom the AI system will impact.

[D3]   Establish clear procedures for ensuring data privacy and offering opt-out options

Data privacy should be at the forefront, particularly when data from marginalized populations is involved. End users should be offered choices about privacy and ethics in the collection, storage, and use of data. Opt-out methods for data collected for model training and model application should be offered where possible.

[D4]   Understand and adhere to data sovereignty praxis

The concept of—and practices supporting—data sovereignty is a critical element in the AI ecosystem. It covers considerations of the "use, management and ownership of AI to house, analyze and disseminate valuable or sensitive data."[12] Although definitions are context-dependent, operationally data sovereignty refers to stakeholders within an AI ecosystem and other relevant representatives from outside stakeholder cohorts to be included as partners throughout the AI-LC. Data sovereignty should be explored from and with the perspectives of those whose data is being used. These alternative and diverse perspectives can be captured and fed back into AI literacy programs, exemplifying how people can affect and enrich AI both conceptually and materially.

---

12. World Economic Forum, A Blueprint for Equity and Inclusion in Artificial Intelligence.

Various Indigenous technologists, researchers, artists, and activists have progressed the concept of, and protocols for, Indigenous data sovereignty in AI. This involves "Indigenous control over the protection and use of data that is collected from our communities, including statistics, cultural knowledge and even user data," and moving beyond the representation of impacted users to "maximizing the generative capacity of truly diverse groups."[13]

[D5]   Recognize relationships between access issues, infrastructure, capacity building, and
       data sovereignty

Access, including cloud and offline data hosting, should be attended to because government and industry generally build and manage these on their own terms. Access is directly connected to capacity building (teams and stakeholders) and data sovereignty issues.

[D6]   Consider context issues and context drift during model selection and development

Context should be taken into consideration during model selection to avoid or limit biased results for sub-populations. Caution should be taken in systems designed to use aggregated data about groups to predict individual behavior as biased outcomes can occur. "Unintentional weightings of certain factors can cause algorithmic results that exacerbate and reinforce societal inequities," for example, predicting educational performance based on an individual's racial or ethnic identity.[14]

Observed context drift in data should be documented via data transparency mechanisms capturing where and how the data is used and its appropriateness for that context. Harvard researchers have expanded the definition of data transparency, noting that some raw datasets are too sensitive to be released publicly, and incorporating guidance on development processes to reduce the risk of harmful and discriminatory impacts:

- In addition to releasing training and validation data sets whenever possible, agencies shall make publicly available summaries of relevant statistical properties of the data sets that can aid in interpreting the decisions made using the data, while applying state-of-the-art methods to preserve the privacy of individuals.

- When appropriate, privacy-preserving synthetic data sets can be released in lieu of real data sets to expose certain features of the data if real data sets are sensitive and cannot be released to the public.[15]

---

13. A. Abdilla et al., "Out of the Black Box: Indigenous Protocols for AI," United Nations Educational, Scientific and Cultural Organization (UNESCO), 2021, https://oldwaysnew.com/s/Final-Unesco-Paper_Designed.pdf.

14. Schwartz et al., NIST Special Publication 1270.

15. J. Stoyanovich and B. Howe, "Follow the Data! Algorithmic Transparency Starts with Data Transparency," *The Ethical Machine*, November 27, 2018, https://ai.shorensteincenter.org/ideas/2018/11/26/follow-the-data-algorithmic-transparency-starts-with-data-transparency.

Teams should use transparency frameworks and independent standards; conduct and publish the results of independent audits; open nonsensitive data and source code to outside inspection.[16]

[D7]   Assess dataset suitability factors

Dataset suitability factors should be assessed. These include statistical methods for mitigating representation issues, the socio-technical context of deployment, and interaction of human factors with the AI system. The question of whether suitable datasets exist that fit the purpose of the various applications, domains, and tasks for the planned AI system should be asked.

[D8]   Document social descriptors when scraping data from different sources and perform
        compatibility analysis

Developers should attend to and document the social descriptors (for example, age, gender, and geolocation) when scraping data from different sources including websites, databases, social media platforms, enterprise applications, or legacy systems. Context is important when the same data is later used for different purposes such as asking a new question about an existing dataset.[17] A compatibility analysis should be performed to ensure that potential sources of bias are identified, and mitigation plans made. This analysis would capture context shifts in new uses of datasets, identifying whether or how these could produce specific bias issues.

[D9]   Improve feature-based labeling and formulate more precise notions about user identity using
        qualitative data from social media sources

Apply more inclusive and socially just data labeling methodologies such as Intersectional Labeling Methodology to address gender bias.[18] Rather than relying on static, binary gender in a face classification infrastructure, application designers should embrace and demand improvements to feature-based labeling. For instance, labels based on neutral performative markers (e.g., beard, makeup, dress) could replace gender classification in the facial analysis model, allowing third parties and individuals who come into contact with facial analysis applications to embrace their own interpretations of those features. Instead of focusing on improving methods of gender classification,

---

16. E. M. Adams, "Bias and AI: Ensuring Inclusive Tech," *Practical Law,* Winter 2022, https://media-exp1.licdn.com/
    dms/document/C561FAQEpU0gdxRmJHg/feedshare-document-pdf-analyzed/0/1668819656532?
    e=1669852800&v=beta&t=ODBqJGBFkuj0jFzFo4nDp_tXDfyWtvee8AAVLu9g7gs.

17. R. Peng, "Context Compatibility in Data Analysis," *Simply Statistics*, 2018. [https://simplystatistics.org/
    posts/2018-05-24-context-compatibility-in-data-analysis/.

18. J. Buolamwini and T. Gebru, "Gender Shades: Intersectional Accuracy Disparities in Commercial Gender
    Classification," in *Proceedings of the 1st Conference on Fairness, Accountability and Transparency,* 2018, https://
    proceedings.mlr.press/v81/buolamwini18a.html.

application designers could use labeling alongside other qualitative data such as Instagram captions to formulate more precise notions about user identity.[19]

Process

In this section we suggest guidelines both for the main stages of the AI system development lifecycle and those that specifically respond to the AI ecosystem's evolutionary and iterative qualities. The guidelines draw on long-standing principles and practices in the human-centered design field, and in some cases adapted for elements pertaining to AI.

Pre-Development Process

[P1]   Practice inclusive problem identification and impact assessment

A project owner (individual or organization) with suitable expertise and resources to manage an AI system project should be identified, ensuring that accountability mechanisms to counter potential harm are built in. It should be decided which other stakeholders will be involved in the systems development and regulation. Both intended and unintended impacts that the AI system will or might have should be assessed in collaboration with stakeholder communities, with additional experts being consulted if necessary.

Incorporate inclusive tech principles such as normalizing inclusion at a systemic level; designing with excluded and diverse communities, not for them; promoting accountability; and enforcing data governance to ensure ethical practices are being met.[20]

[P2]   Establish mechanisms for monitoring and improvement

Mechanisms enabling an iterative process of continuous monitoring and improvement of diversity and inclusion considerations should be established from the outset. These mechanisms will help ensure that all stakeholders' needs are met and that inadvertent harm is not caused. Both team and system performance should be regularly assessed, improvements identified, and changes executed accordingly.

[P3]   Identify possible systemic problems of bias and appoint a steward

At the start of the design stage, stakeholders should identify possible systemic problems of bias such as racism, sexism, or ageism that have implications for diversity and inclusion. Main

---

19. M. K. Scheuerman, J. M. Paul, and J. R. Brubaker, "How Computers See Gender: An Evaluation of Gender Classification in Commercial Facial Analysis Services," presented at the Proceedings of the ACM on Human-Computer Interaction, 2019.

20. Adams, "Bias and AI: Ensuring Inclusive Tech."

decision-makers and power-holders should be identified, as this can reflect systemic biases and limited viewpoints within the organization.

A sole person responsible for algorithmic bias—a steward—should be appointed. This role entails broad oversight over strategic decisions and accountability for mitigating bias (in consultation with team and stakeholders).[21]

[P4]   Consider specific categories relevant to the AI system

For example, before embedding gender classification into a facial analysis service or incorporating gender into image labeling, it is important to consider what purpose gender is serving. Furthermore, it is important to consider how gender will be defined and whether that perspective is unnecessarily exclusionary (for example, nonbinary). Therefore, stakeholders involved in the development of facial analysis services and image datasets should assess the potentially negative and harmful consequences their service might be used for, including emotional, social, physical, and systematic (state or governmental) harms.[22]

Development Process

[P5]   Consider multiple trade-offs

In the design stage, decisions should weigh the social-technical implications of the multiple trade-offs inherent in AI systems. These trade-offs include the system's predictive accuracy, which is measured by several metrics. The metrics include accuracies within sub-populations or across different use cases, as partial and total accuracies, and fairness outcomes for different sub-groups of people the AI systems will be applied to or make decisions for. The other trade-offs could be related to generalizability, interpretability, transparency, or explainability.

Acknowledge the challenges of trading off and balancing fairness and accuracy, especially when they influence high-stakes decisions. For instance, in the field of computational medicine, post-hoc correction methods based on randomizing predictions that are unjustifiable from an ethical perspective in clinical tasks (for example, severity scoring) should be avoided.[23]

Teams should decide how to treat "multiple axes of identities" in the machine learning pipeline to reduce the risk of unfairness or harm. Attention to intersectionality throughout the AI-LC ranges from selecting which identity labels to use in datasets, to deciding how to "technically handle the progressively smaller number of individuals in each group that will result from adding additional

21. E. Bembeneck, R. Nissan, and Z. Obermeyer, "To Stop Algorithmic Bias We First Have to Define It," October 21, 2021, https://www.brookings.edu/research/to-stop-algorithmic-bias-we-first-have-to-define-it/.

22. Scheuerman, Paul, and Brubaker, "How Computers See Gender."

23. I. Chen, F. D. Johansson, and D. Sontag, "Why Is My Classifier Discriminatory?" *Advances in Neural Information Processing Systems* (2018): 31, https://arxiv.org/pdf/1805.12002.pdf.

identities and axes" during model training, and deciding how to perform fairness evaluation as the number of groups increases.[24]

[P6]   Employ model designs attuned to diversity and inclusion

Diverse values and cultural perspectives from multiple stakeholders and populations should be codified in mathematical models and AI system design. Basic steps should include incorporating input from diverse stakeholder cohorts, ensuring the development team embodies different kinds of diversity, establishing and reviewing metrics to capture diversity and inclusion elements through-out the AI-LC, and ensuring well-documented end-to-end transparency on final design choices.

[P7]   Evaluate, adjust, and document bias identification and mitigation measures

During model training and implementation, the effectiveness of bias mitigation should be evaluated and adjusted. Periodically assess bias identification processes and address any gaps. The model specification should include how and what sources of bias were identified, mitigation techniques used, and how successful mitigation was. A related performance assessment should be undertaken before model deployment.

[P8]   Create realistic validation processes

Subject matter experts should create and oversee realistic validation processes addressing bias-related challenges, including noisy labeling (for example, mislabeled samples in training data), using proxy variables, and performing system tests under optimal conditions unrepresentative of real-world deployment context.

[P9]   Follow holistic value-sensitive design principles and methodology

Teams should engage with the complexity in which people experience values and technology in daily life. Values should be understood holistically and as being interrelated, rather than being analyzed in isolation from one another.

[P10]   Construct evaluation tasks that best mirror the real-world setting

Evaluation, even on crowdsourcing platforms used by ordinary people, should capture end users' types of interactions and decisions. The evaluations should demonstrate what happens when the algorithm is integrated into a human decision-making process. Does that alter or improve the decision and the resultant decision-making process as revealed by the downstream outcome?

---

24. A. Wang, V. Ramaswamy, and O. Russakovsk, "Towards Intersectionality in Machine Learning: Including More Identities, Handling Underrepresentation, and Performing Evaluation," presented at the 2022 ACM Conference on Fairness, Accountability, and Transparency (FAccT '22), Seoul, Republic of Korea, June 21–24, 2022, https://arxiv.org/pdf/2205.04610.pdf.

[P11]   Apply fairness analysis throughout the development process

Rather than thinking of fairness as a separate initiative, it's important to apply fairness analysis throughout the entire process, making sure to continuously re-evaluate the models from the perspective of fairness and inclusion.[25] The use of Model Performance Management tools or other methods should be considered to identify and mitigate any instances of intersectional unfairness.[26] For example, a diversity rating audit that combines various attributes including age, gender, and ethnicity can be used to audit datasets used to train AI algorithms.[27]

[P12]   Assess the suitability of human-centered design (HCD) methodology for AI system
         development

A human-centered design (HCD) methodology, based on International Organization for Standardization (ISO) standard 9241-210:2019, for the development of AI systems, could comprise:

- Defining the Context of Use, including operational environment, user characteristics, tasks, and social environment;

- Determining the User & Organizational Requirements, including business requirements, user requirements, and technical requirements;

- Developing the Design Solution, including the system design, user interface, and training materials; and

- Conducting the Evaluation, including usability and conformance testing.[28]

[P13]   Establish diverse partnerships and training populations

Partner with ethicists and antiracism experts in developing, training, testing, and implementing models. Recruit diverse and representative populations in training samples.[29]

---

25. B. Richardson and J. E. Gilbert, "A Framework for Fairness: A Systematic Review of Existing Fair AI Solutions," *Journal of Artificial Intelligence Research* 1 (2021), doi: https://doi.org/10.48550/arXiv.2112.05700.

26. M. Shergadwala, "Detecting Intersectional Unfairness in AI: Part 1," April 4, 2022, https://www.fiddler.ai/blog/detecting-intersectional-unfairness-in-ai-part-1.

27. MIT Sloan School of Management, Human-Centered AI: How Can the Technology Industry Fight Bias in Machines and People? (MIT Sloan School of Management, 2021).

28. Schwartz et al., NIST Special Publication 1270.

29. M. Nyariro, E. Emami, and S. A. Rahimi, "Integrating Equity, Diversity, and Inclusion Throughout the Lifecycle of Artificial Intelligence in Health," presented at the 13th Augmented Human International Conference, 2022.

Post-Development Process

[P14]   Monitor and evaluate during deployment

New or emergent stakeholder cohorts should participate in system monitoring and retraining. Stakeholders should be involved in a final review and sign-off, particularly if their input propelled significant changes in design or development processes. After validation, teams should obtain informed consent on the developed product features from impacted stakeholders, to track and respond to the system's impact on different communities.

When the AI system will have a direct impact on citizens, then public communication regarding possible impacts on lives or services should occur. Announcements should be presented in multiple languages via a range of media to reach the widest possible audience.

[P15]   Undertake holistic monitoring of external impacts

AI systems' learning capabilities evolve. External contexts such as climate, energy, health, economy, environment, political circumstances, and operating contexts also change. Therefore, both AI systems and the environment in which they operate should be continuously monitored and reassessed using appropriate metrics and mitigation processes, including methods to identify the potential appearance of new user groups who may be treated differentially by the AI system. Teams should consider the entire decision-making process, not only the algorithm in isolation. Even if an algorithm satisfies the criteria of fair or accurate and is deemed not risky, it still can have downstream consequences when deployed with human interactions. Software tools monitoring system behavior should be complemented by teams who can assess and respond to impacted stakeholders.

Detailed policies and procedures on how to handle system output and behavior should be developed and followed. Observed deviations from goals should trigger feedback loops and subsequent adjustments to data curation and problem formulation in the model, followed by further continuous testing and evaluation.

[P16]   Monitor and audit changing AI system impacts

It is critical to monitor the use of advanced analytics and AI technology to ensure that benefits are accruing to diverse groups in an equitable manner.[30] The scale of AI system impact can change rapidly and unevenly when deployed. Organizations should build resilience, flexibility, and sensitivity to respond to changes to ensure equitable and inclusive outcomes.

[P17]   Test and evaluate bias characteristics during deployment

The deploying organization and other stakeholders should use documented model specifications to test and evaluate bias characteristics during deployment in the specific context.

---

30. Clark et al., "Health Care Equity in the Use of Advanced Analytics and Artificial Intelligence Technologies in Primary Care."

[P18]   Collect demographic data from users to aid bias monitoring

Monitoring for bias should collect demographic data from users, including age and gender identity, to enable the calculation of assessment measures.

System

AI systems have been defined and classified in different ways. For example, one classification is based on the methods used for development, such as symbolic AI (using logic), probabilistic inference (using Bayesian networks), and connectionist (based on the human brain). Current AI technology is a system that, for a given set of human-defined objectives, typically uses large historical datasets to learn and make predictions, recommendations, or decisions for humans or for other larger systems where AI is a component. In this section, we provide a few guidelines for the AI system in its context of use.

[S1]   Establish inclusive and informed product development, training, evaluation, and sign-off

New stakeholders for iterative rounds of product development, training, and testing should be brought in, and beta groups for test deployments should be recruited. User groups should reflect different needs and abilities. Fresh perspectives contribute to the evaluation of both the AI system's functionality and, importantly, its level and quality of inclusivity. New or emergent stakeholder cohorts should participate in system monitoring and retraining. Stakeholders should be involved in a final review and sign-off, particularly if their input propelled significant changes in design or development processes. After validation, teams should obtain informed consent on the developed product features from impacted stakeholders, to track and respond to the system's impact on different communities.

[S2]   Understand AI systems through a holistic lens

Code is not the right level of abstraction at which to understand AI systems, whether it is for accountability or adaptability. Instead, systems should be analyzed in terms of inputs and outputs, overall design, embedded values, and how the software system fits with the overall institution deploying it.[31]

[S3]   Employ model design techniques attuned to diversity and inclusion considerations

Diverse values and cultural perspectives from multiple stakeholders and populations should be codified in mathematical models and AI system design. Model design techniques are necessarily contextual, related to the type of AI technology, the purpose and scope of the system, how users

---

31. K. Sankar, "AI Bias/Data/Risk: Thoughtful Insights (Beware: Occasionally Counterintuitive!): 3-Day NIST RMF Workshop," *Medium*, May 31, 2022, https://ksankar.medium.com/ai-bias-data-risk-thoughtful-insights-beware-occasionally-counterintuitive-a26bdc950a0c.

will be impacted, and so forth. However, basic steps should include incorporating input from diverse stakeholder cohorts, ensuring the development team embodies different kinds of diversity to reflect the diversity of AI system end users and stakeholders, establishing and reviewing metrics to capture diversity and inclusion elements throughout the AI-LC, and ensuring well-documented end-to-end transparency on final design choices.

[S4]   Evaluate, adjust, and document bias identification and mitigation measures

During model training and implementation, the effectiveness of bias mitigation should be evaluated and adjusted. Periodically assess bias identification processes and address any gaps. The model specification should include how and what sources of bias were identified, mitigation techniques used, and how successful mitigation was. A related performance assessment should be undertaken before model deployment.

Governance

Governance is defined as "a framework of policies, rules, and processes for ensuring direction, management, and accountability."[32] In the larger AI ecosystem, governance occurs at organizational, industry, and project team levels. In this section we include only those governance considerations most relevant to AI project teams because this is the area over which data scientists, team leaders, managers, and stakeholders have direct control.

[G1]   Establish policies for how biometric data is collected and used

Establishing policies (either at the organizational or industry level) for how biometric data and face and body images are collected and used may be the most effective way of mitigating harm to trans people—and also people of marginalized races, ethnicities, and sexualities.[33]

[G2]   Triage and tier AI bias risks

AI is not quarantined from negative societal realities such as discrimination and unfair practices. Consequently, it is arguably impossible to achieve zero risk of bias in an AI system. Therefore, AI bias risk management should aim to mitigate rather than avoid risks. Risks can be triaged and tiered with; resources allocated to the most material risks, the worst problems, and the most sensitive uses, those "most likely to cause real-world harm."[34]

---

32. Schwartz et al., NIST Special Publication 1270.

33. Scheuerman, Paul, and Brubaker, "How Computers See Gender."

34. Schwartz et al., NIST Special Publication 1270; Sankar, "AI Bias/Data/Risk: Thoughtful Insights."

[G3]　Align AI bias mitigation with relevant legislation

Bias mitigation should be aligned with relevant existing and emerging legal standards. These include national and state laws covering AI use in hiring, eligibility decisions (e.g., credit, housing, education), discrimination prohibitions (e.g., race, gender, religion, age, disability status), privacy, and unfair or deceptive practices.

[G4]　Follow AI risk assessment frameworks

Teams should develop diversity and inclusion policies and procedures addressing key roles, responsibilities, and processes within the organizations that are adopting AI. Bias risk management policies should specify how risks of bias will be mapped and measured, and according to what standards.

AI risk practice and associated checks and balances should be embedded and ingrained throughout all levels of the relevant stakeholder organizations. This may require a cultural shift while the AI system is evolving, and an acceptance that neither all questions will be answered necessarily, nor all problems well understood.

AI risk mitigation should not be framed as a quantitative balance but rather as an interdisciplinary qualitative judgment. Stakeholders should consider vetoing a deployment if they foresee potential unintended consequences.

The iterative and continuous AI risk assessment process should be adopted and understood as contributing to an organizational cultural shift. Risk management should be viewed as being beneficial to the organization. The use of methods not necessarily common in the computer science field such as storytelling could be explored.[35]

Regular risk assessment for diversity and inclusion in an AI system should assess the following points:

- Which practices have emerged to date
- Which practices seem no longer relevant
- If the initial vision for diversity and inclusivity has been achieved or is on-track
- If the use case and user group have been equitably defined or require refining
- Whether a proactive approach to inclusivity has been adequately prioritized throughout the development process
- Whose perspectives are or were overrepresented or underrepresented
- If any unforeseen challenges or activities arose and, if so, what measures were taken in response
- How the development process has further informed the understanding of any protected or at-risk groups.[36]

---

35. Sankar, "AI Bias/Data/Risk: Thoughtful Insights."

36. World Economic Forum, A Blueprint for Equity and Inclusion in Artificial Intelligence.

[G5]   Implement inclusive tech governance practices

Organizations should implement responsible AI leadership, drawing on existing resources such as UC Berkeley's Equity Fluent Leadership Playbook.[37] They should engage personnel to implement and monitor compliance with AI ethics principles, and train leaders to operationalize AI and data governance and measure engagement.[38] The governance mechanisms/guidelines should be connected with lower-level development/design patterns. For example, a risk assessment framework can be supported by a continuous risk assessment component in the AI ecosystem.

Conclusion

Diversity and inclusion in AI systems promote a humanist view of product development. Humans must be placed at the center of the AI ecosystem, whether it is within the process (entire AI development lifecycle), for the product (in the context of system use and for those impacted directly or indirectly by AI technology), in data (fair representation of all relevant stakeholders in the datasets), or in governance (legal frameworks, regulations, policies, and guidelines).

The DI-AI guidelines presented in this chapter advise technologists and other professionals in the AI field on *what* should be done to ensure that diversity and inclusion factors are adequately considered in decision-making, software development, and risk assessment throughout the AI lifecycle. At times, we also suggest *who* should be responsible for oversight, implementation, monitoring, and evaluation of the work entailed in the specific guidelines. Various methods exist that would enable the guidelines to be implemented. For instance, the pattern catalogues presented in this book can be adapted to many of the DI-AI guidelines to suggest *how* stakeholders and teams can implement them.

The DI-AI guidelines in this chapter have been organized and presented around the five pillars of the DI-AI definition, while the Responsible AI Pattern Catalogue in the rest of this book has been organized differently and references governance, process, product, and techniques. Moreover, both the DI-AI guidelines and patterns are deliberately open and nonprescriptive to allow them to be used, reused, and adapted to suit the *context and scale* of any AI system. Consequently, those in charge of responsible AI within an organization, project, and/or team can consider a many-to-many mapping of the guidelines and patterns that fits their own purposes. We offer a few examples here under the five DI-AI pillars.

---

37. G. Smith, J. Sanders, and I. Rustagi, *Advancing Belonging in Organizations* (University of California, Berkeley, 2022), https://haas.berkeley.edu/wp-content/uploads/AdvancingBelongingInOrganizations_Berkeley-EGAL.pdf.

38. Adams, "Bias and AI: Ensuring Inclusive Tech."

Human

Integrate diversity and inclusion principles and practice throughout the AI lifecycle [H.1]
This guideline recommends that the composition of different levels of stakeholder cohorts should maintain diversity along social lines and that end users, AI practitioners, subject matter experts, and professionals should be involved to identify downstream impacts comprehensively. It can be mapped to **Stakeholder Engagement [G.20]** in the organization-level governance patterns, and to the **Code of RAI [G.11]** at industry-level governance. Resultant benefits include increased stakeholder trust in the AI project, reduced risk, clear guidance for employees, and the same explicit rules for everyone in the organization.

Data

Involve stakeholders and nonexperts in the selection, collection, and analysis of demographically representative qualitative data [D.2] Diverse viewpoints, including those of nonexperts, should be elicited when collecting and analyzing specific datasets to identify potential problems and risks. This guideline can be mapped to **Stakeholder Engagement [G.20]** and to the technique/ product patterns **Fairness Assessor [T.1]** and **Discrimination Mitigator [T.2].** Fairness metrics could include demographic parity and equal opportunity, and algorithmic discrimination can be addressed by various pre-processing, in-processing, and post-processing techniques.

Process

Assess the suitability of human-centered design (HCD) methodology for AI system development [P.12] This guideline could be addressed by following three requirements of stage process patterns: **Verifiable Ethical Requirement [P.2]**, **Data Requirement [P.3]**, and **Ethical User Story [P.4]**. Business analysts would drive the first two patterns. They would be joined by product managers, AI users, and AI consumers in the creation of ethical user stories.

System

Employ model design techniques attuned to diversity and inclusion considerations [S.3]
Diverse values and cultural perspectives from multiple stakeholders and populations should be codified in mathematical models and AI system design. The design stage process pattern **RAI Design Modeling [P.7]** details relevant practical steps for AI architects, including designing formal models aligned with human values, creating RAI knowledge bases to inform design decisions that consider ethical concerns, and using logic programming to implement ethical principles.

Governance

Triage and tier AI bias risks [G.2] AI bias risk management should aim to mitigate rather than avoid risks. Resources should be allocated to the most material risks, the worst problems, and the most sensitive uses. The organization-level governance pattern **RAI Risk Assessment [G.12]** is relevant to this DI-AI guideline by aiming at management teams and covers both domain-specific risks and emerging risks in constantly evolving AI systems. It recommends that an RAI risk assessment framework be co-designed with key stakeholders, including an RAI risk committee, development teams, and prospective purchasers.

In summary, diversity and inclusion must occupy a special place in the AI ecosystem. Its practices must be acknowledged and valued in all aspects of the AI system development lifecycle, rather than be reduced to merely one of the practices implicitly inferred from the overall understanding of achieving "fairness" in AI. We advocate that diversity and inclusion principles should be at the core of AI ethical principles and embedded in the design, development, deployment, and evolution of all AI systems. We believe that this embedding will in turn accelerate and improve our understanding and practices of diversity and inclusion in society.

PART IV

LOOKING TO THE FUTURE

The area of responsible AI has been evolving quickly and will continue to evolve. In this final part, we provide some insights into the ways in which responsible AI will change and transform in the future.

12

The Future of Responsible AI

Technological developments in artificial intelligence move at a breakneck speed. This book was largely written in the latter half of 2022 and the first half of 2023. Even during that short time, the world witnessed multiple momentous events that have been seen as major milestones for AI. In 2021, OpenAI unleashed its DALL-E text-to-image generator,[1] which was a revelation both to professional artists (who could use it to increase their productivity) and to nonartists, who could, for the first time, produce professional-quality artwork simply by constructing the right prompt to capture the image in their head. DALL-E was quickly followed by a series of text-to-image generation AI tools, including Stable Diffusion[2] and Midjourney.[3]

The real revelation, though, came in November 2022, when OpenAI launched its conversational AI interface, ChatGPT,[4] which allows anyone with a web browser to indulge in back-and-forth conversations with an AI. ChatGPT gained over 100 million users just two months after launching, making it the most rapidly adopted technology in the world *ever*. That's faster than the internet, faster than the most popular social media platforms, and faster than the iPhone. While the technology behind ChatGPT—large language models, and, in particular, GPT—was not new, and those in the AI community had known about such developments for years, the easy-to-use and accessible interface made ChatGPT the first experimental AI of its kind available for anyone in the world to experiment with. It immediately both delighted and stunned users, with its ability to converse in a human way, its ability to remember context from a much earlier part of the conversation, and, although it was

---

1. https://openai.com/product/dall-e-2.

2. https://github.com/Stability-AI/stablediffusion.

3. https://www.midjourney.com.

4. https://openai.com/blog/chatgpt.

certainly not without flaws, it had a much improved set of guardrails that somewhat prevented it from going off the rails and spewing out discriminatory or biased text. The latter made ChatGPT a huge improvement over some earlier experiments at mass adoption of generative AI, such as Microsoft's chatbot Tay, which quickly became racist.

The release of ChatGPT triggered an arms race between big tech companies, each vying to be the best and most widely adopted when it came to generative AI. Microsoft doubled down on its initial investment in OpenAI, announcing a further $10 billion of investment. Google responded by launching its own large language model conversational AI, BARD, although its initial public release was more cautious than OpenAI, limiting it to prescreened users. By February 2023, Microsoft had already incorporated GPT into its search engine, Bing, now called New Bing, and the race was on to steal search market share away from Google, which, for so long, had dominated this space.

Such was the pace of new developments in large language technology that on a single day in March 2023—the fourteenth—there were two major global announcements of new AI technology. In fact, one of those announcements, which on any other day would have been breaking news, was largely ignored. It was the announcement that Google would incorporate its large language model technology into Workspace, thus bringing the power of conversational AI to the most popular Google office products such as Gmail. However, this announcement, made on the morning of the fourteenth, was almost immediately overtaken by OpenAI's latest launch, of GPT-4, its even bigger and even better version of GPT. The hype around GPT was at a fever pitch and led to a daily onslaught of new product announcements from almost all tech companies of any repute, allowing users to use natural language as an interface for producing images, presentations, 3D models, video, and just about anything else you can imagine.

Indeed, the speed of AI developments nowadays is such that, by the time this book is published, it will probably seem quaint to be talking about GPT-4. No doubt by then, the world will have moved on—to GPT-5, or GPT-6, or who knows what?

Despite the fact that the first part of this chapter was likely outdated by the time it was written (and, no, the chapter wasn't written by ChatGPT!), the fever that accompanied these announcements in late 2022 and early 2023 is instructive when it comes to thinking about responsible AI.

Very quickly, popular media divided into two camps of thought when it came to these technologies. There were the revolutionaries, who saw ChatGPT as the dawn of a new age of technological superiority, one in which everyone everywhere would increase their productivity ten-fold, would have their own personal AI assistants to do their bidding, and life, frankly, would never be the same. These revolutionaries were quickly tempered, however, by the doomsdayers, who spoke of how the world would be if AI was allowed to continue to its natural conclusion. They warned not just about the dangers of ChatGPT and related technologies (so-called hallucinations, inability to evidence sources, potential for manipulation of users, scope for the mass dissemination of fake news, and so on) but also about dangers the next generation of AI would bring, describing it as an existential threat to humanity, and one that needed arresting. Indeed, in April 2023, over 1,000 well-known AI experts from around the world, including Elon Musk and Stuart Russell, signed a petition calling for a six-month pause on the development of large language models bigger than GPT-4, and for the community to use that time to come together to agree to a common set of standards and safety protocols for responsible AI. The letter was largely ignored and often ridiculed. And its authors no doubt never really expected such a pause to happen, but they had succeeded in further raising awareness of the issue.

As mentioned earlier, the case of ChatGPT and related events is instructive for responsible AI. Indeed, even the way that ChatGPT was introduced to the world—essentially using the public as beta testers—has been seen by some as highly irresponsible.

All this goes to show just how difficult it is to develop AI in a responsible manner at a global scale. When it comes to responsible AI, the usual mechanisms for addressing it are regulation, education, standards, tools, and public awareness. All these take time and risk being overtaken in the AI arms race. To conclude this book, we briefly consider each of these mechanisms in turn and discuss how effective they are at promoting responsible AI in such a fast-changing world.

Regulation

Perhaps the most effective way of ensuring that AI is developed responsibly is regulation. Legislation has already proven itself as an effective tool when it comes to monitoring and curbing unwanted forms of emerging technologies. The European Union's GDPR is the most well-known example; it provides consumers with protections related to data privacy and applies globally. Breaches can lead to fines as high as 20 million euros or 4 percent of the company's total global turnover from the previous fiscal year, whichever amount is greater.

When it comes to AI, however, legislation is trickier. The most fundamental problem is that there is no clear definition of AI. Any attempt to regulate it must therefore do its best to provide a definition that will then be tested in the courts. The European Union's AI Act defines AI in terms of the technology used to implement an AI system and, therefore, explicitly includes neural networks and other machine learning techniques, as well as more logic-based symbolic approaches to AI. The AI Act's definition has, however, been criticized both for its overly broad interpretation of AI—which includes Bayesian statistics, for example—and for its narrow focus on particular techniques that *currently* implement AI, meaning that new technical developments may not be covered. This looseness of definition when it comes to AI has already led to the demise of some previous attempts to regulate the sector. A task force set up in New York State in 2018 to audit the use of AI in government systems got bogged down trying to decide whether a particular system used by a government agency was actually AI (and, hence, within the remit of the task force) or not. The task force was eventually shut down because it was all just too hard. A similar example is the famous Robodebt scandal in Australia, in which an automated system was used to predict whether benefit claimants owed tax. The Robodebt system sent out automated letters informing taxpayers that they were in debt, wrongly identifying 470,000 people. This debacle led to a Royal Commission. The interesting thing about Robodebt is that, while it concerns the use of automation, it does not concern AI. None of the algorithms used for debt prediction are normally considered part of AI. So, even if there had been any AI regulation enshrined in Australian law at the time, Robodebt would not have been in scope.

The second problem with regulating AI is that legislation takes time. It can take years for a single government to agree on a law, let alone for multiple governments across the world to take the same approach to regulation. The EU AI Act, for example, has spent many years in the European courts.

When it comes to regulating AI, there are two approaches. One is to develop a completely fresh framework for AI regulation. This is the approach taken by the EU AI Act. The second is to rely on the powers of existing regulators, which already cover things such as privacy of consumer data and online safety. The argument goes that most of the issues with AI are already covered by existing laws and perhaps all that is needed is a thin "layer" of AI-specific legislation to coordinate things. This approach should be much faster, of course, although even here, it can take years to get to a finished product. The UK government is currently following this approach to legislation, and this is also the approach preferred by the 2021 Australian Human Rights Commission report on AI and human rights.

What is clear is that there is no easy answer when it comes to regulating AI. Approaches that try to regulate specific technologies are doomed to fail because they will be overtaken quickly. A better attack vector may therefore be to focus on the types of harm that AI could bring and provide protections for them. These types are less likely to change quite as quickly—although it is not inconceivable that a new form of AI will bring a completely new form of harm that wasn't even possible beforehand. Perhaps an even more effective approach is not to try to regulate AI at all. After all, there are many examples of software systems that bring harm to consumers but have nothing to do with AI—Robodebt being a prominent example. An alternative to regulating AI, therefore, is to regulate software that makes automated decisions that affect consumers. This is indeed the approach taken by some jurisdictions, such as GDPR, Australia's Consumer Data Rights (CDR), and California's Privacy Rights Act (CPRA).

Education

One of the more effective strategies for promoting responsible AI—albeit a medium- to long-term one—is education. This education can come in many forms and be targeted to a range of audiences. A key target group is, of course, AI technologists themselves—that is, the software developers, data scientists, and machine learning experts who build AI systems. If this group lacks the motivation or incentives to put responsibility first, we will never get responsible AI. Moreover, if this group has the motivation to implement more responsible AI systems but lacks the skills and know-how, we will also not reach our goal. Technologists are not the only target audience for responsible AI education, however. Another key stakeholder group is board directors and C-suite executives. Boards, in particular, have the power to ensure that a company implements AI responsibly. Boards can introduce governance structures that promote, monitor, and indeed mandate responsible AI. Chapter 4 introduced some of the patterns that boards can use to effectively ensure AI is developed responsibly.

Other stakeholders are important too. Indeed, for responsible AI to be taken seriously, *everyone* needs to be aware of ethics and human values in AI. However, for the sake of brevity, we focus here on the technologists and on the board directors who put in place organizational guardrails.

Most AI technologists have at least one university degree, most commonly—although not always—in computer science, data science, or another STEM subject. Unfortunately, even today, the treatment of computer ethics is somewhat limited in university STEM education. While universities have seen a strong shift toward interdisciplinary thinking in their research, the trend toward interdisciplinary education, although now emerging, has been slower to gain traction. The reason has to do largely with the organizational structures within universities, which tend to make cross-department educational programs more complex. There are some standout examples of interdisciplinary programs in data science, which try to equip students not just with core computer/data science skills but also skills in another domain, including, in some cases, the social sciences. In Australia, good examples (although not the only ones) are the bachelor of applied data science at Monash University and the federally funded Next Generation AI Graduates program, which operates at a national level.

Despite these innovations, however, for the most part, STEM education—and computer science education, in particular—pays little attention to ethics. Accreditation bodies typically insist that students are exposed to computer ethics, but this exposure is usually implemented by offering a mandatory computer ethics course, which all undergraduate students take. Unfortunately, this course is far too little, and is far too siloed, to have much effect on students' mindsets. A computer ethics course is usually perceived as being disconnected from other core courses, often receives poor student evaluations because ethics is not contextualized within other courses, and so, as a result, is seen as a course that students have to get through, and they quickly forget anything they have learned. An alternative approach is needed in which computer ethics—and AI ethics, in particular—is embedded across *all* undergraduate computer science courses. This is not difficult to do in theory. All it takes is for learning objectives on technical courses to be embellished with learning objectives around ethics. For example, a machine learning course might have learning objectives to teach core machine learning algorithms, but it can also include case studies on bias in machine learning. In practice, of course, moving ethics from a single, siloed course to a cross-cutting and holistic consideration requires a radical shift, and it requires the passion and drive of leaders in education to make these changes, which will often be in the face of opposition from more technically oriented colleagues who may lament the fact that teaching ethics takes valuable teaching time away from the core technical material. Note also that, in our opinion, delegating the teaching of ethics to educators from other disciplines, such as the social sciences, is not sufficient. Ethics needs to be taught to STEM students in a particular way that is properly oriented within the context of technical material. This effort requires educators with a STEM background but who also understand enough about ethics and responsible innovation so that they can weave the two subjects together in a seamless way. Doing so is not easy, of course, and it should be fairly clear that we lack educators with such experience and knowledge in the current system.

University education is not the only way to upskill AI technologists. Software professionals routinely continue to learn on the job via informal coaching or through formal short courses, such as micro-credentials, workshops, or certificate programs. These programs also need to embed AI ethics as a core part of what they teach. Again, we believe the key here is not to see AI ethics as a disjoint topic that is taught once in a dedicated short course. Rather, it needs to be embedded across all short courses. AI technology development should start and finish with responsible AI, and that means that in AI courses, responsible innovation needs to be at the start and end, and be a constant primary theme throughout. This is as much true of short courses as of university degrees.

When it comes to education of boards, we know that boards generally lack knowledge of AI, what it can and cannot do, and how to guard against risks. The good news is that history tells us that such a situation can change over time. An analogy is with cybersecurity, which is now embedded as a core part of what most boards do, and most boards will receive cybersecurity and cyber-risk assessment training. While not perfect, it is clear that boards take cybersecurity seriously, and, as such, board directors both individually and as a collective seek out ways to better educate themselves. Another analogy is Environmental, Social, and Governance (ESG) considerations. ESG is a more recent issue of debate in boards and concerns how boards can drive not just a strong financial bottom line but also strong performance when it comes to minimizing the company's impact on the environment, be a good citizen in its communities and in society more broadly, and be an exemplar of good governance to manage risks around ESG. Similarly to cybersecurity, we are now seeing more interest from boards in educating themselves on ESG matters. This interest is driven somewhat by intrinsic motivations of companies that want to "do good," but the real step change is due to extrinsic factors such as the rise in ethical investing as well as compliance legislation, both of which bring bottom-line reasons for a company to change.

When it comes to AI and boards, we are very much at the beginning of the journey. The rapid developments of ChatGPT and other AI tools in 2023 have sped things up somewhat, and many boards are now actively seeking out ways to educate board directors with the skills they need to understand the basics of AI, how AI affects their business, and how the risks of AI can be managed—without sacrificing the business opportunities—within an organization. We expect to see a plethora of new board-level responsible AI courses, responsible AI consulting, and responsible AI frameworks for boards in the months and years to come.

Education—a bit like regulation—is more of a medium- to long-term proposition for addressing responsible AI. It should be clear by now, however, that there are no quick fixes for implementing AI responsibly.

Standards

Commonly agreed-upon standards are a typical way both to provide guidance to companies in a particular technical area as well as to promote compliance of particular ways of doing things. In fact, standards for the responsible development of AI have existed for many years; see IEEE P7000, ISO/IEC JTC 1/SC42. One advantage of standards is that they tend to be global in nature and are often the result of countless hours of cross-border collaboration. This collaboration promotes a standard way of doing things across international borders. Closely related to standards, there are looser principles, such as Australia's AI Ethics Principles, mentioned in Chapter 1. Principles are just that: They tend to be very high level and not so detailed, whereas standards may be documented as many hundreds of pages of detailed specifications. A key advantage of detailed standards such as these is that they often lead to new industries whereby tool vendors develop standards-compliant tools, both supporting companies to follow best practice in an area, but also allowing for interoperability between tools so that companies are less likely to get permanently locked into one vendor. A good example of the latter is the OMG UML Standards, which, for many years, have defined how tool vendors develop software modeling tools.

Standards are, of course, a voluntary mechanism, in contrast to regulation. Standards are managed by standards authorities such as the OMG, IEEE, or Standards Australia. These trusted authorities can lead to wide-scale adoption, as described previously, but are not meant to impose the standards, although this can sometimes occur when the reputational risk of not being standards-compliant is too severe for a particular company in a sector.

When it comes to responsible AI, specific standards have already been developed, such as ISO/IEC 23894 and NIST AI RMF. On their own, however, responsible AI standards are unlikely to lead to a step change in the development of AI in a responsible way. This change would occur only if adoption of the standards is such that any new company entering the market felt pressured to also follow the standards. This is not yet the case for responsible AI and, indeed, it is not clear to what extent these standards have been adopted at all. In the responsible AI space, large tech or consulting companies have often created their own principles or standards for internal adoption. Such companies include Microsoft and Google, as well as consulting companies such as Deloitte and KPMG that may encourage their clients to follow the standards.

Despite all these changes, the use of a standards mechanism to promote responsible AI seems limited currently. This is evidenced by the fact that, although company- and sector-specific responsible AI standards have existed for a long time, companies still routinely launch AI products with questionable adherence to these standards. Unless there is a more concerted effort to work across standards bodies and enforce standards, this situation appears unlikely to change.

Tools

While certainly not a solution in and of itself, effective and appropriate sets of tools are an essential aid to any organization interested in responsible AI. The word *tool* here is intended broadly, to include not just technical development tools but also guidelines, frameworks, and best practices. Indeed, the main topic of this book is to provide you with exactly such a set of tools, in this case formalized as a set of patterns. The general structure used within this book—governance, process, and pattern—is a useful way of classifying responsible AI tools more broadly.

On governance, an organization can use a number of existing risk assessment tools to understand the risks and mitigation strategies associated with the use of AI. On process, an organization will need to implement a set of policies and practices to ensure that its workforce follows best responsible AI practices. On product, technical design patterns and data science tools can be used to help AI technologists understand any emerging risks associated with AI. The full range of tools—whether they be governance, process, or product—is too extensive to be covered within this chapter; however, Australia's National AI Centre has produced a good source for further information.[5]

---

5. https://www.gradientinstitute.org/posts/csiro-gradient-new-report/.

Public Awareness

One powerful influencer is the court of public opinion. A company's bottom line ultimately lives or dies on its reputation with existing and potential customers. If a groundswell of public opinion—positive or negative—rises strongly and fast enough, it can force an organization to fundamentally change its direction of travel. There are many examples of this throughout history, both within and outside the tech sector. Serious loss of life in airline accidents, for example, if attributed to an aviation company's negligence may put the company out of business, or, at least, make it very difficult for the company to continue to attract customers. In the automobile industry, the Volkswagen emissions scandal led to a severe—albeit ultimately temporary—loss in VW share prices and profits due its lack of governance in compliance of monitoring emissions. The tech industry has, to date, been more sheltered from serious public backlash, largely because many tech platforms (such as social media) follow a business model of offering services for free, hooking customers who may then be reluctant to demand radical change. Even here, however, there are some high-profile cases where tech companies have been forced to change the design of their systems due to public opinion. One case in point is Instagram, which eventually changed its content moderation practices in response to the suicide of a British teenager in 2017 when her father attributed her death in part to Instagram serving up problematic content on her feed.

Public opinion on new tech developments is difficult to predict and can take a long time to change. Clearly, the role of the media is paramount in this process. At the time of writing, this process of the public deciding on its view of a new technology, as mediated by the press, is in full play, with the evolving public attitudes toward ChatGPT and similar tools.

Suffice to say, there is a certain responsibility of AI experts to provide a balanced view to the public on AI. Leading AI experts often differ in their views on whether AI is overall a force for good. This difference is, of course, generally a healthy thing, although it can sometimes get out of hand. Commentators with a balanced approach will ultimately win out and can be a powerful voice for helping the public to make up their own minds about the pros and cons of AI. Indeed, one of the authors of this book has made his own attempt to provide such a balanced view, with the Everyday AI podcast,[6] which is a gentle introduction to the topic of AI, aimed at the general public—available on your favorite streaming platform!

Final Remarks

It is undoubtedly a great time to be working in AI. AI is changing just about every industry and is more and more becoming part of all of our daily lives. Thankfully, in the last decade or so, the rapid technological developments in AI have been accompanied by a strong narrative and emerging frameworks for developing AI responsibly. While fraught with many challenges, substantial progress has been made toward the responsible development of AI, and public awareness of the potential benefits and risks of AI has never been greater.

---

6. https://www.csiro.au/en/news/podcasts/everyday-ai-podcast.

We hope in this book that we have made our own—very modest—contribution to promoting responsible AI. We hope furthermore that this book can provide a reference for those working in the field, with concrete guidance on how to develop responsible AI effectively. The patterns provided here are not intended to be complete—and to attempt to reach completeness in such a rapidly changing area would be folly. New patterns will be needed in the future, and we aim to maintain our pattern catalogue and update it as new knowledge becomes available. If you are interested in keeping abreast of these developments, head over to the website accompanying this book.

PART V

APPENDIX

This appendix provides further information about the patterns we introduced in this book as index cards.

APPENDIX

Governance Patterns

G.1. RAI Law and Regulation

- **Type of pattern:** Governance pattern
- **Type of objective:** Trustworthiness
- **Target users:** RAI governors
- **Impacted stakeholders:** AI technology producers and procurers, AI solution producers and procurers, RAI tool producers and procurers
- **Lifecycle stages:** All stages
- **Relevant AI ethics principles:** HSE well-being, human-centered values, fairness, privacy protection and security, reliability and safety, transparency and explainability, contestability, accountability

G.2. RAI Maturity Model

- **Type of pattern:** Governance pattern
- **Type of objective:** Trust
- **Target users:** RAI governors
- **Impacted stakeholders:** AI technology producers and procurers, AI solution producers and procurers, RAI tool producers and procurers

- **Lifecycle stages:** All stages
- **Relevant AI ethics principles:** HSE well-being, human-centered values, fairness, privacy protection and security, reliability and safety, transparency and explainability, contestability, accountability

G.3. RAI Certification

- **Type of pattern:** Governance pattern
- **Type of objective:** Trust
- **Target users:** RAI governors
- **Impacted stakeholders:** AI technology producers and procurers, AI solution producers and procurers, RAI tool producers and procurers
- **Lifecycle stages:** All stages
- **Relevant AI ethics principles:** HSE well-being, human-centered values, fairness, privacy protection and security, reliability and safety, transparency and explainability, contestability, accountability

G.4. Regulatory Sandbox

- **Type of pattern:** Governance pattern
- **Type of objective:** Trustworthiness
- **Target users:** RAI governors
- **Impacted stakeholders:** AI technology producers and procurers, AI solution producers and procurers, RAI tool producers and procurers
- **Lifecycle stages:** All stages
- **Relevant AI ethics principles:** HSE well-being, human-centered values, fairness, privacy protection and security, reliability and safety, transparency and explainability, contestability, accountability

G.5. Building Code

- **Type of pattern:** Governance pattern
- **Type of objective:** Trustworthiness
- **Target users:** RAI governors

- **Impacted stakeholders:** AI technology producers and procurers, AI solution producers and procurers, RAI tool producers and procurers

- **Lifecycle stages:** All stages

- **Relevant AI ethics principles:** HSE well-being, human-centered values, fairness, privacy protection and security, reliability and safety, transparency and explainability, contestability, accountability

G.6. Independent Oversight

- **Type of pattern:** Governance pattern

- **Type of objective:** Trustworthiness

- **Target users:** RAI governors

- **Impacted stakeholders:** AI technology producers and procurers, AI solution producers and procurers, RAI tool producers and procurers

- **Lifecycle stages:** All stages

- **Relevant AI ethics principles:** HSE well-being, human-centered values, fairness, privacy protection and security, reliability and safety, transparency and explainability, contestability, accountability

G.7. Trust Mark

- **Type of pattern:** Governance pattern

- **Type of objective:** Trust

- **Target users:** RAI governors

- **Impacted stakeholders:** AI technology producers and procurers, AI solution producers and procurers, RAI tool producers and procurers

- **Lifecycle stages:** All stages

- **Relevant AI ethics principles:** HSE well-being, human-centered values, fairness, privacy protection and security, reliability and safety, transparency and explainability, contestability, accountability

G.8. RAI Standards

- **Type of pattern:** Governance pattern

- **Type of objective:** Trustworthiness

- **Target users:** RAI governors
- **Impacted stakeholders:** AI technology producers and procurers, AI solution producers and procurers, RAI tool producers and procurers
- **Lifecycle stages:** All stages
- **Relevant AI ethics principles:** HSE well-being, human-centered values, fairness, privacy protection and security, reliability and safety, transparency and explainability, contestability, accountability

G.9. Leadership Commitment for RAI

- **Type of pattern:** Governance pattern
- **Type of objective:** Trustworthiness
- **Target users**: Management teams
- **Impacted stakeholders:** Employees, AI users, AI impacted subjects, AI consumers
- **Lifecycle stages:** All stages
- **Relevant AI ethics principles:** HSE well-being, human-centered values, fairness, privacy protection and security, reliability and safety, transparency and explainability, contestability, accountability

G.10. RAI Risk Committee

- **Type of pattern:** Governance pattern
- **Type of objective:** Trustworthiness
- **Target users:** Management teams
- **Impacted stakeholders:** Employees, AI users, AI impacted subjects, AI consumers
- **Lifecycle stages:** All stages
- **Relevant AI ethics principles:** HSE well-being, human-centered values, fairness, privacy protection and security, reliability and safety, transparency and explainability, contestability, accountability

G.11. Code of RAI

- **Type of pattern:** Governance pattern
- **Type of objective:** Trustworthiness

- **Target users:** Management teams
- **Impacted stakeholders:** Employees, AI users, AI impacted subjects, AI consumers
- **Lifecycle stages:** All stages
- **Relevant AI ethics principles:** HSE well-being, human-centered values, fairness, privacy protection and security, reliability and safety, transparency and explainability, contestability, accountability

G.12. RAI Risk Assessment

- **Type of pattern:** Governance pattern
- **Type of objective:** Trustworthiness
- **Target users:** Management teams
- **Impacted stakeholders:** Employees, AI users, AI impacted subjects, AI consumers
- **Lifecycle stages:** All stages
- **Relevant AI ethics principles:** HSE well-being, human-centered values, fairness, privacy protection and security, reliability and safety, transparency and explainability, contestability, accountability

G.13. RAI Training

- **Type of pattern:** Governance pattern
- **Type of objective:** Trustworthiness
- **Target users:** Management teams
- **Impacted stakeholders:** Employees, AI users, AI impacted subjects, AI consumers
- **Lifecycle stages:** All stages
- **Relevant AI ethics principles:** HSE well-being, human-centered values, fairness, privacy protection and security, reliability and safety, transparency and explainability, contestability, accountability

G.14. Role-Level Accountability Contract

- **Type of pattern:** Governance pattern
- **Type of objective:** Trustworthiness
- **Target users:** Management teams

- **Impacted stakeholders:** Employees, AI users, AI impacted subjects, AI consumers
- **Lifecycle stages:** All stages
- **Relevant AI ethics principles:** HSE well-being, human-centered values, fairness, privacy protection and security, reliability and safety, transparency and explainability, contestability, accountability

G.15. RAI Bill of Materials

- **Type of pattern:** Governance pattern
- **Type of objective:** Trust
- **Target users:** Management teams
- **Impacted stakeholders:** Employees, AI users, AI impacted subjects, AI consumers
- **Lifecycle stages:** All stages
- **Relevant AI ethics principles:** HSE well-being, human-centered values, fairness, privacy protection and security, reliability and safety, transparency and explainability, contestability, accountability

G.16. Standardized Reporting

- **Type of pattern:** Governance pattern
- **Type of objective:** Trustworthiness
- **Target users:** Management teams
- **Impacted stakeholders:** Employees, AI users, AI impacted subjects, AI consumers
- **Lifecycle stages:** All stages
- **Relevant AI ethics principles:** Transparency and explainability, accountability

G.17. Customized Agile Process

- **Type of pattern:** Governance pattern
- **Type of objective:** Trustworthiness
- **Target users:** Project managers
- **Impacted stakeholders:** Development teams, AI users, AI consumers, AI impacted subjects
- **Lifecycle stages:** All stages

- **Relevant AI ethics principles:** HSE well-being, human-centered values, fairness, privacy protection and security, reliability and safety, transparency and explainability, contestability, accountability

G.18. Tight Coupling of AI and Non-AI Development

- **Type of pattern:** Governance pattern
- **Type of objective:** Trustworthiness
- **Target users:** Project managers
- **Impacted stakeholders:** Development teams
- **Lifecycle stages:** Operation
- **Relevant AI ethics principles:** HSE well-being, human-centered values, fairness, privacy protection and security, reliability and safety, transparency and explainability, contestability, accountability

G.19. Diverse Team

- **Type of pattern:** Governance pattern
- **Type of objective:** Trustworthiness
- **Target users:** Project managers
- **Impacted stakeholders:** Development teams
- **Lifecycle stages:** All stages
- **Relevant AI ethics principles:** HSE well-being, human-centered values, fairness, privacy protection and security, reliability and safety, transparency and explainability, contestability, accountability

G.20. Stakeholder Engagement

- **Type of pattern:** Governance pattern
- **Type of objective:** Trustworthiness
- **Target users:** Project managers
- **Impacted stakeholders:** Development teams
- **Lifecycle stages:** All stages

- **Relevant AI ethics principles:** HSE well-being, human-centered values, fairness, privacy protection and security, reliability and safety, transparency and explainability, contestability, accountability

G.21. Continuous Documentation Using Templates

- **Type of pattern:** Governance pattern
- **Type of objective:** Trustworthiness
- **Target users:** Project managers
- **Impacted stakeholders:** Development teams
- **Lifecycle stages:** All stages
- **Relevant AI ethics principles:** HSE well-being, human-centered values, fairness, privacy protection and security, reliability and safety, transparency and explainability, contestability, accountability

G.22. Verifiable Claim for AI System Artifacts

- **Type of pattern:** Governance pattern
- **Type of objective:** Trustworthiness
- **Target users:** Project managers
- **Impacted stakeholders:** Development teams, AI users
- **Lifecycle stages:** All stages
- **Relevant AI ethics principles:** HSE well-being, human-centered values, fairness, privacy protection and security, reliability and safety, transparency and explainability, contestability, accountability

G.23. Failure Mode and Effects Analysis (FMEA)

- **Type of pattern:** Governance pattern
- **Type of objective:** Trustworthiness
- **Target users:** Project managers
- **Impacted stakeholders:** Development teams
- **Lifecycle stages:** Requirements engineering, testing, operation

- **Relevant AI ethics principles:** HSE well-being, human-centered values, fairness, privacy protection and security, reliability and safety, transparency and explainability, contestability, accountability

G.24. Fault Tree Analysis (FTA)

- **Type of pattern:** Governance pattern
- **Type of objective:** Trustworthiness
- **Target users:** Project managers
- **Impacted stakeholders:** Development teams
- **Lifecycle stages:** Requirements engineering, testing, operation
- **Relevant AI ethics principles:** HSE well-being, human-centered values, fairness, privacy protection and security, reliability and safety, transparency and explainability, contestability, accountability

Process Patterns

P.1. AI Suitability Assessment

- **Type of pattern:** Process pattern
- **Type of objective:** Trustworthiness
- **Target users:** Business analysists, architects
- **Impacted stakeholders:** Development teams
- **Lifecycle stages:** Requirements
- **Relevant AI ethics principles:** HSE well-being, human-centered values, fairness, privacy protection and security, reliability and safety, transparency and explainability, contestability, accountability

P.2. Verifiable RAI Requirement

- **Type of pattern:** Process pattern
- **Type of objective:** Trustworthiness
- **Target users:** Business analysts
- **Impacted stakeholders:** Developers, data scientists, testers, operators

- **Lifecycle stages:** Requirements
- **Relevant AI ethics principles:** HSE well-being, human-centered values, fairness, privacy protection and security, reliability and safety, transparency and explainability, contestability, accountability

P.3. Lifecycle-Driven Data Requirement

- **Type of pattern:** Process pattern
- **Type of objective:** Trustworthiness
- **Target users:** Business analysts
- **Impacted stakeholders:** Developers, data scientists, testers, operators
- **Lifecycle stages:** Requirements
- **Relevant AI ethics principles:** HSE well-being, human-centered values, fairness, privacy protection and security, reliability and safety, transparency and explainability, contestability, accountability

P.4. RAI User Story

- **Type of pattern:** Process pattern
- **Type of objective:** Trustworthiness
- **Target users:** Product managers, business analysts, AI users, AI consumers
- **Impacted stakeholders:** Developers, data scientists, testers, operators
- **Lifecycle stages:** Requirements
- **Relevant AI ethics principles:** HSE well-being, human-centered values, fairness, privacy protection and security, reliability and safety, transparency and explainability, contestability, accountability

P.5. Multi-Level Co-Architecting

- **Type of pattern:** Process pattern
- **Type of objective:** Trustworthiness
- **Target users:** Architects
- **Impacted stakeholders:** Developers, data scientists
- **Lifecycle stages:** Design

- **Relevant AI ethics principles:** HSE well-being, human-centered values, fairness, privacy protection and security, reliability and safety, transparency and explainability, contestability, accountability

P.6. Envisioning Card

- **Type of pattern:** Process pattern
- **Type of objective:** Trustworthiness
- **Target users:** Product managers
- **Impacted stakeholders:** Developers, data scientists
- **Lifecycle stages:** Design
- **Relevant AI ethics principles:** HSE well-being, human-centered values, fairness, privacy protection and security, reliability and safety, transparency and explainability, contestability, accountability

P.7. RAI Design Modeling

- **Type of pattern:** Process pattern
- **Type of objective:** Trustworthiness
- **Target users:** Architects
- **Impacted stakeholders:** Developers, data scientists
- **Lifecycle stages:** Design
- **Relevant AI ethics principles:** HSE well-being, human-centered values, fairness, privacy protection and security, reliability and safety, transparency and explainability, contestability, accountability

P.8. System-Level RAI Simulation

- **Type of pattern:** Process pattern
- **Type of objective:** Trustworthiness
- **Target users:** Architects
- **Impacted stakeholders:** Developers, data scientists
- **Lifecycle stages:** Design

- **Relevant AI ethics principles:** HSE well-being, human-centered values, fairness, privacy protection and security, reliability and safety, transparency and explainability, contestability, accountability

P.9. XAI Interface

- **Type of pattern:** Process pattern
- **Type of objective:** Trustworthiness
- **Target users:** Data scientists, UX/UI designers
- **Impacted stakeholders:** Developers
- **Lifecycle stages:** Design
- **Relevant AI ethics principles:** HSE well-being, human-centered values, fairness, privacy protection and security, reliability and safety, transparency and explainability, contestability, accountability

P.10. RAI Governance of APIs

- **Type of pattern:** Process pattern
- **Type of objective:** Trustworthiness
- **Target users:** Developers
- **Impacted stakeholders:** Testers, AI users, AI consumers
- **Lifecycle stages:** Implementation
- **Relevant AI ethics principles:** HSE well-being, human-centered values, fairness, privacy protection and security, reliability and safety, transparency and explainability, contestability, accountability

P.11. RAI Governance via APIs

- **Type of pattern:** Process pattern
- **Type of objective:** Trustworthiness
- **Target users:** Developers
- **Impacted stakeholders:** AI technology procurers, AI solution procurers, AI users, AI consumers
- **Lifecycle stages:** Implementation

- **Relevant AI ethics principles:** HSE well-being, human-centered values, fairness, privacy protection and security, reliability and safety, transparency and explainability, contestability, accountability

P.12. RAI Construction with Reuse

- **Type of pattern:** Process pattern
- **Type of objective:** Trustworthiness
- **Target users:** Developers
- **Impacted stakeholders:** Testers
- **Lifecycle stages:** Implementation
- **Relevant AI ethics principles:** HSE well-being, human-centered values, fairness, privacy protection and security, reliability and safety, transparency and explainability, contestability, accountability

P.13. RAI Acceptance Testing

- **Type of pattern:** Process pattern
- **Type of objective:** Trustworthiness
- **Target users:** Testers, AI users, AI consumers
- **Impacted stakeholders:** Business analysts, developers, data scientists
- **Lifecycle stages:** Testing
- **Relevant AI ethics principles:** HSE well-being, human-centered values, fairness, privacy protection and security, reliability and safety, transparency and explainability, contestability, accountability

P.14. RAI Assessment for Test Cases

- **Type of pattern:** Process pattern
- **Type of objective:** Trustworthiness
- **Target users:** Testers
- **Impacted stakeholders:** Developers, data scientists
- **Lifecycle stages:** Testing

- **Relevant AI ethics principles:** HSE well-being, human-centered values, fairness, privacy protection and security, reliability and safety, transparency and explainability, contestability, accountability

P.15. Continuous Deployment for RAI

- **Type of pattern:** Process pattern
- **Type of objective:** Trustworthiness
- **Target users:** Operators
- **Impacted stakeholders:** Developers, AI users, AI consumers
- **Lifecycle stages:** Operation
- **Relevant AI ethics principles:** HSE well-being, human-centered values, fairness, privacy protection and security, reliability and safety, transparency and explainability, contestability, accountability

P.16. Extensible, Adaptive, and Dynamic RAI Risk Assessment

- **Type of pattern:** Process pattern
- **Type of objective:** Trustworthiness
- **Target users:** Operators
- **Impacted stakeholders:** Developers, business analysts, AI users, AI consumers
- **Lifecycle stages:** Operation
- **Relevant AI ethics principles:** HSE well-being, human-centered values, fairness, privacy protection and security, reliability and safety, transparency and explainability, contestability, accountability

P.17. Multi-Level Co-Versioning

- **Type of pattern:** Process pattern
- **Type of objective:** Trustworthiness
- **Target users:** Operators
- **Impacted stakeholders:** Developers, AI users, AI consumers
- **Lifecycle stages:** Operation

- **Relevant AI ethics principles:** HSE well-being, human-centered values, fairness, privacy protection and security, reliability and safety, transparency and explainability, contestability, accountability

Product Patterns

D.1. RAI Bill of Materials Registry

- **Type of pattern**: Product pattern
- **Type of objective:** Trust
- **Target users:** Architects, developers
- **Impacted stakeholders:** Development teams, RAI governors, AI users, AI consumers
- **Relevant AI ethics principles:** Privacy protection and security, transparency and explainability, accountability

D.2. Verifiable RAI Credential

- **Type of pattern:** Product pattern
- **Type of objective:** Trust
- **Target users:** Architects, developers
- **Impacted stakeholders:** Development teams, RAI governors, AI users, AI consumers
- **Relevant AI ethics principles:** HSE well-being, human-centered values, fairness, privacy protection and security, reliability and safety, transparency and explainability, contestability, accountability

D.3. Co-Versioning Registry

- **Type of pattern**: Product pattern
- **Type of objective:** Trustworthiness, trust
- **Target users:** Architects, developers
- **Impacted stakeholders:** Operators, developers, data scientists
- **Relevant AI ethics principles:** Transparency and explainability, accountability

D.4. Federated Learner

- **Type of pattern**: Product pattern
- **Type of objective:** Trustworthiness
- **Target users:** Architects, data scientists
- **Impacted stakeholders:** Operators, developers
- **Relevant AI ethics principles:** Privacy protection and security, reliability and safety

D.5. AI Mode Switcher

- **Type of pattern:** Product pattern
- **Type of objective:** Trustworthiness, trust
- **Target users:** Architects, developers
- **Impacted stakeholders:** Operators, AI users, AI consumers
- **Relevant AI ethics principles:** Human-centered values, privacy protection and security, contestability

D.6. Multi-Model Decision-Maker

- **Type of pattern:** Product pattern
- **Type of objective:** Trustworthiness
- **Target users:** Architects, developers, data scientists
- **Impacted stakeholders:** AI users, AI consumers
- **Relevant AI ethics principles:** Fairness, reliability and safety

D.7. Homogeneous Redundancy

- **Type of pattern:** Product pattern
- **Type of objective:** Trustworthiness
- **Target users:** Architects, developers
- **Impacted stakeholders:** Data scientists
- **Relevant AI ethics principles:** Reliability and safety

D.8. Continuous RAI Validator

- **Type of pattern:** Product pattern
- **Type of objective:** Trustworthiness
- **Target users:** Architects, developers
- **Impacted stakeholders:** Operators, data scientists
- **Relevant AI ethics principles:** HSE well-being, human-centered values, fairness, privacy protection and security, reliability and safety, transparency and explainability, contestability, accountability

D.9. RAI Sandbox

- **Type of pattern:** Product pattern
- **Type of objective:** Trustworthiness
- **Target users:** Architects, developers
- **Impacted stakeholders:** Data scientists
- **Relevant AI ethics principles:** Human-centered values, fairness, privacy protection and security, reliability and safety

D.10. RAI Knowledge Base

- **Type of pattern:** Product pattern
- **Type of objective:** Trustworthiness
- **Target users:** Architects, developers, data scientists
- **Impacted stakeholders:** RAI governors, AI users, AI consumers
- **Relevant AI ethics principles:** HSE well-being, human-centered values, fairness, privacy protection and security, reliability and safety, transparency and explainability, contestability, accountability

D.11. RAI Digital Twin

- **Type of pattern:** Product pattern
- **Type of objective:** Trustworthiness
- **Target users:** Architects, developers

- **Impacted stakeholders:** Operators, data scientists
- **Relevant AI ethics principles:** HSE well-being, human-centered values, fairness, privacy protection and security, reliability and safety, transparency and explainability, contestability, accountability

D.12. Incentive Registry

- **Type of pattern:** Product pattern
- **Type of objective:** Trustworthiness
- **Target users:** Architects, developers
- **Impacted stakeholders:** Data scientists
- **Relevant AI ethics principles:** HSE well-being, human-centered values, fairness, privacy protection and security, reliability and safety, transparency and explainability, contestability, accountability

D.13. RAI Black Box

- **Type of pattern:** Product pattern
- **Type of objective:** Trust
- **Target users:** Architects, developers
- **Impacted stakeholders:** RAI governors, AI users, AI consumers
- **Relevant AI ethics principles:** HSE well-being, human-centered values, fairness, privacy protection and security, reliability and safety, transparency and explainability, contestability, accountability

D.14. Global-View Auditor

- **Type of pattern:** Product pattern
- **Type of objective:** Trust
- **Target users:** Architects, developers
- **Impacted stakeholders:** RAI governors, AI users, AI consumers
- **Relevant AI ethics principles:** HSE well-being, human-centered values, fairness, privacy protection and security, reliability and safety, transparency and explainability, contestability, accountability

Principle-Specific Techniques

T.1. Fairness Assessor

- **Type of pattern:** Product pattern
- **Type of objective:** Trustworthiness
- **Target users:** Data scientists
- **Impacted stakeholders:** RAI governors, AI users, AI consumers
- **Lifecycle stages:** Design
- **Relevant AI ethics principles:** Fairness

T.2. Discrimination Mitigator

- **Type of pattern:** Product pattern
- **Type of objective:** Trustworthiness
- **Target users:** Data scientists
- **Impacted stakeholders:** RAI governors, AI users, AI consumers
- **Lifecycle stages:** Design
- **Relevant AI ethics principles:** Fairness

T.3. Encrypted-Data-Based Trainer

- **Type of pattern:** Product pattern
- **Type of objective:** Trustworthiness
- **Target users:** Data scientists
- **Impacted stakeholders:** RAI governors, AI users, AI consumers
- **Lifecycle stages:** Design
- **Relevant AI ethics principles:** Privacy protection and security

T.4. Secure Aggregator

- **Type of pattern:** Product pattern
- **Type of objective:** Trustworthiness

- **Target users:** Data scientists
- **Impacted stakeholders:** RAI governors, AI users, AI consumers
- **Lifecycle stages:** Design
- **Relevant AI ethics principles:** Privacy protection and security

T.5. Random Noise Data Generator

- **Type of pattern:** Product pattern
- **Type of objective:** Trustworthiness
- **Target users:** Data scientists
- **Impacted stakeholders:** RAI governors, AI users, AI consumers
- **Lifecycle stages:** Design
- **Relevant AI ethics principles:** Privacy protection and security

T.6. Local Explainer

- **Type of pattern:** Product pattern
- **Type of objective:** Trust
- **Target users:** Data scientists
- **Impacted stakeholders:** UX/UI designers, RAI governors, AI users, AI consumers
- **Lifecycle stages:** Design
- **Relevant AI ethics principles:** Explainability

T.7. Global Explainer

- **Type of pattern:** Product pattern
- **Type of objective:** Trust
- **Target users:** Data scientists
- **Impacted stakeholders:** UX/UI designers, RAI governors, AI users, AI consumers
- **Lifecycle stages:** Design
- **Relevant AI ethics principles:** Explainability

Index

K

Register Your Product at informit.com/register

Access additional benefits and save up to 65%* on your next purchase

- Automatically receive a coupon for 35% off books, eBooks, and web editions and 65% off video courses, valid for 30 days. Look for your code in your InformIT cart or the Manage Codes section of your account page.
- Download available product updates.
- Access bonus material if available.**
- Check the box to hear from us and receive exclusive offers on new editions and related products.

InformIT—The Trusted Technology Learning Source

InformIT is the online home of information technology brands at Pearson, the world's leading learning company. At informit.com, you can

- Shop our books, eBooks, and video training. Most eBooks are DRM-Free and include PDF and EPUB files.
- Take advantage of our special offers and promotions (informit.com/promotions).
- Sign up for special offers and content newsletter (informit.com/newsletters).
- Access thousands of free chapters and video lessons.
- Enjoy free ground shipping on U.S. orders.*

* *Offers subject to change.*
** *Registration benefits vary by product. Benefits will be listed on your account page under Registered Products.*

Connect with InformIT—Visit informit.com/community

 Pearson

Addison-Wesley • Adobe Press • Cisco Press • Microsoft Press • Oracle Press • Peachpit Press • Pearson IT Certification • Que